THE ANTHOLOGY AN̶
RISE OF THE NOV̶

From Richardson to George Eliot

The Anthology and the Rise of the Novel brings together two tradition-ally antagonistic fields, book history and narrative theory, to chal-lenge established theories of "the rise of the novel." Leah Price shows that far from leveling class or gender distinctions, as has long been claimed, the novel has consistently located them within its own audience. Shedding new light on Richardson and Radcliffe, Scott and George Eliot, this book asks why the epistol-ary novel disappeared, how the book review emerged, why eight-eenth-century abridgers designed their books for women while Victorian publishers marketed them to men, and how editors' re-production of old texts has shaped authors' production of new ones. This innovative study will change the way we think not just about the history of reading, but about the genealogy of the canon wars, the future of intellectual property, and the role that anthologies play in our own classrooms.

Leah Price is Professor of English at Harvard University.

THE ANTHOLOGY AND THE RISE OF THE NOVEL

From Richardson to George Eliot

LEAH PRICE

Harvard University

CAMBRIDGE
UNIVERSITY PRESS

PUBLISHED BY THE PRESS SYNDICATE OF THE UNIVERSITY OF CAMBRIDGE
The Pitt Building, Trumpington Street, Cambridge, United Kingdom

CAMBRIDGE UNIVERSITY PRESS
The Edinburgh Building, Cambridge CB2 2RU, UK
40 West 20th Street, New York NY 10011–4211, USA
477 Williamstown Road, Port Melbourne, VIC 3207, Australia
Ruiz de Alarcón 13, 28014 Madrid, Spain
Dock House, The Waterfront, Cape Town 8001, South Africa

http://www.cambridge.org

First published 2000
Reprinted 2001, 2002 (twice)
First paperback edition 2003

Printed in the United Kingdom at the University Press, Cambridge

Typeset in Baskerville 11/12.5 pt [VN]

ISBN 0 521 78208 2 hardback

Contents

Acknowledgments

This study of readers owes a lot to its own. I'm grateful to Ruth Yeazell not just for criticizing several drafts in detail, but for her intellectual generosity during the years they were written; to Peter Brooks, who responded thoughtfully to a dissertation that strayed far from his own interests, and taught me a lot about novel-reading along the way; and to Gillian Beer for trenchant comments on the manuscript as well as various forms of institutional support. For close readings of the entire book, I'm indebted to Ann Gaylin, Steve Monte, David Quint, Alex Woloch, and especially Margaret Homans. David Bromwich, Ian Duncan, Stephen Greenblatt, Sarah Meer, James Simpson, Pam Thurschwell, and Alexander Welsh commented on parts of the project in ways that made the whole better. Most of what follows was argued out with Natalka Freeland, whose criticism has taught me almost as much as her friendship. Thanks also to Elizabeth Eger, Ina Ferris, Kate Flint, Dan O'Neill, Jeffrey Robinson, and Ashley Tellis for bibliographical suggestions, to Nicola Bown, Clíona ÓGallchoir, and Jan Schramm for camaraderie, to Roland Greene for putting me in a position to undertake this project, and to Richard Price and Sally Price for an example of common reading very different from the Bowdler family's. Nor does Linda Bree bear any resemblance (apart from the amount of time that she put into the book) to the monomaniacal editors who populate its pages.

Back in 1992, Roger Chartier's seminar at the Ecole des Hautes Etudes en Sciences Sociales taught me most of what I know about the history of the book, as well as how much I don't. I'm grateful to the Ecole Normale Supérieure, Harvard University, and the Ministère des Affaires Etrangères for funding that year, as well as to the Mellon Foundation, the Beinecke Library, and the Yale Department of Comparative Literature for financial support since then. Thanks also to the Mistress and Fellows of Girton College, Cambridge for granting the

Research Fellowship during which the manuscript was completed, and to colleagues there for making it a stimulating place to work. This book could not have been written without the help of staff at the Bibliothèque de France, the British Library, Cambridge University Library, Sterling Memorial Library, the Beinecke Library, and the National Library of Scotland.

Parts of the following chapters rework material that appeared earlier in *Novel*, *Studies in Eighteenth-Century Culture*, *Women's Writing*, and *Eighteenth-Century Fiction*; I'm grateful to those journals for permission to reprint.

Introduction

Just before the French Revolution, the utopian writer Louis-Sebastien Mercier set out to imagine what libraries might look like in the twenty-fifth century. The only books left on the shelves, as a citizen of 2440 explained to Mercier's hypothetical time traveler, would be neither large nor new.

Those of the greatest judgment amongst us have extracted the substance of thousands of volumes, which they have included in a small duodecimo; not unlike those skilful chemists, who concentrate the virtues of many plants in a small phial, and cast aside the refuse. We have abridged what seemed of most importance; the best have been reprinted; and the whole corrected according to the true principles of morality. Our compilers are a set of men estimable and dear to the nation.[1]

Present-day futurologists continue to predict the disappearance of the book. Yet for the digital technologies that we now picture compacting libraries, Mercier substituted verbal operations: abridgment, expurgation, compilation. The information overload that Mercier projected into our future had already begun in his lifetime. So had an arsenal of devices for containing it – the "shelf or two of BEAUTIES, ELEGANT EXTRACTS and ANAS" which Coleridge estimated sourly at "nine-tenths of the reading of the reading public."[2]

Two centuries on, anthologists have yet to become national heroes. Mercier's utopia stands alone in a tradition where anthologies have more often inspired dystopianism, even paranoia. Writing a few years later, the reformer Hannah More blamed their editors for the decay of morals: to let people assume that you had read the entire work from which an anthology-piece was excerpted, she warned girls, was no better than lying outright. In the 1840s, less predictably, Engels took time out from *The Condition of the Working Class in England* to execrate the poetic albums that littered the sofa-tables of the Manchester bourgeosie.

In the 1980s, the American poet David Antin aphorized that "anthologies are to poets as the zoo is to animals." More recently, Marjorie Perloff called for undergraduates to swear off brand-name mineral water, in the hope that abstainers could afford unabridged books rather than hackneyed fragments.[3]

Few readers listen. In Britain today, anthologies count among the only volumes of poetry that stand even a chance at mass-market success. In North America, where the economics of college survey courses have made "poem" nearly synonymous with "anthology-piece," the canon wars of the 1980s were fought over anthologies' tables of contents. Nor are anthology-pieces confined to the book. Poetic tags have long spilled over the borders of anthologies themselves to decorate billboards, calendars, even playing cards. Anthology-pieces ornament tombstones, inspire advertisements, occasion sermons, vertebrate dictionaries. More immediately (given that no argument about *Clarissa* or *Middlemarch* can appeal to more than synecdochal evidence), extracts underwrite the discipline of literary criticism as we know it. Like book reviews or film previews, the pages that follow depend on a gentleman's agreement to take the parts of a work for the whole.

Not even their most devastating critics have been able to explain how a culture without anthologies would function – to imagine, in Antin's metaphor, what a natural habitat for literature would be. Yet although literary critics spend at least as much time quoting out of context as do literary anthologists, the profession that teaches anthologies has provided few theories of the genre. The energy invested in uncovering subtle intertextual maneuvers correlates logically enough with a lack of interest in more crudely parasitic operations like excerpting, abridging, compiling. Source-study provides even fewer conceptual tools to deal with the hackneyed scraps of verse that litter eighteenth- and nineteenth-century novels; within an esthetics of difficulty, familiar quotations pose either an ethical embarrassment or a hermeneutic dead end. Nor does the language of criticism leave much room for anthologists. The middleman who excerpts cuts across the divisions of labor that make it possible to understand texts, or even to catalogue them: writer and reader, writer and critic, writer and publisher, writer and censor. The modern use of "reader" as a synonym for "anthology" defines anthologies not only as a product of writing but as a trace of reading – though also a device to spare, or prevent, its own readers from reading all the editor did. Compilers elude what

Roland Barthes calls "the pitiless divorce which the literary institution maintains between the producer of a text and its user, between its owner and its customer."[4]

Even more fundamentally, the anthology violates modern readers' expectation that the material unit (the book) should coincide with a verbal unit (the text). As a result, the anthologies which provide a vehicle for literary history have rarely become its object. We know more about the self-confident Renaissance culture of the commonplace than about its self-effacing successors.[5] Although the canon wars have drawn attention to the power of anthologists to shape national identity, a criticism which reduces anthologies to their evaluative function can do little more than catalogue binary oppositions: including or excluding particular texts, over- or under-representing a given category of authors, acknowledging or ignoring new writing.[6] Anthologies are more than a referendum. They determine not simply who gets published or what gets read, but who reads, and how.

Approached as a genre in its own right rather than a container for others, the anthology begins to look like a rather less conservative institution. Where poets and critics interested in the content of anthologies have tended (with good reason) to attack their resistance to change, those few who examine their form – most searchingly Robert Crawford and Barbara Benedict – have argued on the contrary for the liberating potential of the combinatory structure that allows anthologies (in Benedict's words) to "pull language out of legal frameworks and decentralize literary culture . . . by their subversive deferral of a central authority."[7] Benedict's Bakhtinian celebration of anthologies' formal variety is not, I think, irreconcilable with a suspicion of their literary-historical unanimity. At once the voice of authority and a challenge to prevailing models of authorship, the anthology traces its ambiguity to the late eighteenth century, when an organicist theory of the text and a proprietary understanding of authorship gathered force at the same moment as legal and educational changes lent compilers new power. Even biography confirms the contradictory role that the anthology took on at that time: of two of the most influential eighteenth-century collections, William Dodd's *Beauties of Shakespeare* and William Enfield's *Speaker*, one was edited by a future forger, the other by the author of a treatise on intellectual property.

The anthology's effect on reading practices is equally equivocal. The proliferation of schoolbooks that followed the 1774 defeat of perpetual copyright in Britain appears at first to confirm Rolf Engelsing's hypothesis of a late-eighteenth-century shift from the rereading of a few prized texts to the consumption of many ephemeral ones. This is less because anthologists encouraged extensive reading, however, than because of the energy they spent staving it off. Vicesimus Knox, whose *Elegant Extracts* (1783) swelled to enough volumes to create a market for meta-anthologies like *The Prose Epitome* and *The Poetical Epitome, or, Elegant Extracts . . . Abridged from the Larger Volume*, elsewhere claimed that the "superfluity" of books turned every reader into an anthologist: "the art of printing has multiplied books to such a degree, that . . . it becomes necessary to read in the classical sense of the word, LEGERE, that is, to *pick out . . .* the best parts of books." Nearly a century later, Francis Turner Palgrave compiled the *Golden Treasury* to cure a culture in which "everything is to be read, and everything only once."[8] The solution, apparently, was to refrain from reading "everything" – not only to ignore non-anthologized texts, but to pass over all but a few passages in the works that did make it into the *Treasury*. While the rise of extensive reading remains difficult to assign to a specific historical moment, what does seem clear is that generation after generation of anthologists saw their campaign against speed-reading as a losing battle. Far from replicating the move away from intensive reading that its editors registered in the culture at large, the history of the anthology inverts it. The moment to which Engelsing dates that shift is precisely when the early eighteenth-century miscellany – which, as Barbara Benedict has shown, valued variety and novelty – gave way to anthologists' mission not only to reprint older literature, but to revive a style of reading that they situated in the past.[9]

By reproducing scattered fragments while excising much longer stretches, however, even Knox and Palgrave marked the moments of intensive reading that they invited as the exception rather than the rule. Far from substituting extensive for intensive reading, anthologies forced their editors alternately to re-enact and to undo that historical shift by oscillating constantly between the two. Within each source, they distinguished some passages to be read once and immediately forgotten from others to be quoted, memorized, republished, and re-read. The anthology trained readers to pace themselves through an unmanageable bulk of print by sensing when to skip and where to linger. In the process, its editors set an example for the stop-and-start rhythm of reading that made possible new genres like the gothic novel (which punctuated prose narrative with verse epigraphs), the life-and-letters biography (which used narratorial summaries to frame epistolary excerpts), and even the tourist guidebook (which by the 1830s, as James Buzard has shown, came to ornament logistical instructions about the quickest routes with snatches of poetry to recite upon reaching a scenic stopping-place).[10] In each case, the contrast between two paces of reading – a leisured appreciation of beauties and an impatient, or efficient, rush through the plot – allowed critics to project the divided structure of individual texts onto the social makeup of the reading public.

Within a culture of the excerpt, the novel forms a test case. Few genres have been better placed to escape the anthology's sphere of influence. Sheer scale helps define the novel. So do the pace and duration of reading which that scale elicits. But the novel depends just as much on readers' resistance to those demands.[11] Skipping (or anthologizing) and skimming (or abridging) have never been separable from a genre that cracks under its own weight. What has come to be studied in classrooms and endorsed from pulpits is not the novel itself so much as the novelistic anthology-piece, whether actual or potential.

This is not to say that the "rise" of the novel correlates directly with the representation of novels in anthologies. On the contrary, over the course of the nineteenth century editors narrowed their generic range until the anthology-piece became tacitly synonymous with the lyric. Even in late-twentieth-century America, where the intellectual superiority of novel-readers over non-novel-readers appears to be more uncritically accepted than at any other time or place, size alone has sufficed to ensure anthologies' displacement of the novel by the theoretically less canonical genre of the short story. The recent appearance on North American campuses of a series entitled "Norton Anthology Editions" – one-volume novels marketed to buyers of the *Norton Anthology of English Literature* and designed, as the preface to the latter puts it, to "match" the *NAEL* – betrays the supplementary status of a genre that has become central to our imagination of the canon but whose size prevents it from entering that canon's most concrete material manifestation.[12] Norton's urge to make the anthology coextensive with the curriculum suggests how difficult it is to classify a genre resistant to one but essential to the other. The contradiction to which the portmanteau phrase "Anthology Editions" responds raises questions not only about the place of the novel within the canon, but about the relation of the canon to the book.

Until modernism made novels more difficult and didacticism less respectable, however, the novel eluded the anthology for qualitative reasons even more than quantitative ones. The anthology contained moral truths and esthetic touchstones, the novel corrupted morals and taste; one was expected to be memorized and re-used, the other to be devoured and discarded. While novelists gave their name often enough to the individual anthologies examined in the following chapters – from Defoe's *Serious Reflections during the Life and Surprising Adventures of Robinson Crusoe*, to Richardson's *Collection of Moral Sentiments*, to the *Beauties of Sterne*, to the *Wit and Wisdom of Sir Walter Scott*, to George Eliot's *Sayings* and *Birthday Book*, to George Meredith's *Birthday Book* and *Pilgrim's Scrip* – the novel remained largely absent from the more encyclopedic multiply-authored anthologies that defined the canon. When Virginia Woolf congratulated Hardy on his absence from an anthology of English prose, she invoked the commonplace that the two genres have nothing in common: "The great novelists very seldom stop in the middle or the beginning of their great scenes to write anything that one could cut out with a pair of scissors or loop around with a line of red ink . . . One must not go to [novelists] for perfect passages, descriptions, perorations, reflections so highly wrought that they can stand alone without their context." As it happens, by the time Woolf wrote this, Hardy had already been excerpted very publicly in a *Thomas Hardy Calendar* which culled 365 thoughts for the day, but her point stands.[13] For a novelist, to be excerpted is sometimes an honor (as for Richardson), sometimes an embarrassment (as for George Eliot), but always an anomaly. Yet as I'll suggest, precisely because anthologies tend to derive their raw material from more esthetically and morally serious genres (epic, lyric, essay), the novel tests the anthology's power. By salvaging anthology-pieces from their low origins, editors prove their authority to grant personal dispensations from generic rules.

The novel makes visible the anthology's own cult of the anomaly. An anthology-piece is not a random sample any more than an abridgment is a scale model. ("In the case of written composition," one Victorian editor complained, "there are no mechanical appliances, as there are in painting and architecture, for varying the scale.")[14] The anthology's ambition to represent a whole through its parts is always undermined by readers' awareness that the parts have been chosen for their difference from those left out. But anthologies drawn from the novel destabilize that delicate balance by subordinating the representative to the anomalous. In the hands of its editors, the novel rose piecemeal: islands of lyric or didactic or sententious collectibles bobbing up occasionally from a sea of dispensable narrative. The novel could not have become respectable without the tokenism embodied in the anthology – a synecdochal esthetic that corresponds to an equally atomistic model of individual upward mobility. As I'll argue, the novel rose less by challenging the esthetic and social hierarchies which had kept it down than by projecting those stratifications onto its own audience. Far from leveling class or gender distinctions (as hostile critics accused in the eighteenth century, and as celebratory ones from Ian Watt to Margaret Anne Doody have more recently argued), the novel has internalized and even reinvented them.[15]

The size of the novel presents anthologists with the same problem as the size of its audience: good readers need to be sifted from bad ones as urgently as anthology-pieces from forgettable dross. Anthologies' logic of the exception does not simply demarcate quotable passages from the bulk of the novels in which they originally appeared. It also distinguishes anthologized authors from the mass of novelists, and the readers of anthologies (or reviews or criticism) from the novel's mass public. Each process feeds into the other. Eighteenth-century anthologists chose excerpts for truth, nineteenth-century editors for style, but esthetic beauties came to perform the same function that moral "beauties" had earlier filled in the structure of novels. Both punctuated the narrative, interrupted the time of reading, and forced readers to surface periodically from the self-indulgent pleasures of mimesis to a higher, less particularized, more disinterested plane. In that sense, the opposition between fragment and frame cuts across the historical shift from didactic to formalist criticism. Even as the discourses against which narrative was defined changed – from maxims in Richardson, to inset lyrics and landscape descriptions in Radcliffe, to antiquarian collectibles in Scott, to self-authored epigraphs and self-referential generalizations in Eliot – what remained constant was editors' urge to prise narration apart from static, atemporal, self-contained passages of something else. By training women to prefer one and men the other, abridgers and anthologists together exchanged the novel's traditional difference from other genres for a gendered (but constantly shifting) division of labor within its own public. In the century separating Richardson's death from George Eliot's, a culture in which serious critics appreciated timeless truths while frivolous ladies devoured stories gave way to one where women relished ornamental digressions and men demanded the narrative point. Yet both cultures debated what to do with the non-narrative parts of novels, and both freighted that decision with social consequences.

The rise of serious discourse about novels – which required the description and proscription of alternative ways of reading them – can be dated to the years stretching from the first edition of *Clarissa* in 1747–48 to the wave of obituary assessment that followed George Eliot's death in 1880. Within those boundaries, the following chapters oscillate (rather like the texts they discuss) between survey and example, sandwiching an account of the anthology-piece's dislocations at the turn of the nineteenth century with more detailed case studies on either side. Chapter one charts the tension between narrative authority and epistolary compilation that Richardson's novels bequeathed their nineteenth-century successors. Although *Clarissa* credits its coherence to an inscribed editor who compiles, excerpts, and abridges letters – and its moral power to an author/publisher who anthologizes the novel in turn – each successive edition raised more urgent ethical questions about its characters' impulse to appropriate others' writing. Richardson himself excerpted the maxims from *Clarissa* to form an anthology that not only inculcated moral lessons about the outside world, but also, more self-referentially, inoculated its audience against the vice of skipping. The division of labor that later emerged between dangerously entertaining abridgments and strategically boring anthologies further widened the gap which within *Clarissa* itself had already separated the centripetal editorial apparatus from the composite structure of the text that it framed. Not until his last novel did Richardson resolve the contradiction inherent in an epistolary mode which defined writing as collectively produced but privately owned. Yet even in *Sir Charles Grandison*, where the figure of the executor finally disjoins property from authority, competition from rival printers combined with the collaboration of personal friends to threaten the ownership of the book itself.

The changing techniques that editors have used to compress the bulk of Richardson's novels provide an index to shifting assumptions about the most efficient way to convey information – or indeed about what counts as information at all. But nineteenth-century abridgments also shed light on the riddle of the death of the epistolary novel, by providing one of the only clues we have to the way old epistolary novels were being read at the moment when new ones ceased to be written. Paradoxically, as long as the epistolary novel remained in vogue, abridgers transposed letters into retrospective, omniscient narration; conversely, epistolary abridgments began to appear as soon as the novel in letters was no longer a viable form. That second wave of abridgments draws on a tradition of nineteenth-century works in radically different genres – from Sir Walter Scott's edition of Richardson (1824) to his ambivalently epistolary novel *Redgauntlet* (1824, 1832) to J. G. Lockhart's intermittently epistolary *Life of Scott* (1837) – which revive the letter to test the relation of social history to literary scale.

Chapter two examines the range of competing tools that turn-of-the-century editors devised to re-order a threateningly large and shapeless reading public: anthologies, abridgments, expurgations. Unlike late-twentieth-century anthologies that seek to represent diversity through their selection of authors, anthologies published in post-1774 Britain located difference among readers. So did the new novelistic subgenres that made a bid to take over the anthology's mission of constructing a middle-brow, middle-class public. Where Vicesimus Knox reduced the scholarly anthologist to the amanuensis of a consensual audience, Ann Radcliffe's reviewers appropriated the formal conventions of the anthology to distinguish their pace of reading from that which they attributed to an all-too-common reader – a contrast which Radcliffe's own use of the epigraph had already inscribed within the structure of the novel. Shakespearean editors, too, expanded the audience for a single national poet only by packaging his work in a range of different forms calibrated as finely as the market segments that they called into being. In the process of distinguishing stretches to be skimmed from moments to be remembered, they not only set a precedent for the half-hearted canonization of the novel a few decades later, but taught their readers to recognize themselves as members of a class, a generation, a sex. By the early nineteenth century, Susan Ferrier was able to enlist Shakespearean anthology-pieces and indeed Shakespearean anthologies in a campaign against solipsistic novel-reading, producing fictions so riddled with hackneyed quotations as to be barely readable today. Her pedantry repels not because its sources are too difficult for modern readers to recognize, but because their facility stops interpretation short. Ferrier's shallow allusiveness tests the limits not only of intertextual reading but of feminist literary-historical revisionism.

I end with the novels of George Eliot, more ruthlessly excerpted than any since: chopped into anthology-pieces, recycled as calendar decorations, used to test army officers, deployed in a Zionist tract, plastered onto billboards, and quarried for epigraphs to a socialist treatise and even an abridgment of Boswell's *Life of Johnson*. Like Radcliffe, Eliot

disciplines feminine readers' impatience by diluting her narrative with
more static modes of discourse. Punctuated with chapter mottoes attributed or misattributed to other authors and studded with atemporal
generalizations so self-contained as to be universally applicable, her last
novels bear the traces of being written for – and against – the anthologies in which she expected to be repackaged in turn. Those collections
redefined the genre of Eliot's oeuvre and the gender of its author, in
contradictory ways: they canonized her novels by packaging her as a
poet, and bracketed her with male predecessors by marketing her to
women.

Nineteenth-century reviews and twentieth-century criticism characterized her work more explicitly as peculiarly quotable, even as – like
Eliot herself – they questioned the ethics of appropriating others' words.
Their distaste for Eliot's lapidary generalizations reversed traditional
assumptions about the relation between plot and pleasure, replacing the
figure of the self-indulgent female reader about whom eighteenth-
century critics had worried by a new figure of the self-important female
sage. Debates about Eliot's sententiousness reflect reviewers' and critics'
growing doubts about the synecdochal logic of their own practice.
Eliot's shifting place in the canon over the past hundred years reveals
not only evolving assumptions about the structure of literary texts, but
changes in the evidentiary value accorded to quotation. Those worries
gave rise to legal debates: what constitutes fair use? Does obscenity
reside in the parts of a text or depend on the proportions of the whole?
But they have also had more direct consequences for the theory of
literary genres and for the genres of literary criticism.

The work of professional mediators like editors, condensers, and reviewers figures less often in critical text than in scholarly footnotes – or
only, anecdotally, as corruptions that reflect a "horizon of expectations"
against which to measure authorial originality.[16] Yet competing editorial alternatives (anthology, abridgment, expurgation, collected works)
add up to more than a series of accidents in the transmission of
particular texts. They also shape a larger generic system. Shakespearean
editing set a precedent for the power of condensations to scramble
genre: anthologies chopped lower literary forms (first the drama, then
the novel) into pseudo-lyric snippets as mechanically as abridgments
translated verse into quasi-novelistic prose. Richardson's editors, too,
forced readers to choose among methods of miniaturization which
borrowed their formal conventions from opposite ends of the generic

hierarchy. Where anthologies salvaged lyric beauties and moral truths from their dispensable narrative frame, abridgments degraded their raw materials by reducing all literary forms to the lowest common denominator of impersonal retrospective prose narration. Although both strategies responded to a generic landscape increasingly polarized between decorative verse and utilitarian prose, neither simply updated inherited texts to match the literary works being currently produced. On the contrary, editing has more often functioned as a conservative counterweight to esthetic change, providing a space in which discarded formal alternatives can be recycled.

In order to reconstruct the significance of editorial conventions, the following chapters compare editions not simply with other versions of the same text (as studies centered around a particular work have long done) but also with analogous editions of others. On a local level, such comparisons make it possible to trace the triangular relations among different literary careers. Thus, I take Shakespeare's influence on George Eliot to encompass the relation between anthologies of Shakespeare and anthologies of George Eliot, between critics' claims for Shakespeare's difference from other dramatists and critics' claims for Eliot's difference from other women, between Scott's editors' invocation of Shakespearean editing and Eliot's editors' invocation of Scott's marketing – and the list could go on. When Richardson indexed his own novels in the form that Pope's edition of Shakespeare had borrowed from his translation of Homer, he acknowledged the power of such circuitous mediation.

But a history of the conventions through which novels have been reproduced and reduced could contribute more generally to a genealogy of late-twentieth-century academic criticism. Pierre Bourdieu's appeal for critics "to make explicit to [themselves] [their] position in the subfield of producers of discourse about art and the contribution of this field to the very existence of the object of study" can be extended from discourse itself to a wider range of nonexpressive practices: all the acts of textual reproduction and omission, contextualization and juxtaposition, which together construct not only a particular literary tradition but a model of what literature is.[17] Discourses are easier to describe than practices, however. Anthologists' silences furnish a more slippery kind of evidence than do theoretical manifestoes. My project bears traces of that problem. Since close reading provides more tools for interpreting verbal judgments than for describing editorial acts, I devote a disproportionate amount of space to the paratextual apparatus (titles, prefaces, tables of contents, footnotes) where the editor becomes a writer.[18] Although, as I shall argue, those liminary moments rarely provide a reliable description of the editorial practice that they frame – often overcompensating for it instead – they constitute one crucial source for the "critography" that Peter Widdowson has recently proposed: a project that would add to the comparison of individual critical theories or schools a more distanced attention to the unspoken premises and institutional bases that they share.[19]

My focus on the mechanics of the excerpt should provide one alternative to a tradition of reception studies that focuses on the content of readers' opinions – whether on the psychology of experimental subjects' "responses" or on the history of the judgments through which a particular text has been "received" – to the exclusion of the form that those opinions take and the institutions that generated them in the first place.[20] In one case, readers express themselves in the inevitably artificial guise of answers to (leading) questionnaires or tests or interviews. In the other, writings that originated in wildly different contexts are lumped together as "sources," as in Routledge's *Critical Heritage* anthologies, which juxtapose published reviews with private letters and diaries while excising plot summary and illustrative quotation from the former. What readers respond to (at least in forms to which more than telepathy can give us access) is never just a text: they respond to the editor's demand for a review, to the teacher's demand for an exam answer, to the interviewer's demand for a statement, to the publisher's demand for an edition. This book brings reception history together with narrative theory to explore what new literary genres, and new uses for old ones, have emerged from the endeavors of professional readers – editors, publishers, teachers, critics – to predict or prescribe or proscribe the reading of others.

CHAPTER I

Richardson's economies of scale

What Cleanth Brooks anathematized fifty years ago as "the heresy of paraphrase" remains impossible to escape in literary critics' daily practice.[1] Plot summary, on the one hand, and quoting out of context, on the other, continue to underpin our arguments – if only because, for example, it would be impossible for me to reproduce verbatim all eight volumes of *Clarissa* as evidence for what this chapter argues. Sheer bulk lays Richardson open to summary. The impossibility of fitting all eight volumes of *Clarissa* or seven of *Grandison* into the human mind at once turns readers into editors. The first collection of excerpts from *Clarissa* appeared only three years after the novel itself; the first plot summary, four years later. Ever since then, the shifting division of labor between Richardson's anthologists and his abridgers has registered successive generations' unspoken assumptions about the most efficient way to convey information, and indeed about what counts as information at all. Condensations define some modes of discourse as functional, others as decorative. They predict which aspects of a text will provoke curiosity or boredom. They impute to some audiences a vulgar greed for plot, to others a painstaking appreciation of style. In skimming, the former abridge; in skipping, the latter anthologize.

Richardson lived to see *Clarissa* and *Grandison* abridged. He set that process into motion himself by adding an index to the second edition of *Clarissa* in the expectation that readers would have forgotten the beginning by the time they reached the end, and "would not chuse to read seven Tedious Volumes over again." The index was offered as a surrogate memory, "a help to their Recollection."[2] But Richardson's readers have spent as much energy "writing Indexes, . . . abstracting, abridging, compiling" as he himself claimed to.[3]

So do his characters. Each novel takes an anthologist for its heroine. Pamela keeps "a Common-place Book, as I may call it; In which, by her Lady's Direction, from time to time, she had transcribed from the Bible,

13

and other good Books, such Passages as made most Impression upon her, as she read."[4] The double plot of *Sir Charles Grandison* produces two competing collections of excerpts: the hero's rejected lover assembles biblical quotations, while her successful rival copies "consoling" extracts from private letters.[5] Clarissa keeps a commonplace book like Pamela, compiles religious extracts like Clementina, and excerpts letters like Harriet.[6] Richardson never specifies the contents of Pamela's commonplace book, but his later novels grant the anthology more substance: Clementina's and Harriet's excerpts are reproduced in full, Clarissa's archive of letters is presented as the origin of the novel itself, and her "Meditations" are not only inserted in the novel but reprinted later as an independent volume. The heroines' common practice of the commonplace cuts across class, nationality, and religion. It also extends to men. Every major male character in Richardson – Mr. B., Belford, Lovelace, Grandison – excerpts quotations. So do most minor ones: Greville, Brand, Bartlett, Sir Charles' short-hand writer Henry Cotes, even a philistine Anthony Harlowe and a barely literate Richard Mowbray. Together, they set an example of how (and how not) to manipulate texts produced by others.

Richardson's late novels pose a double question: why do their characters spend so much time excerpting texts? And why have the novels themselves been so energetically excerpted? One explanation is that his fictions are already anthologies. Vicesimus Knox's decision to supplement his *Elegant Extracts* by a companion volume of *Elegant Epistles* serves as a reminder that collections of letters, like collections of anthology-pieces, are strung together from self-contained texts signed by multiple authors. Unlike anthologies, though, epistolary novels are also continuous narratives in which – however many different names appear under individual letters – the text as a whole is ultimately attributed to one author at most. The tension between those two facts structures Richardson's fiction. Despite their quotation of letters and in letters, later editions of *Clarissa* began to dramatize the ethical dangers of appropriating others' words. Throughout Richardson's lifetime and after it, each successive edition widened the gap between the centripetal editorial apparatus and the composite form of the text that it frames. Not until his last novel did Richardson find a plot capable of resolving the contradiction inherent in a genre that defines writing as collectively produced but privately owned. And even *Sir Charles Grandison*, in which the figure of the executor finally disjoins property from authority, gave rise to proprietary disputes with both amateur friends and commercial rivals.

The size of Richardson's novels would eventually invite even more radical kinds of appropriation. The competing strategies that successive anthologists and abridgers used to compress them provide a clue to the riddle of the epistolary novel's disappearance in the nineteenth century. This chapter will turn in conclusion to a range of ambivalently documentary nineteenth-century genres – abridgment, biography, historical novel – to explore how old epistolary fictions came to be read once new ones ceased to be written.

WRITING AGAINST THE MOMENT

Scale alone cannot explain the repackaging of Richardson's novels. While some editions shorten the originals, others supplement them, and even those rewritings that do shrink the text change more than size. For over a hundred years after Richardson's death, every abridgment pre-fixed genealogical and biographical information to the courtship plots which Richardson himself had begun *in medias res* before returning belatedly to the heroines' childhoods and origins. All three novels originally open at the moment when an adolescent girl becomes aware of a man's pursuit; their time-frame coincides with what Clarissa calls "the space from sixteen to twenty-two . . . which requires [a parent's] care, more than any other time of a young woman's life." A parent's – but also a reader's. Mrs. Harlowe refuses to credit Clarissa for an exemplary youth, claiming that only "now that you are grown up to marriageable years is the test." In *Pamela*, too, we hear little about the heroine's childhood until Mr. B.'s reminiscences in the third volume. Even then, what he remembers is precisely his impression that Pamela's character was not yet worth noticing: "the Girl's well enough, for what she is; but let's see what she'll be a few Years hence. Then will be the Trial" (*Pamela*, 3.30.241).[7] By realigning the order of story with the order of discourse – and, in the case of *Sir Charles Grandison*, by substituting the hero's birth for the heroine's coming of age as their starting-point – the earliest abridgments matched the boundaries of the plot to the par-ameters of a (masculine) life.

More fundamentally, eighteenth-century abridgments altered epis-tolarity along with length. For a collection of first-person present-tense letters "written to the moment," they substituted a single retrospective, impersonal narrator, temporally and diegetically removed from the events described.[8] No letters appear in *The Paths of Virtue Delineated: or, the History in Miniature of the Celebrated Pamela, Clarissa Harlowe, and Sir Charles*

Grandison, Familiarised and Adapted to the Capacities of Youth (London: R. Baldwin, 1756), which went through many editions both as a whole and in separate volumes before being recycled in 1813 as *Beauties of Richardson*; in *Clarissa, or, The history of a young lady . . . abridged from the works of Samuel Richardson* (London: Newbery, n.d. [1769?]); in *The History of Sir Charles Grandison, abridged from the works of Samuel Richardson* (London: Newbery, n.d. [1769?]); or in J. H. Emmert, *The Novelist: or, a Choice Selection of the Best Novels* (Gottingen: Vandenhoek and Ruprecht, 1792), which combined abridgments of Richardson's last two novels. Paradoxically, abridgers continued to transpose letters into narrative as long as the epistolary novel remained in vogue: from 1756 through 1813, no abridgment published in English retained the novels' original form. Conversely, as we shall see at the end of this chapter, abridgers began to adopt the epistolary mode only in 1868, once the production of new epistolary novels had dwindled to a trickle. Yet even those abridgments – like their successors still in print today – continued to add third-person past-tense plot summaries to replace the letters excised and to frame the epistolary excerpts that remain. As synoptic narrative alternates with synecdochal extracts, each modern abridgment oscillates between the narrative conventions of eighteenth-century epistolary fiction and those of nineteenth-century omniscient narration.

Brevity has no intrinsic connection with narrative distance: a sentence phrased in the past tense and the third person is no shorter than one in the present and the first. Yet the consensus that confuses efficiency with impersonality has remained constant from Richardson's lifetime right down to the present. In a letter, Richardson apologized (or boasted) that "Prolixity, Length at least, cannot be avoided in Letters written to the Moment." The preface to *Grandison*, too, contrasts the epistolary novel before us with a potential past-tense abridgment: "The nature of familiar Letters, written, as it were, to the *Moment*, while the heart is agitated by Hopes and Fears, or Events undecided, must plead an excuse for the *Bulk* of a Collection of this kind. Mere Facts and Characters might be comprised in a much smaller Compass."[9] *Clarissa* is prefaced by an even more explicit discussion of abridgment. The "editor" explains that he was "so diffident in relation to this article of *length*" that he asked his friends "what might best be spared." One "advised him to give a narrative turn to the letters," while others argued that "the story could not be reduced to a dramatic unity, or thrown into the narrative way, without divesting it of its warmth" (*Clarissa*, 35–36). The speaker chooses the second opinion over the first, and both prefaces ultimately reject abridgment. Indeed, their allusions to that possibility call attention to the uncompromising length of the novels that follow. Yet readers of the first editions arrive at the full texts of *Clarissa* and *Grandison* only after passing through prefatory discussions of abridging. The question of how the novels could be condensed comes up even before they begin.

Richardson acted on those speculations. In 1749, the second edition of *Clarissa* added a table of contents summarizing each letter. Once republished as a separate pamphlet later that year, the table of contents became a synecdochal substitute for the novel: a plot summary that could be bought instead of the full text as well as along with it. Richardson's next supplement was quite different, however: *A Collection of such of the Moral and Instructive SENTIMENTS, CAUTIONS, APHORISMS, REFLECTIONS and OBSERVATIONS contained in the History [of Clarissa], as are presumed to be of general Use and Service* (1751), followed in 1755 by a *Collection of the Moral and Instructive Sentiments, Maxims, Cautions, and Reflections, Contained in the Histories of PAMELA, CLARISSA, and Sir CHARLES GRANDISON*. Like abridgments, the *Collections* shorten, but their principles of selection are diametrically opposed. The *Collections* fragment the novels by substituting alphabetical for chronological order; the abridgments unify them by stripping discontinuous digressions away from linear plot. The anthologies excise ephemeral local detail in favor of timeless maxims "of general use and service" (a claim confirmed the next year when Benjamin Franklin inserted twenty-one of them in *Poor Richard's Almanack*); the abridgments keep narrative particulars but cut abstractions, sprinkling gaps through the text like negative anthology-pieces.[10] What was figure becomes ground.

Richardson memorably dubbed his method "writing to the moment," but in the *Collection of Sentiments* we see him editing against the moment. The alphabetical order of the *Collection* substitutes the paradigmatic for the syntagmatic, undoing not only the order of time, but the significance of order. With each successive edition, that contrast between linear summaries and modular collections widened further. Where the table of contents of *Clarissa* promised to "shew the Connexion of the whole," the 1755 *Collection* eventually disintegrated into a "set of entertaining Cards, neatly engraved on Copper-Plates, Consisting of moral and diverting Sentiments, extracted wholly from the much admired Histories of PAMELA, CLARISSA, and SIR CHARLES GRANDISON" produced in 1760, which excerpted from the *Collection* the maxims that the latter had already extracted from the novels.[11]

Transposed from bound pages to cards made to be shuffled, the "sentiments" lost even the arbitrary order that the *Collection* had borrowed
from the letters of the alphabet – and the material connection that the
novel borrows from its binding.

Yet the division of labor between narrative abridgments and sententious anthologies simply makes visible a tension that already structures
the full texts from the beginning. In a letter, Richardson dismissed his
Collection of Moral Sentiments as "a dry Performance – Dull Morality, and
Sentences . . . divested of Story."[12] In *Sir Charles Grandison*, however,
Charlotte contrasts "story" less favorably with the "sentiments" that
give the *Collection of Moral and Instructive Sentiments* its title: "The French
only are proud of sentiments at this day; the English cannot bear them:
Story, story, story, is what they hunt after" (*Grandison*, 6.52.228).[13] In a
departure from Richardson's usual xenophobia, the epigrammatic form
of Charlotte's observation, which lends itself to being generalized and
indeed quoted, implicitly endorses "sentiment" over "story." Boswell
reproduces that preference when he quotes Samuel Johnson saying that
"if you were to read Richardson for the story, your impatience would be
so much fretted, that you would hang yourself. But you must read him
for the sentiment, and consider the story as giving occasion to the
sentiment."[14] That pronouncement itself appears in a biography in the
form of an anthology, Boswell's *Life*, which frames a collection of
Johnson's sayings by the story of Johnson's life. In prescribing how to
read Richardson, Boswell defines his own genre.

Johnson was only one of several critics beginning with Richardson
himself who perceived "read[ing] Richardson for the story" as a dangerous temptation. In *The Progress of Romance* (1785), Clara Reeve acknowledges that "if you have a mind to see an Epitomé of Richardson's
works, there is such a publication, wherein the *narrative* is preserved; but
you must no longer expect the graces of *Richardson*, nor his pathetic
addresses to the heart, they are all evaporated and only the dry *Story*
remains."[15] We have no way of knowing which of the many "epitomes"
Reeve is referring to – though *The Paths of Virtue* seems the most likely –
for her complaint about the elimination of everything except "narrative" applies equally well to every abridgment on the market at that
date. Reeve's and Johnson's scorn for "reading for the story" forms the
corollary of abridgers' unspoken assumption that poor or young or lazy
readers want nothing but plot.

Long before Reeve, Richardson had characterized "the narrative
way" as a "reduction," reporting that the revision of parts of *Clarissa*

"into a merely Narrative Form . . . has help'd me to shorten much," and associating "Story" with "haste": "Was it not time I shd. hasten to an end of my tedious Work? Was not Story, Story, Story the continual demand upon me."[16] Reeve's phrase "dry story," too, reproduces an image of "dry narrative" that first appeared in *Clarissa*, where Belford points out that the heroine is "writing of and in the midst of present distresses! How much more lively and affecting for that reason, must her style be, than all that can be read in the *dry, narrative*, unanimated style of persons relating difficulties and dangers surmounted!" (*Clarissa*, 391.1178, my emphasis). Belford's contrast between "narrative" and "presence" anticipates the logic of eighteenth-century abridgments which adopt a distanced narrator and a retrospective tense. Like abridgers, Richardson, Reeve, and Johnson posit a choice between, on the one hand, "facts and characters," "narrative," "story," "reduction," "haste"; on the other, "sentiment," "presence," "tediousness," "length," "bulk." All but the abridgers agreed in preferring the latter to the former. Yet the fact that Belford applies to "narrative" and Reeve to "story" the same adjective ("dry") which Richardson used to characterize "Sentences . . . divested of Story" suggests that story and sentiment form mirror-images of one another – and that either half of the compound loses its force when separated from the other.

Richardson never determined whether "story" could be purified from "sentiment" as cleanly as his metaphor of evaporation implied, let alone whether it should be. The preface to *Clarissa* warns that if the novel were to be "thrown into the narrative way," "very few of the reflections and observations" (two of the terms later listed in the title of the *Collection*) "would then find a place" (*Clarissa*, 35–36). The preface to the 1751 *Collection of Sentiments*, in contrast, acknowledges that some readers have legitimate reasons to separate the two:

As the narrative part of those Letters was only meant as a vehicle for the instructive, no wonder that many readers, who are desirous of fixing in their minds those maxims which deserve notice distinct from the story that first introduced them should have often wished and pressed to see them separate from that chain of engaging incidents.[17]

Such readers demand the "chain of incidents" to be excised, not because it bores them, but on the contrary because it "engages" them too pleasurably not to distract from the moral. This is the logic of Elizabeth Griffith's argument, in a 1775 anthology of *The Morality of Shakespeare's Drama*, that the sententious passages need to be extracted because "a single line, sometimes a single word, in many instances throughout his Works, may convey a hint, or impress a sentiment upon the heart, if properly marked, which might possibly be overlooked, while curiosity is attending to the fable"; or of a later anthologist's claim, in *The Genius and Wisdom of Sir Walter Scott*, that "the passages in which are developed [Scott's] peculiar notions of morals and philosophy escaped the attention of the generality of readers, in consequence of their minds being absorbed in the contemplation of the different varied incidents of the deeply interesting narrative they were perusing."[18] Although the preface to the 1751 *Collection* congratulates its readers on their self-denial, the reference to "engaging incidents" cannot help reminding them of the existence of other, more frivolous, readers, whom the sentiments presumably fail to "engage."

Reader-response criticism has little to say about those unresponsive readers. We know more about the apocryphal villagers who supposedly rang the church bells to celebrate Pamela's wedding – an anecdote disproved fifty years ago but still retailed as fact by two otherwise meticulous scholars as recently as 1991 – than about the very real people who used abridgments to short-circuit Richardson's prolixity.[19] The critical profession's vested interest in believing that people can be turned on by reading has deprived us of any language with which to describe what happens when books turn readers off. Robert Darnton's pioneering work on pornographic texts and weeping readers has bequeathed to later literary historians an ethical imperative to prove that reading can produce results as tangible as bodily fluids. Conversely, to acknowledge that the length of Richardson's novels has prevented many people from responding or even from reading constitutes critical treason.[20] In an earlier version of this chapter, my reference to "the impossibility of fitting all eight volumes of *Clarissa* or seven of *Grandison* into the human mind at once" incited one anonymous reviewer to testify that "I have read the unabridged CLARISSA about three (or perhaps four) times – and GRANDISON about twice." Even Patricia Meyer Spacks, who takes *Sir Charles Grandison* as a case-study in her recent book *Boredom*, backs down by displacing that boredom at once into the future of the text (as if Richardson bored no one until the twentieth century) and into the past of her readers (who are expected to come away from *Boredom* less bored with *Grandison*). Spacks' subtle analysis ends on a pious anticlimax: "To try to reconstruct the interest of such a book, however hypothetically, . . . reminds us that 'boring books' need not always bore us."[21] Eighteenth-century abridgments suggest a rather different chronology.

As early as 1756, when *The Paths of Virtue* appeared, abridgers acted on Richardson's assumption that anything but third-person past-tense narrative would tempt the young, the ignorant, and the idle to skip. In turn, that prophecy fulfilled itself as eighteenth-century "histories in miniature" – unbroken, or unrelieved, by the original "sentiments" – trained their readers to dismiss non-narrative discourse as digression, interruption, delay.

In a novel published a year before *The Paths of Virtue*, Eliza Haywood personified such a reader under the name of Miss Loyter:

Miss Loyter. As for Novels, I like some of them well enough, particularly Mrs Behn's; but I know not how it is, the Authors now-a-days have got such a way of breaking off in the middle of their stories, that one forgets one half before one comes to the other.
Author. Digressions, miss, when they contain fine sentiments and judicious remarks, are certainly the most valuable parts of that sort of writing.
Miss Loyter. I cannot think so, and could wish the Authors would keep their sentiments and remarks to themselves, or else have them printed in a different letter, that one might know where to begin and where to leave off.[22]

Richardson's novels are as open as any to the charge of breaking off in the middle of the story. Far from printing his sentiments in a different typeface to facilitate skipping, he reprinted his *Sentiments* in a different book to discourage it. Yet this was not for want of anticipating the resistance that Haywood attributes to a young, female reader. Indeed, Richardson's second *Collection*, published in the same year as Haywood's novel, targets not the priggish readers addressed in the preface to the 1751 anthology, but, on the contrary, readers who share Miss Loyter's esthetic: "young People; who are apt to read rapidly wth. a View only to *Story*." "I thought my End wou'd be better answered," Richardson adds, "by giving at one View Ye Pith & Marrow of what they had been reading, perhaps with some Approbation; in order to revive in their Minds ye *Occasions* on which ye Things were supposed to be said & done, ye better to assist them in ye Application of ye Moral."[23] What Richardson elsewhere calls the "demand [for] story" forces not only the writer but his readers to "hasten." "Story" becomes synonymous with speed, "sentiments" with enforced stasis.

In retrospect, Richardson's losing battle against his readers' "engagement" suggests that the sententious passages which pepper the novel itself are designed less (through their content) to inculcate specific moral lessons than (through their structure) to regulate the pace of reading. Far from subordinating esthetic considerations to artless moral seriousness, the maxims obey a formal logic, even an emptily formalist one. The *Moral Sentiments* teach not so much how to live as how to read. Although the anthology claims to cover a whole range of conduct issues, stretching encyclopedically from the advantages of Absence to the dangers of Zeal by way of humaneness to horses and humility to husbands, the only moral virtue that it succeeds in enforcing is, very simply, the self-restraint needed to refrain from skipping. The *Collection* preaches patience under adversity, but teaches patience with boredom.

Like Johnson's opposition between those who read for the story and those who read for the sentiment, like Reeve's implied distinction between "those who have a mind to see an Epitome" and those (including the speaker) who scorn abridgments, like Charlotte's contrast between the English and the French, the prefaces to Richardson's *Collections* compare not only two modes of discourse but two kinds of readers. Yet that difference dissolved once the 1755 *Collection* acknowledged that the same maxims which blocked some readers' impetus tempted others to the even worse vice of skimming. Every reader his own abridger. Richardson's fear of being read "wth. a View only to *Story*" rests on the assumption that the youngest and laziest readers know how to identify different modes of novelistic discourse as systematically as any professional editor. The opposition between those who read for sentiment and those who read for story depends on their shared ability to tell an "incident" apart from a "maxim" – even without the aid of the contrasting typefaces which Miss Loyter proposes. Hence the need for the *Collection*'s counterattack. The harder the young, the ignorant, and the idle try to read "wth. a View only to Story," the more they need "at one View Ye Pith & Marrow" crammed down their throats, undiluted. The repetition of the word "View" defines the anti-narrative organization of the *Collection* as a polemical strategy designed to correct or even to punish readers' putative desires. The anthology saves readers from the vice of impatience only by ensuring that there is nothing to skip ahead to.

The conclusion of the sentence collapses the distinction between those two "Views," however. The phrase "in order to revive in their Minds ye Occasions on which ye Things were supposed to be said and done" suggests that the *Collection* sets out not to divorce generalizable "sentiments" from particular "story," but to anchor one to the other. The novels themselves are also the "Occasions on which ye Things" were previously read: the *Collection of* . . . *Sentiments* depends for its audience on the popularity of the "stories" that it claims to replace. In fact, although the 1755 *Collection* was published only as an independent volume, its predecessor in 1751 had appeared not only as half of a self-contained book but also appended to the third edition of *Clarissa*. Once issued between separate covers, the 1751 *Collection* and the 1749 table of contents shift genres: from back matter to anthology, from front matter to abridgment. Even in its content, moreover, the 1751 *Collection* is less free of "story" than Richardson claims. Its moral generalizations rub up against illustrative statements that verge on plot summary. Under "Repentance" we learn that "Lovelace lived not to repent!"; under "Passion," that "The command of her Passions was *Clarissa*'s glory"; under "Comedies," "Mr. *Lovelace*, Mrs. *Sinclair*, *Sally Martin*, *Polly Horton*, Miss *Partington*, love not tragedies." The *Collection of Sentiments* is also a collection of stories. Conversely, a plot summary can be labeled a collection of beauties: the most popular eighteenth-century abridgment, *The Paths of Virtue*, reappeared in 1813 as *The Beauties of Richardson*.

In the same way that Richardson used the *Collection* to "separate [maxims] from that chain of engaging incidents," he experimented in *Sir Charles Grandison* with a division of labor between two indexes, one of "similes and allusions" and another "historical and characteristical." The second index is dominated by narrative entries, above all by a fifteen-page plot summary *s.v.* "Grandison, Sir Charles" – a heading whose similarity to the title of *The History of Sir Charles Grandison* identifies the entry as an abridgment of the novel. Moreover, the biographical order within each entry clashes with the topical alphabetical order that governs the index as a whole. In the "historical" index, the narrative entries are interspersed with a series of generalizations ranging from "absence of lovers, promotive of a cure for Love" through "Zeal." Conversely, the index of similes – a collection that runs from "Bachelors, old, and old maids, compared To haunted houses" to "Women out of character, To bats" – slips details from the plot of *Grandison* into its list of all-purpose literary commonplaces. Perhaps the most hackneyed simile to be indexed, "L., Earl of, proud of his infant-son, To a peacock," would have fit into the "index characteristical" at least as well as in the index of similes in which it actually appears. The list of "similes and allusions" that sets out to extract stylistic beauties from plot soon becomes indistinguishable from the "index historical" that undertakes to strip plot of stylistic verbiage.

In other words, while each "Epitome" of the novels – abridgment, table of contents, collection of sentiments, index – attempts to resolve the tension between story and sentiment by pulling the texts in one direction or the other, ultimately they reveal instead the impossibility of composing an anthology devoid of narrative order or a plot that does not crumble into anthology-pieces. The *Collection* and the back matter of *Grandison* both end up collapsing "story" with the "sentiment" from which they set out to distinguish it. As E. S. Dallas admits with mock disappointment in the preface to his abridgment of *Clarissa*, Richardson "has so interwoven [his "preaching"] with the story that it is impossible to cut it all out."[24]

That interweaving culminated in Richardson's third supplement to *Clarissa*, the *Meditations from the Sacred Books . . . mentioned in the HISTORY OF CLARISSA as drawn up by her for her own use. To each of which is prefixed, A Short Historical Account, Connecting it with the Story* (1750). This peculiar volume can best be described as an anthology *en abîme*. It excerpts from the novel the devotional texts that the novel represented Clarissa excerpting from what is, as Belford officiously reminds Lovelace, itself already an anthology: "this all-excelling collection of beauties, the Bible" (*Clarissa*, 364.1126). The advertisement presents the *Meditations* as a shorter source for the moral lessons of *Clarissa*, addressed to "those Persons who have not read the Volumes, or think they shall not have either patience or leisure to read them, and who may yet dip into the following Pages."[25] The book sandwiches excerpts with summaries: a "historical account" – what we would call a plot summary – introduces each meditation, and a "very brief account of the Heroine's part in the Work, as given by Mr. Belford" prefaces the whole (*Meditations*, iii). Like anthologies, the *Meditations* selects some portions of the text and excises others; but like abridgments, it addresses readers who lack "patience" or "leisure." More specifically, it provides a formal model for later abridgers' use of third-person editorial summaries to connect first-person excerpts.

The difference is that the *Meditations* amplifies as much as it compresses. At the same time as the collection subtracts everything but the meditations from *Clarissa* (and by isolating Clarissa's writing from Lovelace's, eliminates the hero's "part in the work"), it adds thirty-two meditations absent from the novel itself. By summarizing the plot while supplementing the beauties, the *Meditations* makes the scale of the text as elastic as the size of the material pages which change from duodecimo in one edition to octavo in the next. When Richardson adds to or subtracts from *Clarissa*, he defines it as an aggregate of modular parts rather than an indissoluble whole.

In alternately expanding and contracting the novel, the *Meditations* anticipated the divided structure of the volume in which the *Sentiments ... Contained in the History of Clarissa* later appeared. The *Collection* occupies only the second half of a book whose first part consists of addenda to earlier editions of *Clarissa*. The title of the whole runs *Letters and Passages Restored from the Original Manuscripts of the History of CLARISSA. To which is subjoined, A Collection of ... Sentiments.* The "Passages Restored" reproduce those portions of the text that appeared for the first time in the second and third editions, ostensibly in order to spare owners of the first edition from having to buy another. Although many of those passages have been shown to respond to criticisms made only after the publication of the first edition, the title terms them "restored" – not added.[26] Similarly, even though the *Meditations* appeared two years after the first edition of the novel, Richardson presents it as the full-length original from which the meditations in *Clarissa* itself were excerpted, explaining that "The Editor of the History of Clarissa having transcribed, for the use of some select friends, the Thirty-Six Meditations of Clarissa, only Four of which are inserted in the History, they were urgent with him to give them to the Public" (*Meditations*, 1). Retrospectively defining the original edition as an abridgment, this account positions Richardson as a censor rather than a writer, an "editor" whose task is not to produce texts but to sift them. The autobiographical fiction that the meditations and passages were restored from an original manuscript reinforces the biographical fiction that they were written by the characters. Both present new compositions as found objects; both figure the author as an anthologist.

Like the *Collection of Sentiments*, the *Meditations* defines itself at once as a self-contained anthology and as a supplement whose interest depends on the original narrative. The effect of publishing devotional texts separate from the profane fiction in which they first appeared is undercut by the inclusion of the "Historical Account, Connecting [them] with the Story." Those prefatory accounts of the circumstances under which each meditation was composed make the *Meditations* borrow its chronological order from its inscribed author's biography and its interest from the plot of the novel, in the same way that the promise to "revive in [readers'] Minds ye Occasions on which ye Things were supposed to be said & done" cancels out at once the independence and the anti-narrative agenda of both collections. At the same time, the claim that the plot summaries "connect" the fragments – to *Clarissa*, but also to one another – recalls the announcement that the table of contents to the second edition of *Clarissa* will "shew the Connexion of the whole." Both derive narrative continuity from an editorial apparatus imposed after the fact.[27]

In the process of alternating lyric "meditations" with "historical accounts," the _Meditations_ balances fragment against "connection" and "sentiment" against "story." By interspersing first-person homodiegetic present-tense meditations with third-person heterodiegetic past-tense narratives, it juxtaposes one series of texts that reproduces the immediacy of Richardson's characteristic "writing to the moment" and "instantaneous descriptions" with another that anticipates the narrative distance of the earliest abridgments (_Clarissa_, 36). At the same time, its technique of connecting first-person excerpts by omniscient retrospective summaries shows a striking resemblance to the strategy of nineteenth-century abridgers. The "historical accounts" bear the same relation to Clarissa's excerpts from the Bible that later editors' plot summaries bear to excerpts from _Clarissa_. The fact that each meditation is dated like a letter makes the similarity even more apparent. In the _Meditations_, Richardson anticipated his readers' impulse to bracket signed and dated first-person extracts by summaries in the voice of an unidentified and temporally unsituated narrator – the voice shared by the table of contents to _Clarissa_, the "index historical" of _Grandison_, and the "historical accounts" in the _Meditations_.

The urge to contain letters within more impersonal narrative can be traced back even farther to _Clarissa_ itself. The first edition already frames the letters by a series of third-person paratexts: preface, afterword, list of characters, and a past-tense conclusion "summarily relating" the events following Lovelace's death. Within the text itself, Richardson intersperses some letters with editorial footnotes, summarizes others, and transposes still others into the third person.[28] As the novel nears its end, the editorial apparatus begins to replace the letters instead of simply supplementing them. Italicized "abstracts" are substituted for parts of Clarissa's posthumous letters: "as they are written on the same subject, and are pretty long, it is thought proper to abstract them" (_Clarissa_, 492.1376). The editor characterizes letters ("The posthumous letter to Miss Howe is exceedingly tender and affectionate" [_Clarissa_, 492.1377]); summarizes them in indirect discourse ("She remembers herself to her foster-brother in a very kind manner: and charges [her foster-mother], for his sake, that she will not take too much to heart what has befallen her" [_Clarissa_ 503.1406]); tags them with "says she," "she tells her," "she prays" (_Clarissa_, 492.1376–77); and even provides tables of contents for individual letters: "This letter contains in substance: 'Her thanks to the good woman for her care of her in her infancy; for her good instructions and the excellent example she had set her: with self-accusations'" (*Clarissa*, 503.1406). While the *Meditations* and post-1868 abridgments abandon the epistolary mode, both faithfully reproduce and even accentuate a more basic formal characteristic of *Clarissa*: the structure that pits signature against anonymity, dilation against summary, immediacy against distance.

MEANING AND GAPING

Like its abridgers, *Clarissa* ends up recanting the inscription of authorship. The body of the text, in which each letter is signed, gives way to a "Conclusion supposed to be written by Mr Belford" (*Clarissa*, 1489) – a title which pointedly refrains from endorsing that ascription. The "Postscript" which follows multiplies anonymous authorship. It opens with a description of the debate between author and readers: "The author of the foregoing work has been favoured, in the course of its publication, with many anonymous letters, in which the writers have differently expressed their wishes as to what they apprehended of the catastrophe" (*Clarissa*, 1495). Although the identity of the authors of the postscript and of the letters is not specified, their gender is: "Most of [the letters] directed to him by the gentler sex turn in favour of what they call a *fortunate ending*" (*Clarissa*, 1495). The italics distance the author from the vocabulary of the "gentler sex," which will be immediately countered with the masculine "authority" of Aristotle as summarized by Addison (*Clarissa*, 1498). The difference between the author and his correspondents mirrors the contrast between letters and editorial summaries in the novel itself. They are female, he is male. Their form is epistolary, his is not. He refers to himself in the third person, while at least some of them presumably refer to themselves in the first. There are many of them (each expressing "different" views) and only one of him. Yet despite these contrasts, "the author" has something in common with his correspondents: like them, he refrains from naming himself. Multiple correspondents give way first to a single editor and then to letters with no signature, which in turn are summarized (and rebutted) by an author with no name.

By paraphrasing the letters that it refrains from reproducing, the postscript draws attention to the novel's eleventh-hour repudiation of the epistolary mode. The second and third editions extend that process by swamping the epistolary body of the text in a series of paratextual

frames: table of contents, supplementary footnotes, collection of sentiments, index.[29] Within the covers of the first edition as much as over the
course of its publication history, *Clarissa* set into motion the shift towards
a single impersonal voice that abridgments would eventually complete.

The postscript rejects not just the letter but the anthology. Its speaker
claims an authority unavailable to the narrator of the preface, who
claimed only to compile others' letters. The novel begins by mentioning
only "the editor to whom it was referred to publish the whole," but ends
by alluding to "the author of the foregoing work" (*Clarissa*, 35, 1495). In
1751, that last-minute replacement of "editor" by "author" came to be
reinforced by an equally belated bid to redefine Clarissa from a deriva-
tive reader to an original writer. The third edition supplements the
portrait of Clarissa that Anna provides in the first by the startling new
information that "Altho' she was well re'd in the English, French, and
Italian Poets, and had re'd the best translations of the Latin Classics; yet
seldom did she quote or repeat from them, either in her Letters or
Conversation."[30]

Anna's historical revisionism comes too late to be credible, for quotations riddle Clarissa's letters, and the rape causes her to substitute
quotation for narration altogether. The commonplace-book-like "Paper
X" that she produces immediately afterwards consists almost entirely of
excerpts from Otway, Dryden, Shakespeare, Cowley, and Garth
(*Clarissa*, 261.893). The meditations that appear next are pieced together
from biblical quotations. More loosely, the rape prompts Clarissa's
project of compiling other characters' letters to form the corpus that will
eventually become the novel.[31] Instead of narrating, Clarissa "collects."
"The particulars of my story, and the base arts of this vile man will, I
think, be best collected from those very letters of his," she writes to Anna
(*Clarissa*, 379.1163). Belford borrows the vocabulary of the commonplace
book to refer to the "extracts" from those letters that Clarissa asks him
to transcribe, as well as to the "meditation[s] . . . extracted by the lady
from the Scriptures" (*Clarissa*, 387.1174, 389.1176, 391.1177, 391.1178,
364.1124). As Belford reports, Clarissa "acknowledges that, if all [Love-
lace's] letters are written with equal decency and justice, as I have
assured her they are, she shall think herself freed from the necessity of
writing her own story" (*Clarissa*, 391.1178). "Writing" gives way to
"collection," autobiographical narrative to "extracts." Quotations replace Clarissa's body as easily as her story: when Belford asks Lovelace
"if thou canst relish a divine beauty," the noun refers not to Clarissa but
to the excerpt she has transcribed (*Clarissa*, 364.1124). The "mad papers"

alone would reduce Anna's praise of Clarissa's self-restraint to empty obituary piety.

In a novel whose heroine spends so much of her time copying out others' words, however, it is hard to understand why Anna should assume citation to be incompatible with virtue. Clarissa's refusal to quote sticks out in the list of her more conventional moral attributes like charity and early rising. We can begin to understand its logic only if we remember that at the same time as the third edition dissociates its heroine from quotation, it amplifies the role of a despicable minor character whose letters contain little else. In 1751, Richardson added twenty new pages and two new letters by the pedantic clergyman Brand, who had appeared in the first edition only fleetingly as the author of one short letter slandering Clarissa. In the "passages restored," Brand's verbosity more than compensates for his quick exit from the first edition. The third edition also gives him an ambition to marry Clarissa which the first edition had not even hinted at. Brand's new fantasy of social mobility projects onto the plot itself the editorial logic that allots him twenty extra pages – almost as if he knew that his importance had grown in the three years that separate the first edition from the third, and wanted to translate that textual promotion into its social equivalent.

The twenty "restored" pages signed by Brand appear gratuitous: their comic tone jars in the pages leading up to Clarissa's death, and they contribute nothing to the anti-Lovelacean polemic that motivates the other "passages restored."[32] One of the few critics who attempt to explain their function, Thomas Beebee, identifies Brand as a figure for intertextuality but goes on to dismiss him as a foil for the novel's two "strong readers," Clarissa and Lovelace.[33] The contrast is accurate as far as it goes, but does not mean that Brand should be ignored in favor of the strong readers with whom critics prefer to identify. Brand gains prominence in the third edition, I want to argue, precisely because his vanity and self-consciousness spur him to formulate a theory of what could be called weak reading – a theory that challenges the model of intellectual property on which the novel depends.

Of the countless undesirable suitors who pester Clarissa, Brand may well be the worst. Solmes at least notices her reluctance to marry him, but Brand imagines that they will make a perfect match. The proof is their common sententiousness. "With *these*, Sir, and *an hundred more*, wise *adages*, which I have always at my fingers' ends, will I (when reduced to *form* and *method*) entertain Miss," he exults; "and as she is a *well-read*, and (I might say, but for this *one* great error) a *wise* young Lady, I make no doubt but that I shall *prevail* upon her, if not by *mine own arguments*; by those of *wits* and *capacities* that have a congeniality (as I may say) to *her own*."³⁴ The novel takes care, however, to disprove Brand's claim that the wisdom of his "wise adages" is the same as the wisdom of the "wise young Lady." The third edition makes a point of dissociating Clarissa's writing from masculine pedantry. Anna contrasts Clarissa to scholars who "call [their performances] MASCULINE," "spangle over their productions with *metaphors*," and "sinking into the *classical pits*, there poke and scramble about, never seeking to shew genius of their own; all their lives spent in common-place *quotation*; fit only to write *Notes* and *Comments* upon other peoples *Texts*."³⁵ Coming in the wake of Anna's more explicit comparison, the implausibility of Brand's marriage fantasy exorcizes the worrying possibility that the pedant and the compiler might form a logical pair.

The first edition had made Clarissa's strategy of borrowing others' words a proof of modesty: her substitute for shameful self-exposure in a court of law. But by pairing the denial that Clarissa quotes with the insistence that Brand does, the third edition changes quotation to a sign of self-importance. At the same time, the ludicrously serious notes and commentary that Brand appends to his own letters parody Richardson's project of dignifying his epistolary fictions with the editorial apparatus added (along with Brand's letters and commentary) between the first and third editions. Indeed, Brand describes his letter in the same terms that Richardson applies to the *Collection of Sentiments*:

This is *a Letter*, and not *a Letter*, as I may say; but a kind of *short* and *pithy Discourse*, touching upon *various* and *sundry topics*, every one of which might be a *fit theme* to enlarge upon, even to volumes: If this *epistolary Discourse* (then let me call it) should be pleasing to you (as I am inclined to think it will, because of the *sentiments* and *aphorisms* of the *wisest* of the *antients*, which *glitter thro' it* like so many dazzling *sun-beams*), I will (at my leisure) work it up into a *methodical Discourse*; and perhaps may one day print it, . . . *singly* at first . . . and afterwards in my *Works*.³⁶

Brand's reference to "sentiments and aphorisms" repeats the title of Richardson's *Collection of such of the Moral and Instructive SENTIMENTS [and] APHORISMS . . . contained in the History*. His description of the letter as "pithy" and "fit to enlarge upon, even to volumes" anticipates Richardson's description of the 1755 *Collection* as the "pith and marrow of 19 Volumes."³⁷ Brand defines himself even more explicitly as an anthologizer when he calls attention to his habit of "pointing out to [Mr. Harlowe] many *beauties* of the *authors I quote*, which otherwise would lie concealed from *him*, as they must from every *common observer*."

You will perhaps, Mr. Walton, wonder at the meaning of the lines *drawn under many of the words and sentences* (UNDERSCORING we call it); and were my letters to be printed, those would be put in a *different character*. Now, you must know, Sir, that *we learned men* do this to point out to the readers who are not *so learned*, where the *jet of our arguments lieth*, and the *emphasis* they are to lay upon *those words;* whereby they will take in readily our *sense* and *cogency*. Some *pragmatical* people have said, that an author who doth a *great deal of this*, either calleth his readers *fools*, or tacitly condemneth *his own style*, as supposing his meaning would be dark without it . . . [But] to give a very *pretty tho' familiar illustration*, I have considered a page distinguished by *different characters*, as a *verdant field* overspread with *butter-flowers* and *daisies*, and other summer-flowers.[38]

Brand's anxiety about his use of "underscoring" calls attention to Richardson's addition of copious didactic italics throughout the edition in which his letter first appears.[39] The character's fear of "call[ing] his readers fools, or tacitly condemn[ing] his own style, as supposing his meaning would be dark without it" betrays the author/printer's anxiety about the typographical emphasis used in the third edition to close off the interpretive freedom that the first had offered readers.[40]

Richardson's personal correspondence betrays the same double ambivalence about his use of editorial apparatus in the third edition, and of quotation from the first. One letter shifts from discussing the index of *Grandison* to mocking the paratextual baggage weighing down another book:

We are now fallen into an age of Dictionary and Index-Learning; and a Man must make a Figure that seems to go deeper, and can overcharge the Margins of the Books he writes, with Quotations from Authors of Ancient Date. But then there are always, however sparingly sprinkled, in the grossest, in the laziest Ages, true Genius's, who can, if they will, direct the Public Taste, and expose the *Ventilators*.[41]

Nothing if not "overcharged," *Clarissa* combines pointing fingers in the margins (first edition), index (second edition) and a system of marginal bullets marking revisions (third edition). More strikingly, the book that Richardson is criticizing here, Charles Peters's *A Critical Dissertation on the Book of Job*, takes for its subject the same biblical text from which Clarissa draws nearly half of her meditations. The opposition between "Genius's" and "Ventilators" reappears in another letter of the same year that contrasts "Persons of Genius" with "Commonplace-Men," a phrase that borrows pejorative force from the pun on "placemen," as if quotation were as ethically suspect as political opportunism.[42] Brand's pedantry and Anna's praise of not quoting belatedly bring that anxiety about the appropriation of other texts into the novel itself.

But Brand is not the only one who turns Clarissa's taste for quotation against her. Even Anthony Harlowe, distinguished for neither literacy nor religious zeal, taunts her with biblical quotations (*Clarissa*, 406.1196); meanwhile, Lovelace introduces an excerpt from the Book of Job with the boast that "I can quote a text as well as she" (*Clarissa*, 416:1217). And he can. After intercepting a letter in which Anna advises Clarissa to leave him, Lovelace replaces it with a forgery urging just the opposite, which he pieces together by copying some passages from the original, suppressing others, and adding spurious "connexions" in their place (*Clarissa*, 239.811). His success in recycling Anna's words for his own ends makes clear how much the legibility of each passage depends on its context.

It also suggests that expurgating old texts can be more effective than composing new ones. Not content to excise compromising passages from specific letters, as when he reads aloud bowdlerized epistolary extracts to the women in Hampstead (*Clarissa*, 233.781), Lovelace expurgates the entire correspondence (and indeed the archive on which the novel itself is based) by refusing to receive Clarissa's letter retracting her consent to the elopement – an omission that ultimately leads to her flight, rape, and death (*Clarissa*, 99.399). It may be appropriate, then, that his hand is represented graphically as an instrument not of writing but of editing. When Lovelace uses marginal fingers to mark the passages of Anna's letter that require his "animadversion" or deletion, he literalizes the indexes of *Clarissa* and *Grandison* while parodying the marginal bullets used by Richardson to signal textual variants between editions (*Clarissa*, 229.743).

Lovelace is not the last Richardsonian character to censor a letter, however. The marginal hand reappears in *Sir Charles Grandison* to signal those parts of a letter which the heroine, Harriet Byron, wants her correspondent not to read aloud (*Grandison*, 2.6.290). In turn, Harriet divides a satirical letter from her friend Charlotte Grandison into a half to be copied out and a half to be suppressed:

What a Letter you have written! There is no separating the good from the bad in it . . . I skipt this passage – Read that [aloud] – 'um – 'um – 'um – Then skipt again . . . What are the parts of this wicked Letter, for which I can sincerely thank you? – O my dear, I cannot, cannot, without soiling my fingers, pick them out . . . I will transcribe all the good things in it; and some morning . . . I will transcribe the intolerable passages; so make two Letters of it. One I will keep to shew my friends here, in order to increase, if possible, their admiration of my Charlotte; the bad one I will present to you. I know I shall transcribe it in a violent hurry – Not much matter whether it be legible, or not . . . If half of it *be* illegible, enough will be left to make you blush for the whole . . . In all my future letters, I will write as if I had never seen this your naughty one . . . I may better justify my displeasure at some parts of your Letter, by the observance I will pay to others. (*Grandison*, 6.28.117–20)

Harriet's refusal to acknowledge the "naughty" parts of Charlotte's correspondence has the same effect as Lovelace's refusal to accept the letter left by Clarissa in the garden wall. She expurgates those passages twice: first by omitting to read them aloud and "pick[ing] them out" from the copy circulated to friends; next by copying them to form a deliberately illegible anthology, a collection of negative beauties which is itself only a sampling of extracts ("enough to make you blush for the whole"). Her attempt to split Charlotte's letter down the middle, balancing "displeasure" with "observance" and "some parts of your letter" with "others," suggests that the memorialization which the anthology guarantees some passages is inseparable from the oblivion to which it consigns others.

"You know my meaning by my gaping," Charlotte herself explains (*Grandison*, 7.2.262).[43] For Richardson, expression can rarely be separated from suppression. Brand asks his correspondent to inspect the letters he receives for passages that might offend a third party, and to "paste those lines over with *blue or black paper*" before passing it along to him.[44] That third reader, Belford, himself expurgates the letter from James Harlowe that he copies for Lovelace (*Clarissa*, 494.1381), the letter from Morden that he transcribes for Anna (521.1452), and the letters from Lovelace that he reads aloud to Clarissa (339.1077, 387.1174, 446.1297). "I read to [Clarissa] such parts of [Lovelace's] letters as I *could* read to her," he reports; "and I thought it was a good test to distinguish the froth and whipped-syllabub in them from the cream, in what one *could* and could *not* read to a woman of so fine a mind" (446.1297).

Lovelace's rakish language makes it logical for his letters to require expurgation. What is more surprising is that not even Richardson's moral paragon is safe from it. On the contrary, Sir Charles Grandison's letters are excised more heavily than anyone else's. The trail of twentieth-century abridgers is blazed by the well-named secretary Dr. Bartlett, a sort of scribal publisher who strings together snippets from Grandison's letters with third-person plot summaries as deftly as Lovelace assembles excerpts from Anna's: "transcrib[ing] parts of Sir Charles' letters, adding a few lines here and there, by way of connexion"

(*Grandison*, 3.22.137). Grandison's exemplary letters circulate in so many copies that they come to be edited as thoroughly as any published correspondence. Just as Richardson's popularity creates a market for different versions aimed at different segments of his audience – full texts and abridgments, cheap and expensive editions, *Clarissa* for the general public but the *Meditations* for only a few personal friends – Grandison's letters reach their addressees unabridged but are copied selectively for a voyeuristic public.[45] One letter even passes through two stages of excerpting, when Bartlett shows "some of its contents" to Harriet, who in turn selects a smaller fraction of the text to send to Lucy, after requesting Bartlett's authorization – the editor's, not the author's – to transcribe it (*Grandison*, 4.2.265). The self-willed Olivia, however, dispenses with Bartlett's mediation to expurgate Grandison's letters herself: "Your Letter (for I have erased one officious passage in it) is in my bosom all day. It is on my pillow at night. The last thing, and the first thing, do I read it. The contents make my rest balmy, and my rising serene. But it was not until after I had read it the seventh time, and after I had erased that obnoxious passage, that it began to have that happy effect upon me" (*Grandison*, 5.42.644). Reciprocally, the object of all these editorial attentions expects others to censor what they show him. After their wedding, Grandison tells Harriet that "You must make marks against the passages in the Letters you shall have the goodness to communicate, which you would not have me read" (*Grandison*, 7.5.270). Even within the privacy of the Grandisons' model marriage, letters can neither be received without being reproduced, nor be reproduced without being expurgated.

The very first letter of *Sir Charles Grandison* calls into question the feasibility of that process, however. The novel begins with Greville first reading aloud to Lucy "some passages from the copy of his [letter]," and then giving her the papers themselves with some phrases ineffectually crossed out: he "scratched over two passages, and that with so many little flourishes (as you will see) that he thought they could not be read. But the ink [Lucy] furnished him with happening to be paler than his," the passages remain (*Grandison*, 1.1.8). Although Greville's attempt at censorship opens the novel with the threat that the integrity of texts is always under attack, Lucy's defeat of his stratagem suggests from the outset that texts will resist attempts to fragment them. Harriet's project of "mak[ing] two Letters of" one fails too, because "there is no separating the good from the bad"; and, more concretely, because Mr. Selby detects the pauses in her reading and snatches the letter to examine in full. While the publishing history of Richardson's novels suggests that his readers have often preferred excerpts to full texts, the characters within the novels themselves unanimously resist epistolary abridgment. Mr. Selby's refusal to hear only part of Charlotte's letter repeats the scene in *Clarissa* where Anna Howe seizes a letter from which her mother is reading aloud selections (197.623) – a protest which Mrs. Howe eventually reciprocates by refusing to trust Anna's transmission of extracts from Clarissa's letters (*Clarissa*, 27.132). Lovelace's forgery of Anna's letters ultimately confirms Mrs. Howe's assumption that excerpts distort their originals. Writers like Lovelace and Harriet exploit the slippage from anthology to expurgation that readers like Selby, Anna, and Mrs. Howe suspect.[46] In making the parts misrepresent the whole, Richardson's characters discredit the figure of synecdoche.

"COPY IN OTHER HANDS"

One explanation for Richardson's ambivalence about quotations, then, is their vulnerability to manipulation. Brand's "restored" letter suggests another: that the ownership of quotations lies securely neither with the author who quotes nor with the author quoted. Brand warns that:

If [Belford] insisteth on taking a copy of my Letter (for he, or any-body, that *seeth it*, or *heareth it read*, will, no doubt, be glad to have by them the copy of a Letter so full of the *sentiments of the noblest writers of antiquity*, and *so well adapted*, as I will be bold to say they are, to the *point in hand*; I say, if he insisteth on taking a copy) let him give you the *strongest assurances* not to suffer it to be *printed, on any account*; and I make the same request to you, that *you* will not. For if any-thing be to be made of a *man's works*, who but the *author*, should have the *advantage*? . . . I have been told, that a *certain noble Lord*, who once sat himself down to write a *pamphlet* in behalf of a *great minister*, after taking *infinite pains* to *no purpose* to find a *Latin motto*, gave commission to a friend of *his* to offer to *any one*, who could help him to a *suitable one*, but of one or two lines, a *hamper of claret*. . . . If then *one* or *two* lines were of so much worth (A *hamper of claret!* No *less!*) of what *inestimable value* would *such a Letter as mine* be deemed? – And who knoweth but that this noble P——r (who is now living) if he should happen to see *this Letter* shining with such a *glorious string of jewels*, might give the *writer* a *scarf*?[47]

Brand moves here from his earlier floral simile (italics as daisies) to the lapidary metaphor which provides its most conventional alternative. While the comparison of quotations with jewels equates esthetic with monetary value, the mention of the scarf suggests more specifically that literature can be exchanged for goods. Yet Brand's fantasy of receiving gifts from a patron softens the commercialism of his competing plan to publish his letters for financial "advantage."

Brand's theory of literary property contradicts itself. He claims at once that compilers should own what they quote – since living English scholars, not dead Latin writers, earn the claret or the scarf – and that compilers do not own what they quote, since no one "but the author, should have the advantage." If the second claim were true – that is, if Brand were correct in denying Belford's right to collect and sell his words – then the legitimacy of the novel as a whole would collapse. It is no more problematic for Belford to print the letters of one of Clarissa's suitors (Brand) than for him to print a novel composed largely of the letters of another of her suitors (Lovelace). On the contrary: far from authorizing Belford to show those incriminating documents to Clarissa, let alone to the general public, Lovelace demands his letters back from Belford more insistently than Brand ever does. And although Belford does in fact "make something" of Lovelace's "works," what he makes – the novel – is very far from giving their "author" any "advantage." While Brand imagines that Belford's publication of his letter will inspire a P——r to give him a scarf, Belford's circulation of Lovelace's letters causes the only peer in *Clarissa* to disown him. Belford's growing prominence in the plot combines with Lovelace's concomitant disempowerment to demonstrate an author's punitive eclipse by his editor.

At the same time, Brand's uncertainty about whether the profits of a book should go to the author or the compiler reflects Richardson's own vacillation about which name – author, editor, publisher – to claim his own property under. The texts that we now call Richardson's bear a superabundance of competing signatories: inscribed letter-writers, inscribed editors like Belford and Bartlett, the unidentified "editor" mentioned in the prefaces and on the title-pages of *Clarissa* and *Grandison*, the equally unnamed "author" to whom the postscript of *Clarissa* alludes, and finally the publisher identified as S. Richardson.[48] Richardson's name appears on the title-pages of the first editions, not on the top half of the page, where the author's name conventionally appears – a space filled instead, in the later novels, by "the Editor of PAMELA" and "the Editor of PAMELA and CLARISSA" – but at the bottom, as the printer's name.

Layout makes visible a problem that faced Richardson throughout his career: how to claim ownership of texts while disclaiming authorship of their contents. That dilemma became apparent as soon as the popularity of the first two volumes of *Pamela* prompted others to produce sequels (at least four in the year following its publication). Richardson criticized the publisher of one, in a private letter, for "giving out, that I was not the Writer of the two [volumes] (which, indeed, I wish, and did not intend should be known to more than 6 Friends and those in Confidence)."[49] Richardson's fear that other authors might fill the vacuum left by his anonymity extended to the characters who function as inscribed authors within the novels themselves. The contradictory logic of his protest against rival sequels reappeared in his declaration that "I want not the letters [in *Clarissa*] to be thought genuine" but that "they should not be prefatically owned not to be genuine."[50] Characters became competitors. Eventually, the publication of a pirated Irish edition of *Sir Charles Grandison* forced Richardson to contradict in the back matter the fiction of collective composition constructed by the text itself. The first edition of *Grandison* ends with an "Address to the Public" giving an account of Richardson's battle with the pirates (interspersed, in a continuation of the epistolary form, with "extracts" from their correspondence), whom it attacks for stealing "a property so absolutely his own." In a separately published polemic, *The Case of Samuel Richardson . . . with Regard to the Invasion of his Property in The History of Sir Charles Grandison* (1753), Richardson traces that absolute ownership to his double function as writer and printer: "Never was Work more the Property of any Man, than *this* is his. The Copy was never in any other Hand: He borrows not from any Author: The Paper, the Printing, entirely at his own Expence."[51] By invoking his peculiar status as author/printer, Richardson sidesteps the need to specify whether his "Property" is intellectual or material. His overdetermined claim opposes private property at once to intellectual collaboration in procuring ideas ("he borrows not from any Author") and to financial collaboration in procuring materials ("The Paper, the Printing, entirely at his own Expence"). While the first clause overlooks Richardson's heavy use of quotations, the second denies the collective nature of the publishing industry more generally. *Grandison* was vulnerable to piracy only because it had been, at various points in the printing process, "in other Hand[s]": literally, in the hands of the journeymen bribed to leak the sheets to the Dublin booksellers. The chirographic authenticity invoked by the assertion that "the Copy was never in any other Hand" makes no sense for a printed book.

The generic implications of that claim become more explicit in a letter which again disclaims any "borrowing." "Have I not written a monstrous quantity; nineteen or twenty close written volumes?"

Richardson asks. "And for what? To propagate, instead of virtue, theft, robbery, and abuse from the wild Irish and to be forced to defend *a property all my own; that is to say, neither a compilation, nor borrowed from any body*."[52] Richardson's denial that *Grandison* can be called a "compilation" contradicts the preface which terms it a "collection" – and, even more literally, his use of "compilement" as a synonym for epistolary narrative in *Clarissa*, whose heroine describes the collection of letters as "a compilement to be made of all that relates to my Story" (*Clarissa*, 507.1418). The structure of that novel prefigured the course of its author/publisher's career: just as *Clarissa* moves from an "editor"'s preface to an "author"'s postscript, competition eventually forced Richardson to substitute ever more vehement assertions of absolute ownership for his original self-presentation as an "editor" of a correspondence composed by many others.

Yet commercial rivals were not the only threat to Richardson's authority. His admirers appropriated his novels as prolifically as his enemies did: Aaron Hill suggested titles and prefaces, Solomon Lowe sent Richardson an unsolicited forerunner of the *Collection of Sentiments*, and Lady Echlin composed an alternative ending to *Clarissa*.[53] Her sister, Lady Bradshaigh, accepted Richardson's invitation for friends to write a sequel to *Grandison* which he himself would merely edit, so "that every one of my Correspondents, at his or her own Choice, assume one of the surviving Characters in the Story, and write in it; and that . . . I shall pick and choose, alter, connect, and accommodate, till I have completed from [the contributions], the requested Volume."[54] The collaboration that Richardson proposed mirrors the competition that he feared – rather as Brand's worry that Belford would sell his letter for unauthorized publication had translated into cruder commercial terms Lovelace's awareness that Belford had circulated his letters as part of a narrative very different from the one that he would have chosen to write.

That Richardson's novels elicited continuations from both aristocratic amateurs and commercial competitors does not mean that the two kinds of sequel were interchangeable. Where Lady Echlin's and Lady Bradshaigh's represented personal compliments to the author of *Clarissa* and *Grandison*, the sequels to *Pamela* denied Richardson's authorship altogether. Yet within a model of literary property that assigns every text to a single author, collaboration can appear nearly as criminal as the "theft [and] robbery" to which Richardson compares piracy. In the introduction to her richly-annotated edition of *Grandison*,

Jocelyn Harris explains that she chose the first edition as her copy-text because

almost all of the substantial changes of the revised editions were made not for aesthetic purposes but rather in deference or response to the opinions of Richardson's correspondents. To the extent that he allowed outside pressure to influence his work, each edition is progressively less his own, further removed from the original conception.[55]

Harris's attempt to distinguish "outside pressure" from authorial individuality and textual integrity contradicts the novel's own representation of a world in which interiority is revealed only through correspondence and every piece of writing responds to others. At the same time, however, Harris's attempt to isolate the work of a single author from the "pressure" of multiple correspondents repeats Richardson's own ostentatious refusal to pander to readers' desires. Where the postscript to *Clarissa* criticizes female readers' request for a happy ending, *Grandison* concludes with a letter in which Richardson denies a female reader's authority to suggest a longer ending. The "Copy of a Letter to a Lady, who was solicitous for an additional volume to the HISTORY OF SIR CHARLES GRANDISON; supposing it ended abruptly," hastens to correct that supposition: "[I] hope, when you consider the circumstances of the Story, you will be of opinion, that it ends very properly where it does; tho' at the first perusal it may seem, to a Lady who honours the piece with her approbation, to conclude a little abruptly" (*Grandison*, 7.467). Here again, the "gentler sex" is addressed only to be silenced. By paraphrasing rather than quoting those impertinent letters, both conclusions re-establish the division of labor between readers and writers which the novels themselves broke down. Indeed, both reinforce that opposition by gendering their readers female. Yet ironically, as Harris shows, the "Concluding Note" to *Grandison* silently draws several of its rejoinders to readers' objections from a letter written by another woman, Lady Bradshaigh.[56] The contrast between Richardson's rebuff of the unnamed lady's request for a sequel and his invitation to other ladies to contribute to one suggests the depth of his ambivalence about the competing demands of establishing authority and engaging readers – or of representing epistolary exchange and claiming literary property.

Richardson's use of other writers poses as much of a critical challenge as his relation to readers. Since 1936, when Alan McKillop argued that Richardson drew many of his quotations from Edward Bysshe's *Art of English Poetry* (a popular composition manual that includes a catalogue of beauties), the extent of his dependence on anthologies has given rise to critical controversy. Michael Connaughton has shown that much of Richardson's canon in *Clarissa* overlaps with Bysshe's: more than two-thirds of the English quotations in the novel appear in the *Art* (sixty-nine out of 103), and nineteen of those sixty-nine show errors or omissions also made by Bysshe.[57] In contrast, Harris contends that Richardson must have encountered those passages in the original texts: because "Richardson's references are typically not isolated and ornamental, but organic, connected, and controlled, he cannot have been unlearned."[58] The organicist assumption that dismisses any lack of "connection" as a breakdown of esthetic "control" leaves no room for Richardson's own acknowledgment of the ornamental function of learning or the esthetic value of ornament. While Harris defends Richardson from the charge of "decorat[ing] his work with other men's flowers," the floral metaphor appears more positively in *Clarissa* itself, where Brand enthusiastically compares to an "enameled mead" a page mixing roman text and italicized quotations.[59] Although Brand's taste is anything but exemplary, his appreciation of the typographical variety which advertises the juxtaposition of multiple genres and signatures can serve as a reminder that discontinuity offers esthetic pleasures of its own. Bysshe himself prefaces the *Art* with the promise that a collection of excerpts will "divert and amuse [the reader] better" than would a "Composition . . . on one intire Subject," "for here is no Thread of Story, nor Connexion of one Part with another, to keep his mind intent and constrain him to any Length of Reading."[60]

The identification of Bysshe as one of Richardson's sources does not have to invalidate source study, as Harris fears and even Connaughton implies when he distinguishes Richardson's "mechanical" and "inept" use of the *Art* from his more "subtle" allusions to the texts that he seems to have read in their entirety.[61] If we chose to accept Harris' thesis that every quotation alludes to an entire "context," and that Richardson's works are influenced by their sources "not only locally but structurally," then consistency would require us to take the *Art of Poetry* seriously as a source in its own right.[62] As a series of extracts arranged alphabetically by topic, we could then argue, the *Art* anticipates the structure of the *Collection of Sentiments*. Indeed, Richardson's own description of the *Collection* as "divested of Story" echoes Bysshe's claim that the *Art* has "no Thread of Story." The *Art* provides an even closer generic model for the alphabetical index of similes and allusions that concludes *Grandison*. Richardson's compendium of topoi shares its self-conscious literariness with Bysshe's collection of beauties: a writer who wants to learn what to compare a proud person with can find "peacock" in the index to *Grandison*. No less than Bysshe's poetic toolbox, Richardson's modular *Collection* invites readers like Ben Franklin to reassemble its quotations for their own purposes. *Poor Richard's Almanac* does to the *Collection of Sentiments* what the *Collection of Sentiments* did to Bysshe. Indeed, as a collection signed by multiple authors, *Clarissa* itself owes as much to the structure of Bysshe's anthology as to its content. The fragmentation that leads Harris to dismiss the *Art* as a source is precisely what it shares with Richardson's works. If, as various critics have shown, the drama, from which many of Richardson's quotations are excerpted, forms one of his generic models, it seems equally clear that the anthology, in which many of those same quotations reappear, provides another.[63]

Critics' efforts to distinguish anthologies like the *Art* from other sources betray an ethical agenda as much as an evidentiary or even esthetic one. While Harris assumes that quoting from Bysshe would prove Richardson "unlearned," the critics who argue that Richardson did depend on the *Art* accuse him instead of dishonesty: A. Dwight Culler classes Richardson jocularly among "recipients of pilfered goods," while Michael Connaughton describes the overlap between the *Art* and *Clarissa* as proof that Richardson has not always "read what he pretends."[64] Harris addresses the ethics of reading more obliquely when she reproduces Richardson's own representation of his reading practices. To prove the range of Richardson's learning, Harris paraphrases an autobiographical anecdote seized upon by biographers ever since Anna Laetitia Barbauld in 1810. When he read as an apprentice "for Improvement of my Mind," Richardson reminisces in a letter written late in life, he "took Care, that even my Candle was of my own purchasing, that I might not in the most trifling Instance make my Master a Sufferer."[65] Like Richardson's denial that *Grandison* was "borrowed from any body," the heavy symbolism that Harris invokes dissociates quoting from stealing. Richardson read others, the anecdote suggests, but enlightened himself.

At the same time, though, Richardson's letter implies that an apprentice who reads might be suspected of stealing from his master unless the contrary is specified. Harris' distinction between "isolated" and "organic" quotation repeats Richardson's story of his industrious apprenticeship. Each drags in a kind of crude criminal appropriation from which Richardson can arguably be absolved – cribbing anthology-pieces, pilfering candles – in order to suggest, by contrast, that the reading in which he undeniably did engage had nothing to do with appropriation at all. But the need to distinguish reading books from stealing candles backfires by reminding us that both sources of enlightenment are for sale.

The sequels to *Pamela* and the piracy of *Grandison* exposed Richardson's failure to reconcile the disavowal of authorship with the assertion of "a property . . . absolutely his own." In *Sir Charles Grandison* he finally found a more oblique solution to that problem: a hero who divorces authority from authorship by executing other people's wills. Instead of displacing questions about literary property from a central to a minor character as *Clarissa* does by expanding Brand's role in the third edition, *Grandison* substitutes real for literary property and wills for letters.

The proliferation of executorships in *Sir Charles Grandison* demands some explanation.[66] Grandison executes the will of a man who has tried to kill him, the wills of two men whose lives he has saved, and even a will that does not exist. After his father dies intestate, Grandison takes advantage of the semantic overlap between "will" and "intention" to claim that there is something for him to execute: "that intention will I execute with as much exactness, as if he had made a will" (*Grandison*, 2.21.372). Sir Hargrave Pollexfen asks Grandison to administer his property in the same breath as he asks a clergyman to care for his soul: "Be my executor. And do you, good Bartlett, put me in the way of repentance" (6.31.143). The desire of women throughout Europe to make Sir Charles their husband is matched only by the wish of men throughout England to make him their executor – requests which, unlike the competing demands of four English and two Italian ladies, he never refuses.

In a novel ostensibly about courtship, wills replace women as the means of forging alliances between men and transferring property between families. This explains why so many hapless suitors in *Sir Charles Grandison* decide to bequeath their property to the families of the women who rejected them (as Belvedere does to Clementina's relations, and Pollexfen to Harriet's husband) or even (as does Harriet's second ex-suitor) to the woman herself. Although Richardson claims in the "Letter to a Lady" appended to *Grandison* that the "great and decisive event" of a novel can be either "a *Death*, or a *Marriage*" (3.471), the novel concludes not with Harriet becoming one suitor's wife (an event buried in the sixth volume), but with her becoming the administrator of another suitor's charitable bequest, "a very large Legacy in money and his jewels and plate" (7.61.462). The ending substitutes something very like executorship for rape as the bond between Harriet and her would-be abductor Pollexfen; from sex without familial consent, the novel progresses to a transfer of property between families (including the Pollexfen family jewels and plate) without sex. The bequest to the jilt or her family strips her refusal of any monetary consequences. In turn, this helps explain why the novel is so boring: less because nothing happens than because what does happen makes no financial difference.

In bypassing the woman's consent and the woman's body, Belvedere's bequest renders the incest taboo redundant, opening the way for Sir Charles's "family of love," in which the only woman labelled off-limits is his ward Emily, not because they have any relationship by blood, but because Grandison (not surprisingly, considering the odds) happens to be her dead father's executor. In a society where women are legally dead, men need to die biologically before they can prove their love of a man by surrendering the administration of their property into his hands. Given that only executorship legalizes men's relationships with other men as marriage does men's relationships with women, it makes sense for Richardson's first novel named after a male hero to give wills the prominence that his previous two novels had reserved for wedding clothes and marriage articles. Conversely, though, Grandison's role as a disinterested conduit for other men's property can be counted among his feminine traits, as much as his virginity or his addiction to smelling-salts. Like a woman, the executor makes possible family alliances and property transfers in which he himself never appears as a principal.

Executorship had already played a prominent role in Richardson's previous novel. The end of *Clarissa* leaves Belford with at least five wills to execute. He begins with two even before he undertakes Clarissa's; he and Morden seal their friendship by promising to execute each other's; and Lovelace quite reasonably asks him to be his executor "since thou art so expert, and so ready at executorships" (*Clarissa*, 528.1464, 535.1483). The amount of time that Belford must be assumed to spend executing wills rivals even that spent by Clarissa and Lovelace writing letters. In fact, Belford himself anticipates the problem of verisimilitude when he insists that his executorships "sit light upon me. And survivors cannot better or more charitably bestow their time" (*Clarissa*, 507.1412).

The importance of executorship in *Clarissa* can be measured by the ease with which the heroine's executor, Belford, takes the place of her lover, Lovelace. After appropriating the ellipsis that Lovelace had used to refer to Clarissa's rape ("I can go no farther") to describe her death ("I can write no more"), Belford goes on to replace Lovelace as the object of the Harlowes' financial and affective jealousy. "They both, with no little warmth, hinted at their disapprobation of you, sir, for their sister's executor," Morden tells Belford. "They said there was no need of an executor out of their family . . . They were surprised that I had given up to you the proceed of her grandfather's estate since his death" (*Clarissa*, 258.883, 481.1362, 501.1401). The Harlowes' jealousy is not entirely unfounded, for Belford does end up uniting himself legally to their family – not through marriage to Clarissa, but by the promise that binds him and her cousin to execute each other's wills.

Between *Clarissa* and *Grandison*, however, the executor eclipses the testator: *Clarissa* takes its name from the author of a will, *Grandison* from an executor. The executor Belford is no more the hero of *Clarissa* than the testators Pollexfen, Sir Thomas, and Danby are the heroes of *Grandison*. (The latter is never even mentioned until after his death: he becomes a character only once his will needs executing.) Clarissa's elaborate death is not matched by their briefer exits, and Grandison himself does not die at all. As eponymous executor replaces eponymous testatrix, our attention shifts from the character who produces and signs a document to the character who interprets and enforces it.

Clarissa herself sets this shift into motion when she transfers authority from the writer of a will to its readers. After referring to "some blanks which I left to the very last" in her will, Clarissa adds:

In case of such omissions and imperfections, I desire that my cousin Morden will be so good as to join with Mr Belford in considering them, and in comparing them with what I have more explicitly written; and if, after that, any doubt remain, that they will be pleased to apply to Miss Howe, who knows my whole heart; and I desire that their construction may be established; and I hereby establish it, provided it be unanimous, and direct it to be put into force, as if I had so written and determined myself. (*Clarissa*, 507.1420)[67]

The phrase "as if I had so written myself" bequeaths the testatrix's authority to her executors. And not just her authority to write, but (no less important for Richardson) her power to compile. Clarissa's last words, the inscriptions on her coffin, reach Anna Howe – previously her primary reader – only after being filtered through her executor's transcription. As Morden reports, the coffin "gave [Anna] so much fresh grief, that though she several times wiped her eyes, she was unable to read the inscription and texts: turning therefore to me: Favour me, sir, I pray you, by a line with the description of these emblems, and with these texts" (*Clarissa*, 502.1404). Unlike the biblical texts contained in the meditations, the "texts" excerpted on Clarissa's coffin are illegible until quoted in turn by her executor. In death, Clarissa goes from quoting to being quoted. While one executor, Morden, replaces her as the compiler of the texts that decorate the coffin, the other executor, Belford, replaces her as the editor of the letters that make up the novel.

The ventriloquistic fiction constructed by the words "as if I had so written" occurs once again in *Grandison*. But while in *Clarissa* the testatrix writes that phrase, in *Grandison* it appears instead in the mouth of the executor. After his father dies intestate, leaving nothing to the daughters he hates and everything to his son, Grandison gives £10,000 to his sister with the words "Look upon me only as an executor of a will, that ought to have been made" (*Grandison*, 2.25.383). Echoing Clarissa's "as if," he asks her to "receive these as from your father's bounty" (*Grandison*, 2.25.382). That phrase reappears in a third case of money-laundering when Grandison asks Major O'Hara's wife to "accept, as from the Major, another 100 *l.* a year, for pinmoney, which he, or which you, madam, will draw upon me for . . . For this 100 *l.* a year must be appropriated to your sole and separate use, madam; and not be subject to your controul, Major O-Hara" (4.9.310). Unlike Sir Thomas, Major O'Hara is not yet dead. In both cases, however, the counterfactual "as [if] from" marks the money's ostensible source as a front. And in both cases, the fiction that the money comes from a third party (Sir Thomas, Major O'Hara) hides the fact that Grandison is disobeying that party's instructions (in Sir Thomas's case) or withholding the money from him (in O'Hara's). Grandison's misattribution of his money and his generosity to other men inverts Clarissa's request that Belford, Morden, and Anna declare their decisions hers. In both cases, the will is authored by its executor but ascribed to the dead.

Grandison disguises the authority of an heir as the obedience of an administrator. His power to enforce non-existent bequests to his sisters and his father's mistress depends on his position as heir male. One hardly knows whether to be more surprised that an executor who routinely flouts testators' instructions should remain in such demand, or that a priggish moral paragon should ostentatiously disobey his father's dying wish. And not just his father's. It is Grandison's status as

Danby's heir, not as his executor, that allows him "to amend a will, made in a long and painful sickness, which might sour a disposition that was naturally all benevolence" – an amendment which consists of dividing the money Danby meant to leave him among those very relatives whom the will was designed to punish (*Grandison*, 2.25.455). Already at the end of *Pamela*, Mr. B., to whom Mr. Longman leaves his money, magnanimously transfers the legacy to the relatives whom Longman had gone to such lengths to disinherit. Not content with making executorship a prerequisite for heroism, Richardson requires his heroes systematically to betray the trust of the dead. Feminized in this as in so much else, Grandison seems to have inherited his habit of posing as another's agent from his mother, who, even before Sir Thomas's death,

> would confer benefits in the name of her husband, whom, perhaps, she had not seen for months, and knew not whether she might see for months to come. She was satisfied, tho' hers was the *first* merit, with the *second* merit reflected from that she gave him: "I am but Sir Thomas' almoner: I know I shall please Sir Thomas by doing this; Sir Thomas would have done thus: Perhaps he would have been more bountiful had he been present." (*Grandison*, 2.11.312)

From his father Grandison inherits property; from his mother, the practice of giving away property in his father's name.

Why should an owner pose as an executor? The answer, I think, lies in an ambivalence about the relation of owning to signing that characterizes the epistolary novel. In misattributing his own decisions to fictitious documents – in asserting authority while disclaiming authorship – Sir Charles lends moral weight to the financial equivalent of Richardson's own editorial self-representation.[68] In fact, Grandison's strategic confusion between his roles as his father's heir and his father's executor literalizes the double metaphor that structures the "Advertisement" to the second part of *Pamela*, where the "editor" claims the authority to represent the heroine by figuring himself alternately as her literary executor and her literary heir. After criticizing the authors of rival sequels to volumes I and II which "have murder'd that excellent Lady, and mistaken and misrepresented other (suppos'd imaginary) CHARACTERS," he announces that all the copies of Pamela's writings

> are now in *One Hand Only*: And that, if ever they shall be published, (which at present is a point undetermined) it must not be, till after a certain event, as unwished, as deplorable: And *then*, solely, at the Assignment of SAMUEL

RICHARDSON, of *Salisbury-Court, Fleetstreet*, the Editor of these Four Volumes of PAMELA; or, VIRTUE REWARDED. (*Pamela*, 4.495)

The reference to Pamela's death figures the proprietorship of her character at once as a battle between literary executors and as a contested inheritance. The question of who represents and who "misrepresents" Pamela is answered by whoever ends up with the letters in hand. Yet ironically enough, Richardson seems to have inherited (if not stolen) both images for literary property from the rival sequel with which he disputes it. *Pamela's Conduct in High Life*, published in the previous year, was already introduced by a correspondence between Mrs. Jervis' niece, who has inherited her aunt's letters, and the publisher, who assures readers that the niece will use the cash value of the inheritance to keep alive her aunt's charitable projects, which are in turn represented as merely an extension of Pamela's will: "A Profit will certainly arise from their Sale . . . and as your easy Fortune sets you above applying to your own Use such unexpected Money, you may succeed your Aunt in the Post of Almoner, as you did in that of House-keeper to the illustrious Pamela."[69]

The coincidence of Grandison's efficiency as executor with his power as heir reverses the confusion earlier established between Richardson's knowledge of Pamela's wishes and his possession of her letters. Where Grandison distributes money under cover of interpreting documents, Richardson publishes texts under cover of inheriting property. The father's will which Grandison claims to execute is as nonexistent as the characters' letters that Richardson claims to edit. The executor's relation to the testator figures the compiler's to the author. Grandison's double role as obedient executor and self-willed heir resolves the long-standing tension between Richardson's self-presentation as editor and as author; between the polyvocality of the epistolary form and Richardson's monopoly on the right to produce a sequel; between the collective correspondence that forms the body of each novel and the anonymous editorial paratexts that frame it; or, to put it differently, between the presentation of the epistolary novel as the work of several hands and as the property of "One Hand Only."

The image of letters "in One Hand" would resurface at the other end of Richardson's career in the claim that *Grandison* was "never in any other hand." At the same time, the pains that it costs Lovelace to forge Clarissa's and Anna's handwriting remind us that epistolary collections are also presented as having been written in various hands before being reproduced in a single standard type (*Clarissa*, 229.752, 239.814). Brand devises a typographical equivalent for that chirographic diversity when he uses the contrast between roman and italic print to distinguish other writers' words from his own: "I have considered a page distinguished by *different characters*, as a verdant field overspread with *butter-flowers* and *daisies*, and other summer-flowers." Brand's pedantic appeal to multiple authorities set off by (typographical) "characters" literalizes Richardson's own strategy of ascribing each letter to a different (literary) character. But Brand's absurd comparison of typographical with horticultural variety – a pastoral metaphor for mechanical reproduction – recalls as well Fielding's earlier pun on the "common place," as a term for both literary and real property: "The antients may be considered as a rich common, where every person who hath the smallest tenament in Parnassus hath a free right to fatten his muse."[70] That Brand's appreciation of the page as a many-charactered field leads immediately into his refusal to share with other characters the value of whatever "be to be made" from it suggests the strength of the tension between anthology and authority, compilation and continuity, that generates Richardson's works and the work of his readers.

POSTSCRIPT: SCOTT AND THE LITERARY-HISTORICAL NOVEL

Richardson's fate was extreme, but not unique. Epistolary exchange has always attracted editorial appropriation. *Clarissa*'s most ambitious successor, *La Nouvelle Héloïse* (1761), gave rise just as quickly to Samuel Formey's *Esprit de Julie, ou Extrait de la Nouvelle Héloïse* (1763), which reinvented the modular moralism and the anti-narrative form of Richardson's *Collection of Sentiments*.[71] In the same year, a more comprehensive collection of *Pensées de J. J. Rousseau* appeared, followed by fourteen more editions in Rousseau's lifetime and soon pirated by an *Esprit, Maximes et Principes de Monsieur Jean-Jacques Rousseau* (1764), which in turn would immediately be incorporated into the 1764 Duchesne edition of Rousseau's collected works.[72]

One can understand, then, why the anthology became such a central motif in *Rousseau juge de Jean-Jacques* (1782), Rousseau's dialogue between an imaginary biographer who spies on Jean-Jacques and an imaginary editor who compiles a series of "Extraits" inscribed in the text itself. The anthologist scans Jean-Jacques's work for passages that can be strategically decontextualized to make them more topical – hence more offensive. Or rather, recontextualized, for the categories under which the anthology reclassifies extracts (writers, doctors, kings, women, Englishmen) conflate theme with audience, as if people read only for passages applicable to themselves. The splintering of Jean-Jacques's work into anthology-pieces reflects the fragmentation of the public into special-interest groups. Only the editor in the *Dialogues* is finally converted – ironically, by the contact with Jean-Jacques's writing which his task requires – to a more organicist method of reading that renounces "plucking out separate phrases scattered here and there" in favor of "grasping the whole."[73]

Where Richardson had fought back legally, on the margins of his last novel, Rousseau counterattacked through fiction. *Rousseau juge de Jean-Jacques* conflates decontextualization with personal violence, accusing anthologists of "isolating and disfiguring" the author's words.[74] The *Dialogues* juxtapose Rousseau's parodic auto-anthology not only with the charge that portrait-painters have taken bribes to lend Jean-Jacques an unflattering scowl, but also with the narrator's memory of being hung in effigy while *Emile* was burnt in his place and with an anecdote of another man arrested for crimes committed by a sinister look-alike. The chiasmus where textual mutilation intersects with bodily misrepresentation looks forward to George Eliot's triple fear of anthologists, photographers and autograph-seekers. But Rousseau's attempt to counteract that double violation by circulating signed, handwritten copies of his own text looks back as well to Richardson's futile insistence on never letting the printing process out of "one hand."[75]

Rousseau's novel and Richardson's invite excerpting not simply through their bulk, but through the surplus of signatures built into the epistolary novel. *Clarissa* and *Julie* are prefaced, concluded, and ostensibly abridged (in Richardson's case) or ostentatiously censored (in Rousseau's) by a figure whom both name alternately as their "editor" and "publisher" but implicitly identify as their author. Where the title-page of *Clarissa* gives no author but names Richardson (accurately) as its publisher, *Julie* juxtaposes three authors' names on its title-page. The only one labeled as such is Petrarch, to whom the novel's epigraph is unequivocally attributed; but the title itself, "Letters of two Lovers . . . Collected and Published by Jean-Jacques Rousseau," adds two competing signatures, the letter-writers' on the one hand and the novel-publisher's on the other. Yet that ambiguity is resolved twice over, by the announcement repeated at both ends of the book – in its preface and again in the appended "Entretien sur les Romans" – that "I name myself at the head of this collection, not to appropriate it, but to take responsibility for it [*pour en répondre*]."[76] Put differently, *Julie* and

Grandison each frame first-person letters signed by characters not only
with the name of a publisher, but with the signed first-person statement of a heterodiegetic editor who demands the profits in *Grandison* or
the blame for *Julie*. If Richardson's peculiar position as an author-
printer crystallized the tension between compilation and authority in
his novels, his career-long struggle to reconcile documentary authenticity with narrative unity also reflects a larger contradiction inherent
in the composite structure of epistolary fiction.

One might have expected that problem to disappear as third-person
narration began to dominate nineteenth-century fiction. Yet paradoxically, the dwindling viability of the epistolary mode actually increased its
centrality to the self-definition of the novel. In what remains of this
chapter, I work backward from two abridgments of *Clarissa* published in
1868, to J. G. Lockhart's life-and-letters biography of Sir Walter Scott
(1837), to Scott's own flirtation with the epistolary novel in *Redgauntlet*
(1824, 1832) and his equally ambivalent republication of Richardson's
work in Ballantyne's Novelist's Library (1824), in order to explore how
old epistolary novels came to be read once new ones ceased to be
written. Different as they are in their form and their ambitions, each of
these works uses the letter to stand at once for narrative inefficiency and
historical retrogression – and, by extension, for the historicity of literary
form.

The fate of the epistolary novel after the turn of the nineteenth century
is usually conceived as a steady decline. Certainly fewer new epistolary
novels appeared every year.[77] But if we take the history of the genre to
encompass the reproduction of old works as well as the production of new
ones, then that pattern begins to look rather less linear. As we saw earlier
in the chapter, the first abridgments of *Clarissa* and *Grandison* unanimously
replaced the epistolary mode with a single, retrospective, omniscient
narrator writing not "to the moment" but in a preterite as temporally
unsituated as the present tense of the *Moral and Instructive Sentiments*. At the
height of the epistolary novel's popularity, abridgers equated epistolarity
with wasted words: they transposed the first person into the third and the
present tense into the past as automatically as they substituted one
sentence for many. Conversely, in 1868 two new abridgments of *Clarissa* –
the first to appear since 1813 – suddenly resurrected the epistolary form.
The first epistolary abridgments appeared when the novel in letters was
safely dead. The letter became legible only as a historical relic.

Together, the two abridgments of *Clarissa* published in 1868 mark a
break. I have found no English-language abridgment before them that

preserves the epistolary form, and no book-length abridgment after them that does not. The impersonal mode of earlier abridgments did not disappear on that date, though, for every abridgment from 1868 to now has used third-person past-tense plot summaries to connect the epistolary excerpts with one another. That strategy has remained unanimous from E. S. Dallas's *Clarissa* (London: Tinsley, 1868) to Mrs. Humphry Ward's *Clarissa Harlowe, a New and Abridged Edition* (London: Routledge, 1868) to J. Oldcastle's *Sir Charles Grandison* (London: Field and Tuer, [1886]) to George Saintsbury's *Letters from Sir Charles Grandison: selected . . . with connecting notes* (London: G. Allen, 1895) to Sheila Kaye-Smith's omnibus abridgment *Samuel Richardson* (London: Herbert and Daniel, 1911) to John Angus Burrell's *Clarissa* (New York: Random House, 1950) and George Sherburn's *Clarissa* (Boston: Houghton Mifflin, 1962), still, outrageously, being used in American classrooms.[78] In the process of linking letters, this second wave of abridgments exaggerates the fluctuation between editorial distance and epistolary immediacy already latent in the novels themselves. Indeed, Lovelace shows uncanny literary-historical prescience when instead of sending Belford a full transcript of the letters he has intercepted between Anna and Clarissa, he excerpts the juiciest bits and fills in the gaps by summarizing the rest in indirect (would-be omniscient) discourse (*Clarissa* 198.632–38).

More seriously, abridgers' narratological strategy can be traced to the model of life-and-letters biographies – a genre whose founding example, William Mason's *Poems of Mr. Gray. To which are prefixed Memoirs of his Life and Writings* (1775), anticipated by almost a hundred years Dallas's and Ward's tactic of alternating heavily excised epistolary fragments with retrospective editorial summaries. The reappearance of epistolary abridgments coincided not only with the decline of the epistolary novel, but with the rise of epistolary memoirs which literalized Rousseau's fear of an alliance between the biographer and the anthologist. Like Dallas's and Ward's *Clarissa*s, Victorian biographies used a modern editor's narrative to string together truncated excerpts from letters situated firmly in a historical past. The motives for the two oscillations between editorial summary and epistolary quotation differ sharply, of course: in one case, the need to cram more plot into fewer pages; in the other, the duty to protect the privacy of the dead. But the binary structure of both reflects a common tension between the historical authenticity of excerpts and the modern efficiency of narrative. Where twentieth-century biography inherits its mode of narration from the Victorian novel, Victorian biographers appropriated the composite structure which the

novel had earlier borrowed from published collections of correspondence. Biography memorializes more than dead people; it also provides
a resting-place for obsolete forms. In Frederic Harrison's metaphor, life-
and-letters biographies embed letters "like fossil shells in the chalk cliff
of the editorial big print," the relics of an earlier era.[79] A superannuated
narrative technique commemorates the dead.

The method that Ward and Dallas developed to condense Richardson for a more efficient age bears an even more striking resemblance to
the technique which one of the most successful Victorian biographers,
J. G. Lockhart, had already invented to abridge his own equally massive
Memoirs of the Life of Sir Walter Scott. The title of Lockhart's 1848 abridgment, *Narrative of the Life of Sir Walter Scott*, announces the change worked
on the ten-volume *Memoirs* published a decade earlier. The plural
"memoirs," which can refer to autobiography as easily as biography,
encompasses fragments in Scott's own voice as well as the narrative by
Lockhart that frames them. In the condensed *Life*, the "Narrative" of
the title displaces those first-person "Memoirs": as editorial summaries
replace the original letters, the narrator's voice comes to form a growing
proportion of the shrinking text. Even those excerpts that remain are
typographically assimilated to their frame, as the *Narrative* substitutes a
uniform typeface for the two font sizes which the original *Memoirs* used
to set off Scott's writings – rather as red-letter Bibles distinguish Christ's
words from those of the evangelists.

In isolation, Lockhart's abridgment could be explained by the self-
aggrandizing desire to encroach on Scott's share of the text. Yet the
convention goes beyond personal vanity, for a different abridger, in
1869, promises not only to excise large stretches of Scott's diary and "the
letters not strictly biographical," but to "shorten the work by omitting
the extracts from Scott's prefaces (which will be found in his works)."[80]
With each new edition, the *Life* differentiates itself more sharply from
the "works" – or more precisely, from an anthology of elegant "extracts" from them. Even the correspondence that remains changes its
function from a collection of stylistic models to a source of "strictly
biographical" information. As Lockhart's preface to his abridgment
acknowledges, quantitative changes enforce esthetic choices: "in the
case of written composition there are no mechanical appliances, as there
are in painting and architecture, for varying the scale."[81] In fact, the
abridgment opens by acknowledging that Lockhart's decision to subordinate the quotations to the narrative could just as easily have been
reversed:

If I had been to consult my own feelings, I should have been more willing to produce an enlarged edition; for the interest of Sir Walter's history lies, I think, even peculiarly, in its minute details – especially in the details set down by himself in his letter and diaries . . . [The publisher], however, considered that a book of smaller bulk, embracing only what may be called more strictly narrative, might be acceptable to certain classes of readers.[82]

Although his substitution of narrative for letters anticipates the procedure of Richardson's Victorian abridgers, Lockhart's rhetoric also looks backward to Richardson's own. His assumption that "smaller bulk" implies "what may be called more strictly narrative" repeats Richardson's claim that rewriting *Clarissa* "into a merely Narrative Form . . . has help'd me to shorten much."[83] The contrast between Lockhart's reluctance to write a "strictly narrative" abridgement and the putative desire of "certain classes" to read one echoes Richardson's condescension to "young People; who are apt to read rapidly wth. a View only to *Story*."[84]

Yet Lockhart's attempt to shift responsibility for the abridgment onto "classes of readers" (or onto his publisher's greed for a larger share of the market) obscures the role that abridgment plays in the *Memoirs* from the beginning. Already in the first edition, the narrator pauses periodically to point out his omissions. "I abstain from transcribing the letters," he announces at one point; at another, "I regret, that from the delicate nature of the transactions chiefly dwelt upon in the earlier of these communications, I dare not make a free use of them; but I feel it my duty to record the strong impression they have left on my own mind." Halfway through the first edition, he interrupts himself to warn that "the editor has, for reasons which need not be explained, found it necessary to omit some passages altogether – to abridge others."[85] Lockhart's choice of "abridge" as a euphemism for "expurgate" suggests how little divides the condenser's narratological manipulations from the original biographer's moral agenda. The revised *Life* simply changes the abridger of another man's correspondence into an abridger of his own work.

Lockhart's biographical method banishes letters at once to the private sphere and to the prehistory of literary composition. The abridged *Narrative* modernizes and popularizes the *Memoirs* by cutting even more letters. In retrospect, the intermittently epistolary original *Memoirs* – published but still unable to reach "certain classes of readers" – can be situated halfway between the undigested private correspondence to which only the narrator has access and the single-voiced summary that will eventually reach that mass market. The full-length *Memoirs* already projects that publication history onto the time of reading, for Lockhart's decision to retitle the abridged *Memoirs* as a *Narrative* simply repeats the progression from a framed memoir to a frame narrative which structures the original text. The first volume of the first edition opens with an "autobiographical fragment" by Scott, which Lockhart claims to have "discovered in an old cabinet": the same antiquarian conceit that his hero invokes in the postscript to *Waverley*, which traces Scott's novelistic career to an abandoned manuscript "found again among other waste papers in an old cabinet."[86] Over the course of the *Memoirs*, we move from the false start provided by Scott's memoir – an autobiographical document longer than all but one of the subsequent fragments – to an extradiegetic narrative punctuated with ever-shorter epistolary snippets, concluding ten volumes later (like *Clarissa*) in the editor's voice.[87] Put differently, Lockhart's *Memoirs* recapitulates the shift away from epistolary narrative that shaped the novel in the previous decades. So did the history of its composition; so did its successive editions. From the beginning, the *Life of Scott* marked the death of the letter.

One can only speculate whether those parallel histories are causally related: whether "a certain class of readers" – or even a certain class of editors – became impatient with correspondence as the habit of reading epistolary novels receded further into the past. But a more direct analogue for the *Memoirs'* recapitulation of literary history can be found in the work of Lockhart's hero. The shift from autobiography to biography in the original *Memoirs* combined with the replacement of letters by narrative in successive editions to repeat the structure of *Redgauntlet* (1824), Scott's most extended experiment with the epistolary mode. Backdated to the eighteenth century and riddled with Richardsonian allusions, *Redgauntlet* opens as an epistolary novel; but the correspondence that makes up the first volume of the text eventually gives way to a "Journal" with no inscribed reader, interrupted in turn by a narrative with no inscribed author. By the end of *Redgauntlet*, third-person narration has displaced not only the epistolary "I" but the epistolary "you." The conclusion of the novel opens not, like the first volume, with a first-person character writing to a second-person character, but with an impersonal narrator addressing a third-person reader: "The reader ought, by this time, to have formed some idea of the character of Alan Fairford."[88] In turn, the "Letter to the Author of Waverley" tacked on to the end of that "Narrative" recapitulates the novel's shift away from epistolarity by taking us from a first-person salutation ("I am truly sorry, my worthy and much-respected sir") to a third-person conclusion which breaks off without even the signature that would normally conclude a letter. In concert with the "Introduction" added to the Magnum Opus edition of 1832, this last-minute swerve to an epistolary conclusion overlays the novel's progression from letter to omniscient narrative by a more symmetrical pattern which alternates the two. As if to underscore that contrast, the writer of the concluding "Letter to the Author" – a counterpart to the letters to the editor which Richardson attaches to the other end of *Pamela* – is as different as possible from the narrator of the preceding section. Far from being omniscient, he barely remembers the characters' names. Like Lockhart's *Life*, then, *Redgauntlet* sandwiches its retrospective summaries with an ever-dwindling proportion of journals and letters "written to the moment" a generation ago.

Set sixty years since, subtitled "A Tale of the Eighteenth Century," and signed by the Author of Waverley, *Redgauntlet* is instantly recognizable as historical fiction. But what emerges more gradually is a less identifiable genre that could be called literary-historical fiction. Progressing from the epistolary conventions of the mid-eighteenth century to the heterodiegetic narrative popular in the 1820s, the form of *Redgauntlet* spans a much longer historical trajectory than does its action (an abortive Jacobite rebellion that fizzles before being properly begun). As Nicola Watson has noted, the novel gradually moves from a narrative mode contemporary with the historical period being represented to a different set of conventions associated instead with the moment of representation.[89] As ontogeny recapitulates phylogeny with a bravura equalled only by the "Oxen of the Sun" chapter in *Ulysses*, the historical gap distancing the novel's style from its readers gives way instead to anachronism relative to its characters.

Redgauntlet juxtaposes literary history with dynastic succession as ostentatiously as it parallels political history with the time of reading. Its plot pivots on a fictional 1765 Jacobite rebellion organized by veterans of the (historical) rising of 1745; indeed, we can date its action largely through the hero's reference to "those fanatical Jacobites whose arms, not twenty years since, had shaken the British throne, and some of whom, though their party diminished daily in numbers, energy, and power, retained still an inclination to *renew* the attempt they had found so desperate" (*Redgauntlet*, 206, my emphasis). By staging a rebellion only to defuse it and adopting the epistolary form only to abandon it, the novel makes the impossibility of re-enacting the Forty-Five rebellion in

'65 (or, by extension, of reviving the Stuart cause in 1745 or even 1715) stand for the impossibility of transplanting mid-eighteenth-century narrative conventions to 1824. In each case, a relic of the 1740s is revived in order to lay it to rest.

Yet however energetically the novel gestures at synchronizing its narrative conventions with the action represented, the correspondence is never in fact so neat. Oddly, the novel situates the epistolary form not in the 1760s, but in the decade stretching from the first publication of *Pamela* (1740–41) to the appearance of *Clarissa* (1747–48). The characters read novels written twenty years since; the text as a whole never echoes the publications of 1765. The resulting time-lag undermines the homology of literary form with historical content that the novel elsewhere takes such pains to establish. Scott's allusions skip a generation to Richardson and, more obliquely, to Fielding – that is, to literature contemporary with the real rising of '45 rather than with the later rebellion represented in the novel. In fact, the correspondence of Scott's protagonists quickly becomes a dialogue between competing novelists of the previous generation. When Alan Fairford writes to Darsie Latimer that his father has taxed him with reading *Tom Jones*, Darsie retorts that "it is well for thee that, Lovelace and Belford like, we came under a convention to pardon every species of liberty which we may take with each other" (*Redgauntlet*, 21, 26). However, Scott's hero turns out to be less "Lovelace-like" than Pamela-like and Clarissa-like (or even Grandison-like, once his cross-dressing and passivity come to the fore). Spied on and served by a namesake of Clarissa's treacherous maid Dorcas, imprisoned like Clarissa by a family determined to break his reluctance to cooperate with their dynastic ambitions, and abducted like Pamela to the house of a reactionary "Squire" who promises to substitute love for cruelty as soon as his prisoner submits to his desires, Darsie also sings the same psalm in his captivity that Pamela does in hers, and, in a blatant echo of *Pamela*, replaces his letters by a journal hidden "about my person, so that I can only be deprived of [it] by actual violence" (*Redgauntlet*, 221, 181). More fundamentally, although the epistolary false start of *Redgauntlet* can at first be taken to refer to any of a number of eighteenth-century novels, Scott's move away from that initial form eventually narrows the field to *Pamela*. Both novels begin with a correspondence but use the abduction of the protagonist to interrupt it. Both follow that break first by an editorial explanation and then by a first-person journal, before replacing that journal in turn by an even more distanced omniscient conclusion. *Pamela* anticipates not only the epistolary form with which *Redgauntlet* begins, but every stage of Scott's move away from it.

Although the presence of *Pamela* is nowhere more ostentatious than when Darsie's kidnapping forces the correspondence to give way to an omniscient narrator, Scott's transition between the two modes swerves instead to invoke a rival precedent.

The advantage of laying before the reader, in the words of the actors themselves, the adventures which we must otherwise have narrated in our own, has given great popularity to the publication of epistolary correspondence, as practised by various great authors, and by ourselves in the preceding chapters. Nevertheless, . . . it must often happen that various prolixities and redundancies occur in the course of an interchange of letters, which must hang as a dead weight on the narrative. To avoid this dilemma, some biographers have used the letters of the personages concerned, or liberal extracts from them, to describe particular incidents, or express the sentiments which they entertained; while they connect them occasionally with such portions of narrative, as may serve to carry on the thread of the story. (*Redgauntlet*, 140)

While the placement of this voice-over at the end of a correspondence echoes the structure of *Pamela*, its editorial "we" and its position at the beginning of a volume recall instead the narrator (also first-person-plural, also mock-theoretical) of the chapters that introduce each book of *Tom Jones*. Like the exchange between Alan's letter referring to *Tom Jones* and Darsie's response alluding to *Clarissa*, Scott's shift from a narrative mode borrowed from Richardson to a narratorial persona taken from Fielding carefully balances the invocation of an epistolary novelist against the non-epistolary narrative of an anti-epistolary polemicist.

Moreover, although its allusions to *Pamela* and *Clarissa* radically outnumber Alan's one explicit mention of Fielding, *Redgauntlet* repeats the plot of *Tom Jones* even more closely than that of *Pamela*. In both, a young man is banished from his adoptive home to wander unwittingly into a Jacobite rebellion; en route, each hero's ignorance of his parentage leads to a narrow escape from real or imagined incest.[90] (Scott's departure from one key aspect of Fielding's plot, however, reflects the passivity that Alexander Welsh has shown to characterize Scott's heroes: where Allworthy banishes Tom for wenching and drinking, the only crime that motivates Darsie's expulsion is the negative one of lacking an interest in the law – and Mr. Fairford attributes even that fault less to Darsie's preference for other activities than to the inheritance which forces him to idle.)[91] By invoking the Forty-Five as a precedent for his 1765 rebellion, Scott positions his use of (bogus) history as a successor to Fielding's innovative inscription of the Forty-Five within his plot. Indeed, Redgauntlet's crazed conviction that Darsie's pro-Hanoverian upbringing conceals his real Jacobite potential harks back to the more comic incident in *Tom Jones* where a landlord briefly mistakes Tom's beloved Sophia for the Pretender's mistress.[92]

Ultimately, *Redgauntlet*'s references to Fielding undermine its Whig literary history. The "Narrative" replaces the epistolary form of the first volume not by pastiching Richardson's non-epistolary successors – as the structure of the novel leads us to expect – but rather his anti-epistolary contemporary. While the introduction quoted above places epistolarity and omniscient narration at opposite ends of a historical progression, its formal debt to Fielding disrupts that teleology by situating both in the 1740s. Competition replaces evolution. Just as Redgauntlet challenges the history that places the Stuarts in the past and the Hanoverians in the future, so Scott's allusions to *Tom Jones* make it impossible to project alternative narrative modes onto a chronological axis as neatly as the novel invites us to do. Fielding's presence suggests that, far from progressing from the epistolary form of the 1760s to the narrative conventions of the 1820s, the novel never gets past the controversy about epistolarity waged twenty years before its action begins.

Yet even in his Fieldingesque volume introduction, Scott lends the terms of that debate an unmistakably modern inflection. In the mock-historical language of eighteenth-century fiction, the "biographer" would have designated a novelist – like Richardson, whose acknowledgment that "Prolixity, Length at least, cannot be avoided in Letters written to the Moment" anticipates Scott's self-referential claim that letters generate "prolixities and redundancies." By 1824, however, those "biographers" could also be taken literally to refer to more recent authors of life-and-letters biography, which did in fact use "narrative" to "connect" epistolary "extracts." The "dead weight" of letters, too, could be read either as a pun on the necrological function of biography or as a reference to the obsolescence of the epistolary novel. Or even, more literally, to the heft of Richardson's volumes. The letter becomes a bloated corpse whose burden the "narrative" must "carry."

The strategy that Scott describes of "connecting" extracts from letters with "occasional . . . portions of narrative" not only recalls the editorial summaries that replace the letters truncated at the close of *Clarissa*, but anticipates the alternation of epistolary excerpts with third-person summaries which Mrs. Humphry Ward would later develop to counteract what she calls, in an echo of Scott, "the redundancy of Richardson's style." *Redgauntlet's* rewriting of Richardson prefigures more than the form of post-1868 abridgments: it also sets into motion their project of historicizing the epistolary novel. Instead of simply implying, as does the structure of *Redgauntlet*, that the letter is incompatible with modernity, Ward declares boldly that large novels must go the way of small dogs: "The redundancy of Richardson's style had a charm for the readers of his day, when time hung heavy on the hands of fine ladies shut up in country houses, or dawdling over fancy work and pug-dogs, with small interest in passing events, and dead to the delights of that earnest work for good which all may find who seek it."[93] More explicitly than *Redgauntlet*, Ward's abridgment revives the letter only to dismiss it more conclusively as a relic of the past.

In reminding readers of the existence of a longer text, Ward's preface departs sharply from the front matter of earlier, cheaper abridgments such as *The Paths of Virtue*. Given how many earlier abridgments evade any acknowledgment of their omissions – for good commercial reasons – why should a preface deliberately draw readers' attention to the gaps in the text? The answer, I think, is that relative incompleteness had come to replace absolute brevity as abridgments' selling point. While literary critics studying abridgment have usually focused on the specific content of what gets omitted, what mattered to readers of late-nineteenth-century *Clarissas* was rather the sheer fact of omission itself.[94] If Richardson's *Collection* is *Moral* less because of the information it contains than because of the modes of discourse that it excises (and the ways of reading that it rules out in the process), conversely Ward's abridgment updates Richardson less by discriminating those passages likely to interest modern readers from those that have lost their relevance, than by differentiating the efficient readers of abridgments in the present from the lazy readers of complete texts in the past.

Where Haywood equates skipping with "Loyter[ing]," Ward finds no kinder term than "dawdling" to characterize the reading of unabridged novels from cover to cover. The pace of reading retains its moral value, but impatience goes from a symptom of idleness to a mark of industry.[95] For Ward, epistolary narrative is to "events" what "fancy-work" is to "earnest work": the letter against the newspaper. Narrative means business. And that prophecy fulfilled itself. Where Ward claimed to respond to modern readers' need for an abridgment like hers, reciprocally such an abridgment interpellated a new kind of impatient, plot-oriented reader. The supply of abridgments created its own demand. The distaste for sententious matter and epistolary form which Ward identifies as the cause of her editorial strategy can also be explained as its by-product.

In that sense, Ward simply extended to Richardson's readers a historical model which the contemporary journalist R. H. Hutton applied instead to Richardson's characters. According to Hutton, the distance "from the lively rattle of our railway novels to the solemn coach-and-six of Richardson's fulldress genius" makes clear that "in that less busy age, the leisurely classes made a great deal more of one purpose than we do of many, and hence the characters themselves were less mobile than now." One wonders, he adds, whether "any family nowadays could by any chance devote the *time* to breaking in a refractory girl to a disagreeable alliance which the Harlowes devoted to attempting to force Mr. Solmes on Clarissa."[96] Yet Hutton's invocation of the railway novel undercuts itself by reminding his audience that modern time-saving technologies have also created the need to kill time – as ever, by reading. The "railway novels" to which he refers had come into being at mid-century precisely because the faster people could travel, the more they had to travel, and the more time they found on their hands in which it was impossible to do anything more productive than reading a one-volume reprint of a three-volume novel. That contradiction forces Hutton to shift the charge of "leisurely" idleness from fiction-readers to fictional characters. Because the former (slothful by definition) cannot easily be shown to have become more efficient in modern times, the latter must become businesslike on their behalf.

Ward's literary history is even more glaringly wrong. Long novels never stopped being written in the mid-nineteenth century, let alone read. Ward herself went on to produce several didactic novels as oversized and maxim-packed as anything that Richardson ever wrote. She may have cut Richardson down to size, but showed no urge to censor herself. Paradoxically, her own novels return obsessively to the problems that she raised at the beginning of her career in the preface to *Clarissa*, while severing those thematic concerns from the formal corollary that she took for granted there. While her novel *Robert Elsmere* (1888) is structured by the hero's progress from a contemplative to an active life, and *Marcella* (1894) circles back even more uncannily to the question of whether ladies should waste their lives on novels and lapdogs, or engage in what Ward had earlier called "earnest work for good," both of those plots stretch out to three leisurely volumes. Where Ward's abridgment promises to abbreviate an eighteenth-century form to fit the attention span of modern readers, *Marcella* – published at the very moment when the triple-decker was giving way to the one-volume novel – couches self-consciously modern problems in an anachronistically lumbering form.

That biographical paradox is already foreshadowed by the internal structure of Ward's abridgment. A preface relegating the letter to the dustbin of history undermines her decision, in the body of the edition, to restore the epistolary form which earlier abridgers had transposed. The efficiency that Ward's preface attributes to impersonal, retrospective narration paradoxically allows the text that follows to rehabilitate the epistolary as one of the few excuses left for the conspicuous consumption of paper and time. Her edition resuscitates the letter not as a functional form, but a stylized relic. Hutton's tone, too, hovers between sociohistorical triumphalism and literary-historical nostalgia. But another hundred and thirty years since, it has become easier to see that *Clarissa's* putative outdatedness provides part of its force – not only for the Victorians, but for us. Once modern efficiency forbids characters to waste on domestic politics, or writers to waste on epistolary narration, the time that both should be saving for "earnest work," it becomes natural to turn to old novels for the emotional depth that we can no longer enjoy (by bullying our own daughters or sisters in real life), nor even experience vicariously by reading new novels.

Hence the need to reprint, reread, and rewrite Richardson. Scott did all three. At the same moment as he reworked *Pamela* in *Redgauntlet*, Scott reproduced Richardson more literally by including all three of his novels in Ballantyne's Novelist's Library. As editor of Ballantyne's collection, Scott republished epistolary novels; but by ending the series with Radcliffe, he inscribed them within a historical progression leading up to the non-epistolary novel no less irreversibly (even if less explicitly) than Ward would later claim.[97] Scott's preface to Richardson already anticipates the sense of inertia conveyed in *Redgauntlet's* image of narratological "dead weight," in Hutton's metaphor of characters' emotional "[im]mobility," and in Ward's charge of readerly "dawdling." Whatever appeal the epistolary mode presents, Scott argues, "is at least partly balanced, by arresting the progress of the story, which stands still while the characters show all their paces, like horses in a manege, without advancing a yard."[98] Where Hutton figures the epistolary novel as a slowcoach, Scott refuses to acknowledge that it moves at all. Scott names Richardson less openly in *Redgauntlet* than in the Ballantyne's preface, of course, but the novel's form opposes letters just as clearly to "the progress of the story" – a term that conflates narrative pace with political change. Yet the clumsy gap that *Redgauntlet* leaves between the politics of the 1760s and the literary conventions of the 1740s suggests what a weak bridge literary history provides between social and narrative progress. Hence Ward's need to replace that missing link by the more direct connection of readers' work rhythms. In the process of relegating the epistolary novel to the past, Richardson's belated readers politicized his understanding of the letter as a delaying tactic. Scott's novel, Scott's preface, Hutton's essay, and Ward's abridgment all encouraged contemporaries to re-read the epistolary novel only in order to measure their difference from the readers of the 1740s – and the irreversibility of the social transformations which shifting narrative conventions made visible.

The ambition to historicize genre which *Redgauntlet* shares with Ballantyne's Novelist's Library – or indeed with Scott's *Border Minstrelsy* – sets it sharply apart from the mass of the Waverley novels. *Ivanhoe* is more typical in coupling historical nostalgia with literary-historical amnesia: its dedicatory epistle asserts that the novelist's "knights, squires, grooms, and yeomen may be more full drawn than in the hard, dry delineations of an ancient illuminated manuscript, but the character and costume of the age must remain inviolate; they must be the same figures, drawn by a better pencil, or, to speak more modestly, executed in an age when the principles of art were better understood."[99] Like the ancient Rome of early Hollywood, the eighteenth century allowed Scott's self-consciously modern medium to test its historical reach. Although the characters in *Redgauntlet* confine their reactionary politics to words – the Jacobite toasts of "gray-haired lairds over their punch," or old ladies' stories of "having led a dance down with the Chevalier," or the Jacobite joke displayed at the bottom of Justice Foxley's tankard (*Redgauntlet*, 206, 204) – the Waverley novels as a series show even less interest in reviving literary forms than in reviving anything else. Explicitly classified within a modern genre (Waverley Novels, not Romances) they represent past political struggles without re-enacting past literary forms. Or rather, those genres – notably the ballad – remain safely contained within the modern prose frame that they decorate. In *Redgauntlet*, the letter takes over that position and that function. Like the ballads interpolated in other Waverley novels, the letters inscribed in *Redgauntlet* turn back the march of literary history while delaying the progress of the narrative.

Conversely, the ballad first appears in *Redgauntlet* as a substitute for the letter. No sooner does Darsie's confinement cut him off from the post than his solipsistic journal-writing is interrupted by the sudden re-appearance of Wandering Willie, the blind fiddler whose tunes carry coded messages. Darsie soon "trust[s] to my own and my *correspondent's* acuteness, in applying to the airs the meaning they were intended to convey" (*Redgauntlet*, 221, my emphasis). The metaphor makes the illiterate's music interchangeable with the letters which it must now replace as Darsie's link to the outside world. The songs provide an oral equivalent not only for written correspondence, but for Lilias's equally oblique message conveyed to Darsie in the form of a poem "in a beautiful Italian manuscript," and for the schoolboy Latin tags which will later provide Alan and Nanty Ewart with a code (*Redgauntlet*, 223, 299).

Yet while the novel's hero experiences his feudal retainer's songs as part of an oral tradition, its readers can recognize them only because of the scholarly project of publishing that tradition which lends the Scottish Enlightenment its distinctive editorial cast. As Kathryn Sutherland has documented, Wandering Willie's tunes can all be found in earlier anthologies such as Allan Ramsay's *Tea-Table Miscellany* (1723), James Johnson's *Scots Musical Museum* (1787–1803), and Joseph Ritson's *Scottish Songs* (1794) – not to mention Scott's own *Minstrelsy of the Scottish Border* (1802–3). Indeed, *Redgauntlet* reproduces not only the content but the structure of Ritson's anthology. Where Scott's novel represents a failed re-enactment of the Forty-Five through an abortive revival of epistolary conventions, Ritson's preface juxtaposes an elegy for Jacobitism with an elegy for "Scottish song." Toward the end of the preface, Ritson asserts that "the aera of Scottish music and Scottish song is now passed . . . All, therefore, which now remains to be wished, is that industry should exert itself to retrieve and illustrate the reliques of departed genius." Fifty pages earlier, he had defended his inclusion of Jacobite songs in similar terms: "The rival claims of *Stewart* and *Brunswick* are not more to the present generation than those of *Bruce* and *Baliol*, or *York* and *Lancaster*. The question of RIGHT has been submitted to the arbitration of the SWORD, and is now irrevocably decided: but neither that decision, nor any other motive, should deter the historian from doing justice to the character of those brave men."[100] Despite their radically different attitudes toward the Jacobite cause, Ritson's anthology and Scott's novel both use the defeat of Jacobitism as an image for the obsolescence of an eighteenth-century literary form – the song in one case, the epistolary novel in the other – which becomes open to appropriation precisely at the moment when it ceases to be anything more than a "relique" of a past era.[101]

Where Wandering Willie's first appearance prompts Darsie to the "frolic" of playing second fiddle at a fishermen's dance, "assuming an office unworthy of a man of education," his re-appearance in the following volume turns the truant instead into a gentleman-scholar (*Redgauntlet*, 125). The fiddler's intrusion prompts Darsie's journal to take on an uncharacteristically antiquarian note: "It is well known that, in Scotland, where there is so much national music, the words and airs of which are generally known, there is a kind of free-masonry amongst performers . . . I ventured to sing a verse, which, in various forms, occurs so frequently in old ballads" (*Redgauntlet*, 220–23). Darsie's repetition of "known" glosses over the difference between the listeners to whom the music is "generally known" and the readers by whom their knowledge is "well known" in turn. In the same way that the conspirators use tunes as a disguise for verbal messages, the invocation of performance masks the resemblance of those explanatory asides to editorial annotations. When Darsie slips another piece of ethnographic information into his account of "intimat[ing] my speedy departure from my present place of residence, by whistling the well-known air with which festive parties in Scotland usually conclude the dance," he neglects to add that the air is also used to conclude printed collections of songs (*Redgauntlet*, 222; see Sutherland's note, 448). The scene as a whole reduces popular performance to a protective noise, as Darsie "heard a clattering noise of feet in the court-yard, which I concluded to be Jan and Dorcas dancing a jig in their Cumberland clogs. Under cover of this din, I endeavoured to answer Willie's signal by whistling" (*Redgauntlet*, 221). Just as the inarticulate racket made by the ethnographically-attired dancers camouflages Darsie's conversation, so Scott's invocation of oral folklore draws attention away from the print culture in which ballads are collected and novels read.

The shift from Alan's letters to Wandering Willie's airs reverses the career of Scott himself, who began by collecting, translating, and imitating ballads and only belatedly turned to his anomalous pastiche of the epistolary novel. In fact, Darsie's last ballad forms a variant of one that had already appeared in Scott's *Border Minstrelsy*.[102] Not surprisingly, the path from the compilation of the *Minstrelsy* to the composition of the Waverley novels left traces in the latter. Divided by chapter mottoes, annotated with antiquarian excerpts, embellished by ballads, appended with documents, each novel points outward to a range of older genres. Scott's cultural project of reconciling civilized blandness with raw authenticity corresponds to a formal oscillation from the historical and stylistic discontinuities of the anthology to the glib, even, inexorable flow of the narrative, and back again.

Robert Crawford has argued that the "synthetic and eclectic" structure of the Waverley novels comes out of a Scottish literary tradition whose paradigmatic figures "were as much major collectors as major creative artists . . . Sometimes, as in the case of the Ossianic works, collection and creation became so confused as to be virtually inextricable."[103] Scott himself defines authorship in terms of that confusion. The *Minstrelsy* glosses the Scots term "maker" as a synonym for "troubadour," which Scott translates in turn as "finder": "the French Trouvers, or Troubadours, namely, the Finders, or Inventors, has the same reference to the quality of original conception and invention."[104] By invoking the etymology of "invention," the gloss erases any distinction between the original "maker" and the compiler of found objects. Later, Scott boasted of misrepresenting his "made" epigraphs as "found" ones: according to a pivotal scene of Lockhart's *Memoirs*, he

happened to ask John Ballantyne, who was sitting by him, to hunt for a particular passage in Beaumont and Fletcher. John did as he was bid, but did not succeed in discovering the lines. "Hang it, Johnny," cried Scott, "I believe I can make a motto sooner than you will find one." He did so accordingly; and from that hour, whenever memory failed to suggest an appropriate epigraph, he had recourse to the inexhaustible mines of "old play" or "old ballad," to which we owe some of the most exquisite verses that ever flowed from his pen.[105]

While his critics attacked the heterogeneous structure of the Waverley novels on ethical grounds – what Hazlitt calls "patch-work and plagiarism, the beggarly copiousness of borrowed wealth" – Scott forestalled the accusation of plagiarism by presenting himself on the contrary as a forger.[106] Far from claiming others' words as his own, Lockhart's hero passes off "original" poems as "borrowed." Each novel masquerades as an accretion of fragments written at different times by different persons – or rather non-persons, as long as the Author of Waverley still shared the anonymity of "Old Ballad." The epigraphs riddle Scott's work with inscribed signatures as fictitious as those in any epistolary novel. In retrospect, Lockhart's narrative of compilation motivates the novels' composite form. Even within *Redgauntlet*, the proliferation of inscribed ballads and inset tales makes clear that Scott's eventual turn away from the epistolary novel did not end the characteristically eighteenth-century strategy of presenting the work of one author as the work of many.

The modular structure of Scott's novels can perhaps best be measured by anthologists' urge to break them back down into fragments.

Popular, prolix, and plotted, the Waverley novels might logically be expected to resist the anthology. Carlyle posited an inverse ratio of quantity to quotability: "no man has written as many volumes [as Scott] with so few sentences that can be quoted." Bagehot, too, measured the immediacy of the novels by their resistance to quotation: "nobody rises from [Scott's] works without a most vivid idea of what is related, and no one is able to quote a single phrase in which it has been narrated."[107] Yet the epigraphs collected in *The Poetry contained in the Novels, Tales and Romances of the Author of Waverley* (1822) soon gave way to more miscellaneous compilations ranging from *The Genius and Wisdom of Sir Walter Scott* (1839) to *Beauties of Sir Walter Scott* (1849) to the *Waverley Poetical Birthday Book* (1883, immediately imitated by a *Waverley Proverbial Birthday Book* and a *Scott Birthday Record*) to albums that reduced textual excerpts to captions for engravings for (and of) women: *Portraits of the Principal Female Characters in the Waverley Novels; to which are added, Landscape Illustrations* (1833), *The Waverley Gallery of the Principal Female Characters in Sir Walter Scott's Romances* (1841), *Female Portraits from the Writings of Byron and Scott, with poetical illustrations* (1845), and *The Waverley Keepsake* (1853).[108] Where collections of epigraphs severed verse fragments from the prose narrative that bound them together, albums of engraved "scenes" and "portraits" froze the narrative itself into a series of self-contained stills.

The Waverley novels' ridicule of women readers like Mrs. Mailsetter in *The Antiquary* and Martha Buskbody in *Old Mortality* and *The Heart of Midlothian* never prevented publishers from reducing them to raw material for ladies' gifts. The bindings and engravings of those collections of verbal, topographical, and human "beauties" showcased the latest technologies for drawing attention to the materiality of the book.[109] Visual special effects placed them even farther opposite Scott's invocation of a dying oral folklore than the Magnum Opus edition of the novels themselves. The metonymic title of Allan Ramsay's *Tea-Table Miscellany* had already transferred an oral tradition into the drawing-rooms of readers defined at once by their gender and by the luxury goods that they consumed. Scott's anthologists, too, showed readers how far they had come from the ballad and even from the more recent past connoted in *Redgauntlet* by the epistolary novel. Darsie's shift from writing letters to collecting ballads makes clear that by 1824 the inscribed fragment had come to stand for modishness as surely as the inscribed letter for obsolescence. Coffee-table albums completed the progress of romance set into motion at Ramsay's tea-table.

CHAPTER 2

Cultures of the commonplace

The kind of anthology most familiar to academic literary critics today –
delimited by nationality, arranged by chronology – was unknown in
Richardson's lifetime. The anthology itself is much older, as we have
seen. But the defeat of perpetual copyright in 1774 changed the use to
which the form was put. Only once the legal status of earlier works came
to diverge from that of new ones did English-language anthologies
take on the retrospective function (and the academic audience) that they
maintain today. Timely miscellanies of new works gave way to timeless gleanings from the backlist. On or about 1774, as the research of
Barbara Benedict and Trevor Ross has shown, literary history became
anthologists' job.[1]

A generation of late-eighteenth-century anthologies established not
only the content of the canon to date, but also the rules by which future
literature would be transmitted, notably the expectation that every
anthology-piece bear a signature and that its signatory be dead.[2] Even
more important than their ambition to consolidate a national tradition,
however, was the near-monopoly that a few school anthologies achieved
by the end of the century, allowing large numbers of schoolchildren to
share the experience of reading not just the same anthology-pieces but
the same anthologies. Looking back on the *Elegant Extracts: or Useful and
Entertaining Passages in Prose Selected for the Improvement of Scholars in Classical
and other Schools* first published by Vicesimus Knox in 1784, an 1816
edition could boast that the "*uniformity of English books*, in schools" which
enabled "*all the students of the same class*, provided with copies of the same
book, . . . to read it together" would have been logistically unthinkable a
few generations ago. The class reciting in unison provided an image for
a culture cemented not only by the affordability but by the ubiquity of a
few standard collections.[3]

Like other late-eighteenth-century traditions, however, those anthologies backdated their own invention. A companion volume of

Elegant Extracts: or Useful and Entertaining Pieces of Poetry, Selected for the Improvement of Youth in Speaking, Reading, Thinking, Composing; and in the Conduct of Life (1784) vests editorial responsibility with everybody and nobody, displacing Knox's originality at once by the anthologists who preceded him and by the readers forced to ratify his decisions. "There was no occasion for singular acuteness of vision, or of optical glasses," the preface intones heavily, "to discover a brightness which obtruded itself on the eye."

> The best pieces are usually the most popular. They are loudly recommended by the voice of fame, and indeed have already been selected in a variety of volumes of preceding collections . . . Almost any man, willing to incur a considerable expense, and undergo a little trouble, might have furnished as good a collection . . . It was the business of the Editor of a school-book like this, not to insert scarce and curious works . . . but to collect such as were publicly known and universally celebrated . . . Private judgement, in a work like this, must often give way to public.[4]

An anthology that reproduces the words of poets also records the voice of fame. An amanuensis rather than a creator, its editor represents a community instead of expressing a self. In the same way that each anthology-piece functions (at least in theory) as a representative synecdoche for the longer text from which it is excerpted, the anthologist claims to stand within – and for – the same audience that he addresses. Samuel Johnson had positioned himself within that public when he professed in the *Life of Gray* (itself prefaced to one of the volumes which together make up an anthology writ large of *Works of the English Poets*) to "rejoice to concur with the common reader; for by the common sense of readers uncorrupted with literary prejudices . . . must be finally decided all claim to poetical honours."[5] Johnson's "common sense" anticipates Knox's "public judgement" as closely as the latter's lumbering antitheses imitate the former's measured periods, but the *Extracts* go farther to silence Johnson's critical "I" altogether. Caught between the readers for whom he speaks and the writers from whom he copies, the editor dwindles to a vanishing point. In the last moment of the book marked as Knox's own – since the "extracts" themselves change him from author to compiler – the speaker writes himself out of existence. The preface ends with a quotation: "I will, therefore, conclude my preface with the ideas of Montaigne: – *'I have here only made a nosegay of culled flowers, and have brought nothing of my own but the thread that ties them.'*"[6] By substituting Montaigne's signature for Knox's, this conclusion prefigures the transition from the preface where the editor speaks to the body of the text where other authors' voices displace his. The editor abdicates his individuality as a reader together with his originality as a writer. Far from standing above the undifferentiated passivity of the reading public, the anthologist exemplifies it.[7]

Knox's self-conscious sacrifice of "private" or "singular" to "public" or "popular" taste erases not only the editor's superiority to his audience but any difference between one reader and another. The only readers whom his ostentatiously inclusive public excludes are precisely those who try to distinguish themselves: antiquarians whose expertise on what he calls "scarce and curious works" challenges the cohesion of his audience. The *Elegant Extracts* record a double series of discriminations – texts to be represented from texts to be ignored and, within the former, passages to be reproduced from passages to be excised. Yet Knox keeps the act of evaluation decorously offstage. His preface alternately banishes from the "public" those readers who attempt to act upon their "private" judgments and displaces his own editorial responsibility onto the "preceding collections" to which he defers. That precedent itself recedes endlessly, since the preface accuses earlier anthologies of borrowing in turn: "the freedom of borrowing [from other anthologies], it is hoped, will be pardoned, as the collectors, with whom it has been used, first set the example of it."[8] Knox's deference to tradition lends moral significance to the longstanding tension between the demand for new editions to edge older ones out of the market, on the one hand, and the economic incentives to recycle earlier editorial principles or even to re-use old plates, on the other. Indeed, the *Extracts* exclude not only living authors, but new assessments of dead ones. In a characteristically negative formulation, the tenth edition promises that its contents will be "selected from writers whose characters are established without controversy."[9] With what their characters are established remains unspecified, for the anthology defines not only the production but the evaluation of literature as *faits accomplis*.

Knox's disclaimer of originality kept his anthology in print, his selection plagiarized, and his impersonal persona imitated long after more polemical competitors like Hazlitt's ephemeral *Select British Poets, or New Elegant Extracts from Chaucer to the Present Time* (1824) disappeared from sight. Hazlitt broke not only the rule against including living poets – a decision that landed him in immediate copyright difficulties – but the equally unwritten taboo on invoking individual taste. Beginning with the remark that "if it had not been thought that [Knox's] work admitted of considerable improvement . . . the present publication would not have been" undertaken, Hazlitt goes on to overturn not only the content, but the consensuality, of Knox's selection. "Young is a poet who has been much over-rated," his introductory note declares (too blasphemously not to be contradicted by the frontispiece, in which Young's portrait features prominently); and the polemical tone is heightened, rather than toned down, by the mock apology "at least, it appears so to me."[10] Although Hazlitt's self-conscious quirkiness has found occasional successors (most recently, Jerome Rothenberg's and Pierre Joris's *Poems for the Millennium* [1995–98]), Knox's editorial voice won the day. His invocation of an already established consensus has remained formulaic from Kearsley's *Beauties of Shakespeare* (published in the same year as the first volume of the *Extracts*), which apologizes for "dwell[ing] on perfections which every one confesses," to Francis Turner Palgrave's *Golden Treasury* (1861), which calls "its fittest readers those who already love Poetry so well, that [the editor] can offer them nothing not already known and valued," through to Cleanth Brooks and Robert Penn Warren's influential American textbook *Understanding Fiction* (1943), which promises to include only "stories which are popular and widely anthologized." Knox's fantasy of editing by plebiscite was realized two centuries later in Columbia University Press's anomalously explicit *The Classic Hundred: All-Time Favorite Poems* (1990) and *Top 500 Poems* (1992), which select their contents by frequency of appearance in earlier U.S. anthologies as measured by *Granger's Index to Poetry*. When a U.S. Education Secretary's neoconservative *Book of Virtues* (1993) made hackneyed anthology-pieces the vehicle to bring a reluctant public "back" to basics, his declaration that "we don't have to reinvent the wheel" lent political point to the reinvention of tradition that has become traditional among anthologists.[11] Repeated with the same unanimity that they describe, these editorial disclaimers not only imply that texts transmit themselves – that as John Hollander's and Frank Kermode's preface to the *Oxford Anthology of English Literature* put it more thoughtfully in 1973, "English literature has generated its own history" – but present the anthology as the effect of an audience's cohesion rather than its cause.[12]

KNOX'S SCISSOR-DOINGS

Knox's disclaimers of novelty obscure the role of his *Extracts* in defining a specifically middle-class public which owes more to the endurance of the anthology than to the rise of the novel. By dismissing as "private" the elite that prizes authorial obscurity and critical originality, Knox reduces the "public" to the anthology-reading classes. Yet the relation of that audience to its classically-educated betters remains strategically ambiguous. Where the first edition of Knox's *Elegant Extracts* (1783) addresses "school-boys," the tenth (1816), advertised "for the use of both sexes," presents itself as a corrective to the gender gap embodied in the absence of the "mother tongue" from the schoolbooks of "our fathers." "What ENGLISH book similar to this volume, calculated entirely for the use of young students at schools, and under private tuition, was to be found in the days of our fathers?" the preface asks. "None, certainly. The consequence was . . . neglect [of] that mother tongue, which is in daily and hourly requisition."[13] Knox's claim for the novelty of an "ENGLISH" anthology (like his announcement that "this collection may be usefully read at ENGLISH SCHOOLS, just as the Latin and Greek authors are read at the *grammar-schools*") at once acknowledges and dismisses his debt to the centuries-old machinery developed to teach ancient languages to boys.[14]

Collections of classical excerpts designed to exemplify grammatical principles, such as the *Gradus ad Parnassum*, provided a model for the more androgynous vernacular anthologies which began to supplement them in this period. William Enfield, whose academy in Warrington helped institutionalize that shift, uses the preface of his *Speaker* (1774) to reassign the pedagogical function of ancient literature to the moderns: "Without having recourse to the ancients, it is possible to find in modern languages valuable specimens of every species of polite literature."[15] The title's invocation of an oratorical training specific to boys overcompensates for the *Speaker*'s attack on the ancient/modern opposition which had traditionally helped shape children's gender identity. Indeed, Anna Laetitia Barbauld's *Female Speaker* (published thirty-seven years later) opens by regretting the disappearance of that difference between women's education and men's: "It is, perhaps, an error in modern education, liberally conducted as at present it is toward females, that . . . when they have gone through their course of education, they have a general acquaintance with, perhaps, three or four languages, and know little of the best productions of their own."[16] Barbauld's fear that women's eagerness for the prestige of masculine learning would eliminate students' "own" literature from the curriculum reverses Enfield's attempt to construct a national canon by teaching men to read like women. Yet both locate gender difference among consumers, rather than, like Sandra Gilbert and Susan Gubar's *Norton Anthology of Literature by Women* two centuries later, among producers. Even the inclusion of seven token women – Catherine Talbot, Frances Brooke, Lady Mary

Wortley Montagu, Lucy Aiken, Hannah More, Hester Chapone, and
Maria Edgeworth – fails to make *The Female Speaker* significantly more
gender-balanced than Enfield's collection, which had already included
one in the person of Barbauld herself. Barbauld's interpellation of
readers differs sharply from Gilbert and Gubar's representation of
writers; the limits of her anthology depend not on who wrote its
contents, but who edits and reads them. By making clear that the
"Female Speaker" of her title refers only to the audience who recites
from it, Barbauld rules out the possibility that speech might encompass
original self-expression.

The *Extracts'* bid to replace the classical curriculum of "our fathers"
by its equivalent in the "mother tongue" reinforces the feminization of
bourgeois culture that Knox exploits in his equally assonant *Elegant
Epistles*, whose preface reassures readers that "merchants, men of business, and particularly the ladies" write better letters than scholars.[17] In
the *Extracts*, too, the language of gender slips easily into commercial
metaphors. The 1816 preface's description of "the days of our fathers"
concludes:

Persons who had never extended their views to ancient and classic lore, but had
been confined in their education to English, triumphed in the common intercourse of society, over the academical scholar . . . It became highly expedient
therefore to introduce more of English reading into our classical schools; that
those who went into the world with their coffers richly stored with the golden
medals of antiquity, might at the same time be furnished with a sufficiency of
coin from the modern mint, for the commerce of ordinary life.[18]

While adjectives like "common" and "ordinary" describe the same
community that earlier editions invoke, the 1816 preface transposes
them from words denoting evaluation ("universal celebration," "public
judgement") to terms of exchange ("common intercourse," "the commerce of ordinary life"). Knox had already defended his lack of originality by analogy with the circulation of coins: "the stamp of experience
gave ["whatever was found in previous collections"] currency." Here,
too, the scholar's "scarce and curious works" are to the anthology-
reader's "commerce of ordinary life" what ancestral "stores" are to the
exchange of "coins." Aristocratic inheritance and bourgeois commerce
stand for two competing models of literature: one compares it with
heirlooms valuable for their rarity, the other with a currency whose
worth depends on its circulation.[19]

Knox makes even more global claims for the circulation of literature
in his later essay collection, *Winter Evenings: or Lucubrations on Life and*

Letters (1788), which amplifies the *Extracts'* concern with the relation of culture to commerce. The introduction to the *Evenings* defends the proliferation of new publications by describing the widening social and geographical field through which popular English literature "flows":

The world is wide, and readers more numerous at present than in any preceding age. A liberal education is more general, and is likely to be still more extensively diffused . . . The English language is the language of a vast continent of people . . . connecting themselves in commercial and other engagements with all nations. English literature is of course the literature of America. The learning of England has long been flowing from the Thames to the Ganges. The late amicable connection with our neighbours, which reflects so much honour on the liberality and wisdom of the present times, will contribute greatly to extend the language and learning of Great Britain.

The new audience to which Knox appeals here is not only English but British, not only commercial but colonial or post-colonial. Like the audience of the *Extracts*, it derives authority from shared ignorance rather than specialized knowledge. Knox insists, in fact, that the value of learning varies inversely with its rarity:

The erudition which is confined to a few libraries, or locked in the bosom of a few professors . . . may be compared to a stagnant pool; large perhaps and deep, but of little utility; while the knowledge which displays itself in popular works may be said to resemble a river, fertilizing, refreshing, and embellishing whole provinces through which its meanders roll their tide.[20]

The analogy of the river alludes to economic circulation as well, for Knox specifies that the "flow" of English learning depends on "commercial engagements." His celebration of global exchange differs not only from antiquarian projects like Thomas Percy's *Reliques of Ancient English Poetry* (1765), which define literature as a national inheritance, but even more radically from the factionalism of Ritson's ballad collections.

The fact that the *Elegant Extracts* happen to be edited by a conservative Anglican clergyman – not, like the *Speaker* or the *Female Speaker*, by a woman, a radical, or a dissenter – suggests how little its commercial model of literary circulation and feminized vision of the literary public depend on any individual anthologist's identity (what Knox himself dismisses as "private judgement") but how inexorably they follow from the genre of the anthology itself.[21] The anthologist speaks *ex officio* or not at all. Conversely, Knox's self-consciousness about the relations among money, gender, and the circulation of literature reflects more than a biographical mismatch between his own classical education and his readers' presumed lack of it (or between his gentlemanly pretensions and his anthologies' commercial success). Knox's ambivalence looks back to the ambiguous gender of the figure who oversees the transmission of texts and of property in *Sir Charles Grandison*, and forward to George Eliot's hesitation about being excerpted in gift books marketed to girls. Eliot associates anthologies with private exchange among female consumers, Knox with the international trade carried out by classically illiterate men. Both take the anthology as a limit case for the entanglement of esthetics with money.

The convergence that anthologies like Knox's and Enfield's celebrated between the feminization of schooling and the commercialization of literature was soon turned against the genre, however. Hannah More's charge in *Strictures on the Modern System of Female Education* (1799) that "the swarms of *Abridgments, Beauties,* and *Compendiums,* . . . form too considerable a part of a young lady's library" did not so much reflect facts (since the formal education of boys guaranteed condensers their most centralized and captive audience) as literalize the gendered language that Knox and Enfield had used to define their audience's class position. More adds:

A few fine passages from the poets (passages perhaps which derived their chief beauty from their position and connection) are huddled together by some extract-maker, whose brief and disconnected patches of broken and discordant materials, while they inflame young readers with the vanity of reciting, neither fill the mind nor form the taste; and it is not difficult to trace back to their shallow sources the hackney'd quotations of certain *accomplished* young ladies, who will be frequently found not to have come legitimately by any thing they know: I mean, not to have drawn it from its true spring, the original works of the author from which some beauty-monger has severed it . . . If we would purchase knowledge we must pay for it the fair and lawful price of time and industry.

That attack on "the hackney'd quotations of certain accomplish'd young ladies" recalls Richardson's revisionary claim that "seldom did [Clarissa] quote or repeat from" poets – and, more immediately, More's insistence in *Coelebs in Search of a Wife* that her own feminine paragon, Lucilla Stanley, "does not say things to be quoted."[22] In the *Strictures,* however, More's concern is epistemological as much as moral. Quoting reflects not simply feminine vanity, but feminine imposture. More's argument draws on three turn-of-the-century esthetic concepts that have fueled the backlash against anthologies well into the present: originality (the "true spring," the "original works"); organic structure ("position and connection" opposed to "broken and discordant materials"); and, most of all, the fear of a mass public.

Yet More protests anthologists' appeal to a frivolous feminine audience only at the expense of naturalizing it. Compilation is to complete works as women to men: both secondary rather than "original," both decorative but "shallow." Indeed, More's attack on the "disconnected" structure of anthologies echoes her description elsewhere of the female mind: "Both in composition and action [women] excel in details; but they do not so much generalize their ideas as men . . . Women have equal parts, but are inferior in *wholeness* of mind, in the integral understanding." That taste for detail, including textual beauties, extends from women themselves to feminized men. More's caricature of a fop

> . . . studied while he dress'd, for true 'tis
> He read Compendiums, Extracts, Beauties
> Abregés, Dictionnaires, Recueils,
> Mercures, Journaux, Extraits, and Feuilles.[23]

Attention to anthology-pieces undermines masculinity as much as does attention to dress.

More appropriates not only Knox's assumptions about gender but his metaphors of community. Her image of the "swarm" neatly inverts the picture of the busy editorial beehive that decorates the title-page of his *Extracts*. In Knox, the commonplace stands not only for the hard work involved in culling literary "flowers" but for the sociable character of that project. One contemporary editor's conventional defense of the "extract" makes clear how well the beehive emblematizes Knox's subordination of the editorial self to the literary community: "if like the industrious bee I have cull'd from various flowers my share of Honey, and stored it in the common Hive, I shall have performed the duties of a good citizen of the Republic of letters."[24] But More's substitution of a swarm for a hive turned the apiary image against itself, replacing the republic of letters by the mob. In 1782 the *London Magazine* had already characterized anthologists as a "swarm of servile imitators" guilty of "invasion of property."[25] More went farther to hint that unwillingness to pay a "fair" or "legitimate" price made anthology-readers receivers of pilfered goods.

More's nervousness about readers' dependence on anthologies provides one measure of their success. Another can be found in Jane Austen's complaint that critics take novelists less seriously than "the man who collects and publishes in a volume some dozen lines of Milton,

Pope, and Prior, with a paper from the Spectator, and a chapter from Sterne."[26] Like Coleridge's, More's and Austen's hostility testifies to the power which anthologists modestly disclaimed. By the turn of the nineteenth century, what Lonsdale calls "the hypnotically influential way in which the eighteenth century succeeded in anthologizing itself" had provoked an equally powerful reaction against anthologists and their audience – a public which, like novel-readers, ranked scarcely above illiterates in critics' estimation.[27]

The difference, however, is that novel-reading went on to become respectable, as anthologies have yet to do. More than a century later, More's scorn for commercial "beauty-mongers" and mechanical "extract-makers" could still be recognized in Laura Riding's and Robert Graves's attack on "the all too numerous trade-anthologies that turn poetry into an industrial packet-commodity." But their *Pamphlet Against Anthologies* proposes no alternative except a kind of hypertrophied anthology: a self-sufficient corpus of self-contained *oeuvres*.

This full Corpus would include all poets who had a certain recognizable minimum of credibility . . . If there were any disagreement at all about whether or not a poet should be included, he would naturally be included. When it was agreed to include a poet, disagreement as to his relative merit would not matter, as each poet would be printed entire.[28]

Something close to the "Corpus" imagined by Riding and Graves has finally been realized in the form of Chadwyck-Healey's *English Full-Text Poetry Database*, arranged like theirs by author, and delimited by the "recognizable minimum of credibility" borrowed (with scattershot additions) from the *New Cambridge Bibliography of English Literature*. Yet both corpuses are "full" only in the sense that they exclude œuvres wholesale rather than piecemeal, omitting minor poets instead of minor poems. Riding's and Graves's metonymic demand for "each poet entire" simply displaces the canon of anthology-pieces by a catalogue of signatures. The life replaces the poem as the smallest unit that can stand on its own. That substitution depends in turn on the exclusion of anonymous texts, which became conventional in literary anthologies (as opposed to antiquarian ones) at the same moment in which collections like Knox's *Extracts* systematically began to disclaim their editors' individuality. Like the *Extracts*, the *Pamphlet* makes authorial subjectivity the precondition of editorial objectivity. Their doubly impersonal reference to a "recognizable credibility" spares Riding and Graves from specifying who recognizes "merit" and who is expected to "credit" that recognition. Both arguments project the editor's taste onto readers

(Riding's and Graves's "recognizable minimum of credibility," Knox's "voice of fame" and "public judgment") at the same time as they replace the editor's individuality with the identity of the authors who sign their raw materials.

At a moment when the editors of the *Norton Anthology of English Literature* are experimenting with a *salon des refusés* on the Web – a supplementary collection of texts too unwieldy to fit within its covers – it is tempting to imagine that the electronic database will eliminate the economic constraints which have so long rendered the excerpt unavoidable. But the needs to which the anthology responds are hermeneutic, not just logistical. So far at least, Margaret Ezell's hope that exhaustive full-text databases will render anthologies of women's writing obsolete looks as utopian as the idea that genetically modified crops can end famine. Anthologies more often respond to a surfeit of accessible texts than to their shortage: what they omit is as crucial as what they include.[29] Indeed, anthologies like Knox's defined only the minimal limit of an emerging tradition whose maximal form had already been marked by the encyclopedic reprint series beginning with Hugh Blair's *British Poets* (forty-four volumes published between 1773 and 1776).[30] The speed with which Knox's necessary canon followed upon Blair's sufficient one reveals how quickly information overload creates a demand for editors, even for censors – not simply to limit the data available, but to order it. What Paul Duguid has argued of the codex remains even truer for the anthology: "If books [as opposed to digital media] can be thought of as 'containing' and even imprisoning information, that information must, in the last analysis, be understood as inescapably the product of bookmaking."[31]

BOWDLER'S PRIVATE PUBLIC

Knox's hope that anthology-reading could undergird an empire proved short-lived, for the dissemination of a national poet in the decades that followed failed even to unify the new United Kingdom. On the contrary, by enlisting gender difference to justify the proliferation of competing editions, the Shakespeare industry eliminated the common reader whom its promoters invoked. Paradoxically, a national public could be brought together by shared reading of Shakespeare only once that name attached to a range of genres wide enough to distinguish one market niche from another. The public for Shakespeare cracked under its own weight as fast as the plays themselves splintered into rival spin-offs – anthologies, novelizations, prequels, expurgations – which together taught readers to know their place within it.

If the industry devoted to editing and adapting Shakespeare shaped a national identity, as critics from Gary Taylor to Margreta de Grazia to Jonathan Bate to Michael Dobson have recently shown, it also established a more oblique precedent for the Victorians' half-hearted canonization of fiction.[32] Shakespeare set the first example of genius trumping genre: his plays were admitted to anthologies without opening the floodgates for other dramatists. What he did open the way for, instead, was novelists such as George Eliot, whose anthologization a century later did not ennoble the novel so much as reclassify her as a prose poet. In replacing narrative continuity by lyric fragmentation and sententious atemporality, Shakespearean editors proved the power of anthologies to cleanse their raw material of its generic origin. At the same time, though, that precedent created a demand for a wider range of editorial manipulations – novelized plays, narrative abridgments, dramatic expurgations – by heightening each reader's consciousness of her or his difference from others. In representing such self-awareness as painful but morally necessary, those editions made sexual embarrassment inseparable from gendered identity, and both dependent on the publishing industry.

Over the course of the eighteenth century, Shakespeare's oeuvre disintegrated into anthology-pieces. By 1765, Samuel Johnson worried that it was too quotable for its own good: his "Preface to Shakespeare" qualifies the hackneyed observation that Shakespeare's plays are filled with "axioms" by warning that "his real power is not shewn in the splendour of particular passages, but by the progress of his fable, and the tenour of his dialogue; and he that tries to recommend him by select quotations, will succeed like the pedant in *Hierocles*, who, when he offered his house to sale, carried a brick in his pocket as a specimen."[33] Johnson's distrust of textual "specimens" responded to his contemporaries' habit of quarrying Shakespearean "dialogue" for self-contained speeches or maxims arranged alphabetically by theme rather than in the chronological order of "the progress of his fable." Charles and Mary Lamb took action against that habit in the *Tales from Shakespeare* (1807), paraphrasing the plot rather than quoting the beauties in order to set a counterexample of how to read for the "fable." Charles Lamb complains that "to be or not to be" are no longer Shakespeare's words but Enfield's, thanks to the ubiquity of "those speeches from Henry the Fifth, &c, which are current in the mouths of school-boys from their being found in *Enfield Speakers*, and such kind of books. I confess myself utterly unable to appreciate that celebrated soliloquy in Hamlet, beginning 'To be or not to be,' . . . torn so inhumanly from its living place and principle of continuity in the play.''[34] Lamb's failure to specify which speeches he has in mind from *Henry V* suggests that he expected every reader to have memorized the same snippets – and to remember their place in Enfield.

In contrast, Jane Austen predicates the power of Shakespearean fragments on readers' ability to forget where they found them. Although readers often remember *Mansfield Park* as a novel about plays, it is rarely thought of as a reflection on anthology-pieces. This is hardly surprising, given Austen's own association of excerpts with oblivion. Halfway through the novel, after the Bertram family's uproarious play-acting gives way to a quiet evening of reading aloud, Henry Crawford confesses: "I do not think that I have had a volume of Shakespeare in my hand before, since I was fifteen . . . But Shakespeare one gets acquainted with without knowing how. It is part of an Englishman's constitution. His thoughts and beauties are so spread abroad that one touches them every where.''[35] In this osmotic model, Shakespeare's role as a national poet depends on the interplay of learning with ignorance – not only with boys' innocence of the unquotable bits of the plays, but with men's amnesia about just how they learnt their quotable "thoughts and beauties." For anthology-pieces to be memorized, the anthology needs to be forgotten.

Henry's denial that he has read Shakespeare "since I was fifteen" reinforces Austen's observation in *Northanger Abbey* that future heroines "from fifteen to seventeen" must presumably read much Shakespeare "to supply their memories with those quotations which are so service-able and so soothing in the vicissitudes of their eventual lives.''[36] Quoting forms part of adult sociability, and part of the novel; yet the necessary preliminary to it – learning – remains outside the time-frame of fiction. *Mansfield Park* banishes drama at once to the anthology and to the schoolroom, contrasting both to the dangers of private theatricals. Tom Bertram is accused of disingenuity when he argues that his father must approve of acting because he forced his sons to recite Shake-spearean soliloquies: "How many a time have we mourned over the dead body of Julius Caesar, and *to be'd* and *not to be'd*, in this very room, for his amusement! And I am sure, *my name was Norval*, every evening of my life through one Christmas holidays.''[37] Austen's confidence that readers would recognize Tom's joke – a misquotation of one of the few dramatic anthology-pieces *not* to come from Shakespeare, the speech beginning "My name is Norval" which Knox and Enfield both excerpt from John Home's otherwise forgotten tragedy *Douglas* (1756) – suggests that she expected her audience to remember memorizing the passage themselves. And they did. Two generations later, George Eliot still assumed that her readers' names were Norval once, or more than once: Tom Tulliver disclaims any ambition "to spell without forethought, and to spout 'My name is Norval' without bungling," though even when a classical education promises to rescue him from the English anthology-pieces of Mr Jacobs' Academy, his bad Latin is punished by having to learn "ever so many lines of 'Speaker'."[38] As late as 1926, Hugh MacDiarmid could still invoke the name "Norval" to allude to allusion:

> My name is Norval. On the Grampian Hills
> It is forgotten, and deserves to be.
> . . .
> This is the sort of thing they teach
> The Scottish children in the school.
> Poetry, patriotism, manners– [39]

Paradoxically, the obsolescence of *Douglas* onstage makes its one surviving line all the more recognizable as an anthology-piece.

Indeed, Edmund Bertram retorts that Tom is wrong to classify "My name is Norval" and "To be or not to be" as drama at all. "It was a very different thing. You must see the difference yourself. My father wished us, as school-boys, to speak well, but he would never wish his grown-up daughters to be acting plays." Edmund's insistence on the "difference" between elocution exercises and dramatic dialogue literalizes Fanny Price's more loaded declaration that "It is not that I am afraid of learning by heart; but really I cannot act."[40] The Bertram children's eventual conversion of the schoolroom into a rehearsal-room and the study into a green-room avenges their father's pedagogical appropriation of plays. *Mansfield Park* stages the question that contemporary anthologies raised: how to bring drama into the family, and into the novel.

But while Kotzebue competes with Shakespeare to infiltrate the Bertrams' home and the novel in which it appears, early-nineteenth-century editors overwhelmingly chose Shakespeare, rather than any more contemporary dramatist, for their experimental subject. William Dodd's *Beauties of Shakespeare* (1752) not only set a precedent for two centuries' worth of anthologies ranging from Kearsley's namesake of 1783 to the Prince of Wales's rather less successful compilation in 1995, but supplied a template for dozens of subsequent *Beauties* devoted to other authors or no author. The Lambs' *Tales from Shakespeare* established an equally durable prototype for collections from *Tales from Chaucer*

(1833) to *Tales from Scott* (1894).[41] *Beauties of* are to *Tales from* what Richardson's *Collection of Sentiments* is to *The Paths of Virtue*. Where synecdochal anthologies lift sublime fragments (usually in verse) out of their narrative context, synoptic abridgments translate dramatic dialogue into impersonal, retrospective narrative prose. In both cases, changes of scale occasion changes in genre.

Anthologies attack the drama from two directions. First, editors strip the dialogue away from soliloquies and songs to produce snatches of lyric self-expression, and away from maxims to produce universally applicable truths. In that sense, Shakespeare is "improved" not simply by the taste with which any particular anthologist selects and omits, but by the fragmentation inherent to the anthology as a form. And second, anthologists quarantine Shakespeare from other playwrights as systematically as they unmoor selected passages from their dramatic context. Knox's under-representation of drama matches his over-representation of Shakespeare: the *Extracts* of 1783 includes 112 pages of Shakespeare against only twenty-three from other dramatists, while Knox's second-degree anthology, the *Elegant Extracts . . . Abridged*, cuts the latter twice as sharply as the former. The proportion of drama is even lower in William Enfield's *Exercises in Elocution* (1780), as if an anthology designed for oral performance needed to distance itself all the more strenuously from the theater. Their imperative is Edmund's: "You must see the difference." The absence of drama calls attention to Shakespeare's presence. The generic rule proves the authorial exception. Novel-readers were quick to recognize this strategy. When Richardson indexed his novels on the model of Pope's edition of Shakespeare – or later, when Alexander Main invoked Shakespeare in his *Sayings of George Eliot* – they made Shakespearean editing into a precedent for rescuing a few authors, and a few passages, from low company. (Read together, Richardson's *Collection of Sentiments* and indexes to *Sir Charles Grandison* take on a self-aggrandizing resemblance to the indexes of characters and "Sentiments" in Pope's edition of Shakespeare, which Pope claimed in turn to model "upon the plan of mine to Homer.")[42]

In their project of generic whitewashing, however, anthologies soon encountered competition from two rather different editorial strategies: the abridgment and the expurgation. Like photographic negatives, each retains what the other discards. Plot summaries from the Lambs' onward skip the lyric and sententious digressions to which anthologies had lent a new prominence. In contrast, expurgations cut indelicate passages as ruthlessly as anthologies omit dull ones. Abridgers and expurgators both sprinkle gaps through the text like inverted anthology-pieces. More fundamentally, bowdlerizations borrow the atomistic logic of anthologies: the patches of immoral language that the former excise are no less self-contained than the snatches of moral wisdom that the latter reproduce. Both locate moral value in the parts rather than the whole. As a result, all three miniaturizing strategies fed the antitheatricality that Gary Taylor and Terence Hawkes have shown to pervade eighteenth-century editions of Shakespeare: a "shift from stage to page," in Taylor's phrase, that rescued texts from the corruption of performance.[43] Where expurgations omitted verbal obscenities and anthologies salvaged textual beauties, plot summaries attacked vice more obliquely by domesticating Shakespeare's audience.

Yet the project of translating drama into narrative created more problems than it solved, since the solitary reading of fiction posed moral dangers of its own. Elizabeth Macauley's non-Shakespearean *Tales of the Drama* (1822) smuggled plays into Evangelical homes only at the price of transposing them from one suspect genre to another. Her preface promises "to change the acted Drama to the more popular form of narrative, for the purpose of rendering the real beauties of the British stage more familiar . . . and even of extending that knowledge to family circles where the drama itself is forbidden."[44] Neither Macauley's reference to "beauties" nor her liberality with epigraphs, however, succeeds in masking a structure that owes less to the model of Dodd's *Beauties* than of the Lambs' *Tales* – and, through their intermediary, the novel. Her *Tales* follow theirs in borrowing the conventions of that "popular form of narrative": third-person past-tense omniscient prose narration punctuated with an occasional quotation from a character or from a poet. Even the Shakespearean verse epigraphs that interrupt her prose do not recall the form of the plays themselves so much as the chapter mottoes adorning the three Waverley Novels published that year.

No less than the self-contained soliloquies and impersonal maxims collected in anthologies, the omniscient narrative of the plot summary crowds dialogue out. The Lambs and Macauley both expected readers to prefer narrative: in the words of the former, "I have made use of dialogue too frequently for young people not used to the dramatic form of writing. But this fault . . . has been caused by my earnest wish to give as much of Shakespear's own words as possible."[45] That apology for diluting omniscient narrative with direct discourse draws attention to the tension between the efficiency of the Lambs' impersonal editorial voice and the generic authenticity of the dialogue in which they quote

Shakespeare quoting characters. Yet like Macauley's, their strategy of decorating narration with dialogue does not resemble "dramatic form" itself so much as the alternation between scene and summary, zooming in and panning out, that structures the novel.

Abridgment contributed to define prose narrative as the transparent medium into which all other genres could eventually be translated (or, as we shall see in Radcliffe's novels, in which excerpts from other genres could be reframed). The Lambs and Macauley act out Vicesimus Knox's confident assertion that "Poetry is not one of the necessaries of life. The information it conveys may be conveyed in prose."[46] Charlotte Lennox's source-study *Shakespear Illustrated: or the Novels and Histories on which the plays of Shakespear are founded* (1753–54) projects that hierarchy into time by conflating "novella" with its modern English cognate, to derive Shakespeare's plays from originary "Novels." Her literary genealogy gives way to biographical etiology in Mary Cowden Clarke's *Girlhood of Shakespeare's Heroines* (1850–52), a series of children's stories that raid at once the form of biography and the conventions of the bildungsroman to find private antecedents for the public events of Shakespeare's plays. Like Richardson's abridgers, Cowden Clarke replaces Shakespeare's beginnings *in medias res* (and the recapitulation which they make necessary) by narratives *ab ovo* (sometimes literally beginning with prenatal experiences) which realign the order of story with the order of discourse. Like Richardson's abridgers, too, Cowden Clarke reaches backward for genealogical origins: Ophelia's madness is traced to the childhood experience of witnessing the seduction of her friends, Lady Macbeth's unwomanliness explained by her pregnant mother's desire for a son. Personal histories function in Cowden Clarke's prequels as literary history does in Lennox's source study. Both position drama as an after-effect of "Novels." Yet Lennox's omniscient summary of each play's "Fable" simultaneously uses the latter to update the former: seventeenth-century drama becomes raw material for modern narrative. The literary history of *Shakespear Illustrated* comes full circle to derive the plays from the same genre whose conventions it borrows to summarize them.[47] The novel supplies Shakespeare's plots (in Lennox) or characters (in Cowden Clarke) with a past as well as a future.

In short, where expurgators learned from anthologists to censor piecemeal, abridgers showed less interest in pruning the plays' contents than in altering their context. As a result, plot summaries moralized Shakespeare more seamlessly than did the contemporary expurgations whose feminine market they competed for. Thomas Bowdler's *Family*

Shakespeare, in which . . . those words and expressions are omitted which cannot with propriety be read aloud in a family (1818) pushes out to a programmatic preface the antitheatricality which Lennox, the Lambs, Macauley and the Cowden Clarkes weave into the narrative itself. Bowdler begins by relocating Shakespeare's audience from the urban public theater to the private rural home, announcing that "I can hardly imagine a more pleasing occupation for a winter's evening in the country, than for a father to read one of Shakespeare's plays to his family circle."[48] Like Macauley's *Tales*, which "render the real beauties of the British *stage* more *familiar*," Bowdler's expurgation promises to displace the stage by the family. Yet where Macauley changes the genre of the plays, from drama to "the form of narrative," Bowdler does nothing of the sort: on the contrary, he invokes the precedent of theatrical abridgment to justify textual expurgation, dismissing the complete text (with reason) as a scholarly fiction never performed in full on the stage.[49]

The retrospective narrative mode into which Macauley and the Lambs translate the plays appears nowhere in the *Family Shakespeare* except in the paratextual apparatus that frames it. Bowdler attacks the theater not as an editor but as an autobiographer. His title anticipates a footnote which defines the public as a family *manqué*:

In the perfection of reading few men were equal to my father, and such were his good taste, his delicacy, and his prompt discretion, that his family listened with delight to Lear, Hamlet, and Othello, without knowing that those matchless tragedies contained words and expressions improper to be pronounced; and without having any reason to suspect that any parts of the plays had been omitted by the circumspect and judicious reader. It afterwards occurred to me, that what my father did so readily and successfully for his family, my inferior abilities might, with the assistance of time and mature consideration, be able to accomplish for the benefit of the public.[50]

Thomas Bowdler matches Tom Bertram's glibness in invoking the memory of a conveniently absent father to defend his project of bringing the drama into the home. Where his namesake recalls reciting Shakespeare to his father, Bowdler remembers a father reading Shakespeare to him. More specifically, while the sisters in both families favor textual cuts – Henrietta Bowdler in her heavily-expurgated 1807 forerunner to her brother Thomas's adaptation, Maria Bertram in her assurance that "a very few omissions" will make the play decent – the sons promise instead to neutralize the evils of the drama by cutting down its audience to what both call the "family circle."[51] Even the scene in which Tom sets his father's endorsement of drama (a country house "one Christmas holidays") anticipates Bowdler's "winter's evening in the country," which in turn recalls Knox's distinction in *Winter Evenings* between the "summer-reading" (usually novels) which spoilt misses borrow from circulating libraries and the improving books (such as Knox's) that families read "round the parlour hearth" when "the length of the evenings in Winter renders it necessary to find some sedentary and domestic diversion."[52]

Surprisingly, however, by including himself in the "Family" duped by a patriarchal editor, Bowdler identifies with the feminine audience invoked in his promise "to exclude from this publication whatever is unfit to be read aloud by a gentleman to a company of ladies."[53] So does his most charitable reviewer, Francis Jeffrey, in an article first published in the *Edinburgh Review* of 1821 but appended to subsequent editions of the *Family Shakespeare*:

There are many passages in Shakespeare which a father could not read aloud to his children – a brother to his sister – or a gentleman to a lady: – and every one almost must have felt or witnessed the extreme awkwardness, and even distress, that arises from suddenly stumbling upon such expressions, when it is almost too late to avoid them, and when the readiest wit cannot suggest any para-phrase which shall not betray, by its harshness, the embarrassment from which it has arisen. Those who recollect such scenes, must all rejoice that Mr. BOWDLER has provided a security against their recurrence.[54]

In Jeffrey's hands, the "pleasing" picture of patriarchal reading that prefaces the *Family Shakespeare* turns instead into a fraught image of the "distress" that sexual difference brings into the family. Yet that differ-ence breaks down as soon as Jeffrey's tortuous syntax invites us to ascribe female listeners' "embarrassment" to the male readers (of Shakespeare and of the *Edinburgh*) whom he addresses. The former simply "witness" what the latter "feel." Indeed, a conduct book of 1869 reverses Bowdler's original scenario by instructing women to use hypothetical male listeners as a test of decency. "If you come to a passage which you could not read aloud to your father or brothers without a blush," the author instructs girls, "lay down the book, it is not fit for you."[55] All three writers trace embarrassment not to readers' own experience of the text but to their speculation about its potential effect on other readers.[56] Shakespeare becomes legible only over someone else's shoulder.

We can recognize in Bowdler's edition the same triangular model of reading that made possible the growing power of the review in the early nineteenth century. Jeffrey's endorsement of the *Family Shakespeare* reflects not only the resemblance of the reviewer's function to the expurgator's, but his own notorious inability, as editor of the *Edinburgh Review*, to read without putting himself in someone else's place. Bowdler's intended readers share the compulsion to predict other readers' reaction which Bagehot attributes to Jeffrey in his essay "The First Edinburgh Reviewers": " 'Why does Scarlett always persuade the jury?' asked a rustic gentleman. 'Because there are twelve Scarletts in the jury-box,' replied an envious advocate. What Scarlett was in law, Jeffrey was in criticism; he could become that which his readers could not avoid being." Carlyle would later couple Bagehot's analogy of the jury with the well-known anecdote of Molière reading aloud to his housekeeper: "[Jeffrey] was always as if speaking to a jury . . . [He] may be said to have begun the rash reckless style of criticising everything in heaven and earth by appeal to *Moliere's maid*: 'Do *you* like it?' "[57] But where a master reading to a maid crosses class as well as gender lines, while the advocate who may differ from the jurymen in his class position must share their gender, Bowdler substitutes family roles for social structure by refusing to recognize any difference among readers except gender and age. For Bowdler as for Jeffrey, reading requires the presence (real or fantasized) of readers of the opposite sex, as much as sexual morality depends on the embarrassed "distress" which results. Identification with other readers reinforces the sexual difference that it appears to bridge.

When Dodd proves Shakespeare's genius by his appeal to audiences who have nothing else in common, he suggests that the literary unanimity celebrated more ingenuously by Knox can acquire significance only in the context of an otherwise fragmented culture:

"When persons of different humours, ages, professions, and inclinations, agree in the same joint approbation of any performance, then this union of assent, this combination of so many different judgments, stamps a high, and indisputable value on that performance, which meets with such general applause." This fine observation of Longinus is most remarkably verified in *Shakespear*, for all humours, ages, and inclinations, jointly proclaim their approbation and esteem of him.[58]

The greater the differences among readers, the higher the "value" of Shakespeare. Far from claiming that the shared appreciation of great art reflects a deeper commonality among human beings (as some recent defenders of the canon would have it), Dodd makes it impossible to measure a writer's greatness without recognizing how much separates the members of his audience. Like the *Family Shakespeare* – and like many interventions on both sides of the late-twentieth-century canon wars – Dodd's *Beauties* assume at once the premise of difference within the reading public and the promise that literature can abolish it. But where Dodd ascribes this effect to the Shakespearean text itself, Bowdler makes it contingent instead on a particular mode of editorially mediated reading: an oral performance that erases the distance (but not the difference) between men and women or fathers and sons.

The *Family Shakespeare* cements the British public less through the common experience of reading Shakespeare than the common memory of being embarrassed. The retrospective "distress" that Bowdler's female readers share with the masculine public of the *Edinburgh* extends even to professional reviewers: Bowdler ends his response to a more hostile review by invoking (with the masculine pronoun) "those blushes on the cheek of modesty, which ought, on mature reflection, to redden the countenance of every person who employs his talents and his pen in defence of obscenity." But *not* reading provides no guarantee from embarrassment either. According to the same letter, "there is no person in this generation, nor will there be any in future generations as long as the English language is in existence, who would not be ashamed of being unacquainted with [Shakespeare]."[59] Female listeners' embarrassment, male readers' distress, reviewers' blushes, ignoramuses' shame, all acknowledge the existence of other readers.

The idealization of reading aloud that I have been describing is doubly surprising: first, because editors represent that activity as a source of sexual tension; and second, as I shall argue in a moment, because oral performance reproduces the theatricality that adaptors set out to supplant. If reading in mixed company produces such "distress," why do moralists encourage it? Bowdler's preface dwells nostalgically on the cross-gendered linguistic embarrassment that he excises from the text itself, where Katherine's obscene language-lesson is cut cleanly from *Henry V*.[60] The conduct book goes farther, by advising girls to conjure up imaginary male listeners even when actually reading alone. And the Lambs are equally careful to insist that their wish for girls to read different editions of Shakespeare from boys does not preclude communal reading. On the contrary, after shaming boys away from the *Tales*, their preface immediately enlists them in the same dramatic performance that the plot summaries replace:

Boys are generally permitted the use of their fathers' libraries at a much earlier age than girls are, they frequently having the best scenes of Shakespear by heart before their sisters are permitted to look into this manly book; and therefore, instead of recommending these Tales to the perusal of young gentlemen who can read them so much better in the original, I must rather beg their kind assistance in explaining to their sisters such parts as are hardest to understand . . . then perhaps they will read to them (carefully selecting what is proper for a young sister's ear) some passage which has pleased them in one of these stories, in the very words of the scene from which it is taken; and I trust they will find that the beautiful extracts, the select passages, they may chuse to give their sisters in this way, will be much better relished and understood.[61]

Like the title of *The Family Shakespeare*, the preface to the *Tales* represents their audience as a domestic unit. In both cases, however, the image connotes less a family resemblance than a gulf between the sexes and the generations. The internal differences which structure the family naturalize the marketing strategy that creates multiple audiences for competing editions. (That strategy departs sharply from eighteenth-century or indeed twentieth-century anthologists' tendency to hedge their bets by not specifying – and therefore limiting – their audience.)[62] Reciprocally, the tension of communal reading cements the family – not simply, as Bowdler suggests, by drawing its members into a common space, but also by training them to distinguish themselves from each another. Yet the Lambs' worry that boys will be tempted to read the *Tales* in their sisters' absence suggests how much vigilance is needed to maintain the sexual difference between audiences. Not even Bowdler is exempt from the dangers of which the Lambs warn, for his preface undermines the division of labor between vicariously embarrassed men and directly embarrassed women by identifying himself with each in turn. That men can read only to women or as women suggests that the same niche marketing which shapes gender identities also threatens them.

If the need to multiply markets explains editors' insistence on mixed company, however, it still leaves the fantasy of reading aloud unaccounted for. What Jeffrey calls the "scene" of family reading (an oddly theatrical term in this context) is at once unlike and like a play. Bowdler's parlor is more private than a theater but also more sociable than the father's library mentioned by the Lambs, where no "young sister's ear" is admitted.[63] Bowdler's nostalgia for his father's "ready" improvisation makes the anonymous buyers of the printed edition ghosts of the remembered family gathered together to hear a living voice now dead. The Lambs' preface, too, overcompensates for the printed form of the text that follows. Even though the *Tales* transpose play-texts to third-person narrative, their editors represent that project not only as a substitute for dramatic performance but as a preliminary to reading aloud: to a later moment ("then") when readers' brothers will recite "the beautiful extracts, the select passages" that the preface describes in the language of the *Speaker*. Like Lennox, the Lambs make narrative a precondition for drama. The beauties withdrawn from their original theatrical setting need to be recontextualized by a plot summary (and a representation of other readers) before they can be either "relished" or "understood."

Although Bowdler introduces his excerpts by an autobiographical account rather than a plot summary, he shares the Lambs' strategy of framing the drama within a narrative of literary exchange. Both prefaces invoke communal audiences and oral performance as eagerly as both editions displace the theater itself. The scene of fathers reading to families or brothers reciting to sisters charts a narrow course between the licentiousness of the public theater and the self-indulgent solipsism induced by printed narrative. Abridgments and expurgations combine with collections of elocution exercises like the *Speaker* to shape an alternative at once to the theater and to the solitary reading which Knox calls even more dangerous than public entertainments: "In vain is youth secluded from the corruptions of the living world. Books . . . pollute the heart in the recesses of the closet, inflame the passions at a distance from temptation, and teach all the malignity of vice in solitude."[64] The self-indulgent solitude of the young, ignorant, and idle novel-reader paradoxically comes to resemble the scholar's "stagnant pool" of private knowledge (rather as Knox's model of national progress excludes in one stroke the stasis of classical learning and the ephemerality of fashionable fiction). Self-indulgence, but also self-abuse: Knox's masturbatory images of "pollution" and "vice in solitude" bring the sexual dangers of the drama into the home. In the *Family Shakespeare*, too, the parlor displaces the "recesses of the closet" as forcefully as it does the publicity of the stage. The resistance to the Romantic association of reading with solitude that Bowdler's preface shares with the Lambs' lends a more literal force to Knox's dictum that "private judgment must give way to public."

Yet the alternatives to literary self-absorption remain distanced in time. The *Family Shakespeare* presents itself as a printed surrogate for the dead father's voice, and the *Tales* as a stimulus to future recitations once readers have outgrown printed plot summary. Neither situates a community of readers in its own present. Both displace the theater more successfully than they replace it with any convincing model of how printed books can bring together an audience. Even Bowdler finally concedes defeat and disperses the inhabitants of the parlor to their separate rooms, acknowledging that the obscenity of *Othello* is so difficult to localize in any particular passage that "I would advise the transferring it from the parlour to the cabinet."[65] Once the father is provided with his collected works, the sister with her *Tales* or her *Girlhood*, the brother with his *Beauties* or his *Speaker*, the parlor empties. Editors' prefatory rhetoric overcompensates for the power of editions themselves to join each reader not with other members of her or his own family, but with strangers who occupy the corresponding position in others. The *Girlhood*'s exclusion of both male heroes and adult characters implies that girls should read about girls: that identification (or decorum) requires the content of a text to mimic the circumstances of its consumption. Like the sinister anthologist in *Rousseau juge de Jean-Jacques*, or like Amelia Edith Barr's *The Young People of Shakespeare's Dramas: For Youthful Readers* (1882), Cowden Clarke equates topic with audience. By a woman, for women, about women, and translated into the genre most closely associated with women, the *Girlhood of Shakespeare's Heroines* set out to protect its readers from a childhood like Lady Macbeth's.[66] But the girls who identified with "Shakespeare's Heroines" were also identifying with other girlish buyers of the *Girlhood* and against the boyish readers of the *Speaker* or the adult readers of the *Works*. Rather as the division of the "family newspaper" into sections addressed to mutually exclusive audiences later made it possible for an entire household to read a single daily at once, the *Family Shakespeare* industry taught readers to recognize themselves as part of a market whose size depended on its demographic subdivisions.[67] As niche marketing substituted analogy for contiguity, the common canon drove apart the family that it had promised to draw together – and the public for which that family stood.

RADCLIFFE'S UNCOMMON READERS

Compilers like Knox and Enfield raided novels even less frequently than non-Shakespearean drama – with good reason. Like plays, novels threatened anthologists' attempt to grant literature a pedagogical function or even a moral one. The planned obsolescence of late-eighteenth-century fiction challenged anthologists' equation of reading with memorization, book with monument. Characteristically, in the competition between synecdochal anthologies and synoptic abridgments which the divided structure of Richardson's novels set into motion, the abridgment finally won out. *The Paths of Virtue* continued to be reprinted, plagiarized, and even exported to America when the *Collection of Sentiments* was no more than a historical curiosity. By the time the popular *Beauties of Sterne: Including all his Pathetic Tales, and Most Distinguished Observations on Life, Selected for the Heart of Sensibility* appeared in 1782, the selections were already longer, less lapidary, and more narrative than those that composed the *Moral Sentiments*. Even in the index, abstractions that would not have looked out of place in Richardson's collection ("Charity," "Compassion," "Consolation," "Death") rubbed up against entries alluding to narrative particulars ("The Story of Le Fever," "Corporal Trim's Reflections on Death"). By 1813, when *The Paths of Virtue* reappeared under the title *The Beauties of Richardson*, the noun once used to designate atemporal anthology-pieces had come to mean a plot summary.

Where Richardson had tried to enter the anthology, his successors could only enter into competition with it. Nearly every fictional subgenre to emerge at this moment borrowed the discontinuous structure of the anthology – and made a bid, at least, for its social functions. Some took on its ambition to compile a national literary memory, others its project of disciplining narrative greed, others its campaign against solipsistic reading. The gothic novel turned narrative into a hook to hang anthology-pieces on. So did verse like Charlotte Smith's, punctuated just as regularly by short inset lyrics. The historical novel and the national tale of the following generation reduced plot to a filler for the interstices between verse epigraphs, snatches of oral lore, and excerpts from antiquarian documents.[68]

By the turn of the century, chapter mottoes were already ubiquitous enough to lend a polemical edge to those few novels – like Austen's – where they failed to appear as often as chapter numbers. As if to get a novel's worth of epigraphs over with at once, Austen opens *Northanger Abbey* with a parodic catalogue of quotations. In her childhood,

provided they were all story and no reflection, [Catherine Morland] never had any objection to books at all. But from fifteen to seventeen she was in training for a heroine; she read all such works as heroines must read to supply their memories with those quotations which are so serviceable and so soothing in the vicissitudes of their eventual lives.
From Pope, she learnt to censure those who
   "bear about the mockery of woe."
From Gray, that
   "Many a flower is born to blush unseen,
   And waste its fragrance on the desert air."

From Thompson, that
  "–It is a delightful task
  "To teach the young idea how to shoot.'"
And from Shakspeare she gained a great store of information – amongst the
rest, that
  "–Trifles, light as air,
  Are to the jealous, confirmation strong,
  As proofs of Holy Writ."
That [another quotation]. And that [another quotation].

Catherine's developmental progress from reading for "all story and no
reflection" to reading "to supply [her] memory with quotations" confirms the assumption of Richardson's abridgers that a childish enjoyment of plot must be prior (and therefore inferior) to a search for
quotable maxims. Yet the banality of her miniature anthology, an-
chored to the narrative only by a string of "that"s, implies that novelistic "quotation" and "reflection" are actually no less silly – or less
feminine – than novelistic "story." Austen's commonplace ridicule of
teenaged girls' hunger for plot gives way to a less conventional satire
on their taste for platitudes. Conversely, by pointing out that our
frivolous reading of romances presupposes characters' laborious memorization of the anthology-pieces which punctuate their dialogue, Austen challenges the conventional opposition between gothic novel and
pedagogical anthology invoked in *Emma*, where Harriet establishes
Robert Martin's seriousness at once by his familiarity with Knox's
Elegant Extracts and by his ignorance of Radcliffe's *Romance of the Forest*.
Surprisingly, the presence of quotation – rather than the content of the
narrative – gives us the earliest clue to the gothic intertext of *Northanger
Abbey*.[69]

Austen was unusual in eschewing the epigraph, but not in distrusting
it. The inscription of verse fragments in prose narrative which first took
shape in Radcliffe's novels satisfied no one: some readers attacked her
inset lyrics for slowing down the story which frames them, while others
complained that the plot distracted from the beauties. Why, then, did
that alternation find so many imitators? One answer is precisely that it
allowed readers to disagree. At a time when the lack of a stable
consensus about the status of prose fiction was forcing reviewers (for
example) to differentiate themselves from the mass of novel-readers,
Radcliffe projected that discrimination between audiences onto the
structure of the novel itself. Their form trained readers to distinguish
themselves from others in the process of differentiating poetry from

prose, "reflection" from "story," description from narrative, and stylistic display from the plot that occasions it.

A verse anthology marked the end to Radcliffe's novelistic career. By excerpting the lyrics originally inscribed within *The Romance of the Forest* (1791) and *The Mysteries of Udolpho* (1794), *The Poems of Mrs Ann Radcliffe* (1816) undid the metrical mixture promised by the subtitle that the novels share: *A Romance, Interspersed with Some Pieces of Poetry*. In retrospect, the unauthorized *Poems* makes clear how self-contained the "pieces" are. Yet this does not make the poems superfluous to the structure of the "romance." On the contrary, verse vertebrates both novels. Even their most basic unit, the chapter, depends on the introductory mottoes that force readers to pause and withdraw from the action at regular intervals. The chapters themselves are punctuated with original and quoted verse – the former inapposite and the latter anachronistic, as the narrator pedantically acknowledges. Thus, in *Udolpho* a description of Morano's lute-playing concludes: "To him, indeed, might have been applied that beautiful exhortation of an English poet, *had it then existed*: 'Strike up, my master'"; and in *The Romance of the Forest*, the narrator apologizes for describing Theodore's impression of Adeline in the words of a poem not yet written: "Her charms appeared to him like those *since* so finely described by an English poet: 'Oh have you seen, bathed in the morning dew, / The budding rose its infant bloom display?'"[70] Radcliffe's usual insouciance about historical accuracy makes her conscientious acknowledgment of literary-historical anachronism all the more striking. The quotations' ostentatious violation of historical order draws attention to their power to interrupt narrative progress. So does Radcliffe's heavy-handed italicization of misquotations where a pronoun or verb tense has been transposed to align the allusion with the narration that frames it.[71] Together, anachronism and misquotation make readers aware of the reflex to "apply" lyric verse to narrative prose. Both lay painfully bare the division of labor which requires poems to retard and decorate prose, prose to frame and contextualize poems.[72]

Radcliffe's verbatim quotation from recent poetry counterbalances a silent repudiation of the formal conventions dominating recent prose narrative. Yet her abandonment of epistolary fiction does not imply the disappearance of dialogism itself so much as of the plot devices that earlier motivated it. Radcliffe's epigraphs and inset poems allow *Udolpho* and *The Romance of the Forest* to juxtapose as many different signatures as any epistolary novel. By studding third-person narration with descriptive set-pieces and lyric epigraphs, Radcliffe substitutes the collection of beauties for the collection of letters as a model for the novel's composite structure. But by using those epigraphs to punctuate much longer stretches of omniscient narrative, Radcliffe reverses the proportion that Richardson's letters (written, like lyrics, in the first person and "to the moment") bear to their third-person past-tense narrative frames: prefaces, afterwords, indexes, tables of contents. Where the scene of writing forwards Richardson's plots, it interrupts Radcliffe's.

Verse points outward from the gothic novel, breaking and braking the narrative with a kind of centrifugal force. Even the inset poems ascribed to characters are only perfunctorily occasioned by the plot: as one early critic complains, the lyrics "assume a ludicrous air from their contrast with the situations under which they are produced. Under all situations of alarm and anxiety . . . paper, pencils, and poetical enthusiasm are never wanting to her heroines."[73] All that splices Radcliffe's inset lyrics to their prose frame is a transition repeated as monotonously as "that" in *Northanger Abbey*: "she composed the following lines," "she commemorated in the following address," "she expressed the feelings of the moment in the following / SONNET." William Beckford hardly exaggerates in his parody *Modern Novel Writing; or, the Elegant Enthusiast . . . A Rhapsodical Romance; Interspersed with Poetry* (1796), whose Radcliffean subtitle prefigures eighteen quotations introduced as "the following lines," occasionally varied by a desperate periphrasis like "the subsequent verses." And since Radcliffe's characters quote as profusely as they compose, it comes as no surprise to find the same all-purpose formula introducing quotations from other authors: "she recollected the following stanzas," "she repeated the following lines." In both cases, by reducing the relation between prose and verse to a purely spatial one (what comes next on the page), "the following" undoes the confusion of consecution with cause that Roland Barthes identifies as the basis of narrative.[74] Like an anthologist, Radcliffe juxtaposes without justifying. The anachronism of her quotations and the slackness of her transitions call attention to the gulf separating decoration from motivation, style from plot: the rules of the anthology from the rules of the novel.

Fittingly, an anthologist was the first to notice that tension. In a review in the *Monthly*, the editor of the *Speaker* complains that the plot of *Udolpho* distracts from the poems:

The embellishments of the work are highly finished . . . If the reader, in the eagerness of curiosity, should be tempted to pass over any of them for the sake of proceeding more rapidly with the story, he will do both himself and the author injustice . . . Several of the pieces of poetry are elegant performances, but they would have appeared with more advantage as a separate publication.[75]

Enfield can praise Radcliffe's poems only by transferring them from the novel to an imaginary anthology. Although such a collection did not materialize until twenty years later, the review already anticipates the *Poems'* impulse to "separate" "embellishment" from "story." That strategy responds in turn to Enfield's fear that readers will separate the two themselves, not by collecting the poems but, on the contrary, by "passing over" them. The editor of the *Female Speaker*, too, expects readers to resist the generic mixture of Radcliffe's novels: as Barbauld argues, "the true lovers of poetry are almost apt to regret its being brought in as an accompaniment to narrative, where it is generally neglected; for . . . the common reader is always impatient to get on with the story."[76] Like Enfield's contrast between "elegance" and "curiosity," Barbauld's opposition between "true lovers of poetry" and "common readers" associates the interpolated verse with an elite audience.

Both anthologists express that difference less in the traditional language of class or even gender, however, than in terms of the pace of reading. The same is true of Radcliffe's first biographer, who glosses generic mixture as a failure of her "art," observing that "the verses, scattered through all the romances, are so inartificially introduced, that they have little chance of being estimated by an impatient reader."[77] Another review of *Udolpho* agrees:

We have had occasion to observe that the introduction of verses in publications like the present is becoming a fashion, but we confess that they appear to us to be misplaced. However fond the reader may be of poetry, and however excellent the verses themselves, we will venture to assert that few will choose to peruse them whilst eagerly and anxiously pursuing the thread of a tale, a plain proof that, in such a situation, at least they are impertinent. Having said this, we are ready to confess that Mrs Radcliffe's poetical abilities are of the superior kind, and we shall be glad to see her compositions separately published.[78]

A third, by Coleridge, acts on that suggestion by transposing one of Radcliffe's inscribed poems into the equally prosaic frame of the review. Coleridge justifies the inclusion of the excerpt by the need to counteract readers' presumed preference for "adventure" to "beauties": "We cannot resist the temptation of giving our readers the following charming [piece of poetry], especially as poetical beauties have not a fair chance of being attended to amidst the stronger interest inspired by such a series of adventures. The love of poetry is a taste; curiosity is a kind of appetite, and hurries headlong on, impatient for its complete gratification."[79] A quotation immediately follows – shielded, in its new context, from the "[un]fair" competition of the narrative which had originally framed it. For the same reason that Richardson feels the need to excerpt atemporal *Sentiments* from a "Story" too exciting not to distract from them, Coleridge uses the reviewer's privilege of quotation to extract – or rather extricate – the poems from the plot.

In the opening scenes of Radcliffe's following novel, *The Italian*, a boat draws to a halt as "the boatmen rested on their oars, while their company listened to voices [singing]."[80] For Radcliffe's reviewers, too, appreciating lyric seems incompatible with moving forward. All five critics perceive the poems as a series of textual speed-bumps that obstruct the "rapidity" of readers' progress through the narrative. When in the 1830s, as James Buzard has uncovered, guidebooks began to punctuate their prosaic instructions about how to get most efficiently from one point to another with verse anthology-pieces designed to be savored once the tourist reached a picturesque stopping-place, they simply projected onto literal topography the stop-and-go rhythm that commonplaces had already imposed on the readers of gothic novels.[81] Like the massy doors that block so many subterranean passageways in the course of so many gothic heroines' escapes, the epigraphs and inset poems cut readers off from the next chapter or the next event. Yet while all three reviews of *Udolpho* capitulate to readers' putative impatience by urging that the poems be excerpted in a "separate" anthology (or, in Coleridge's, by excerpting them himself), all three reviewers disclaim and even condemn the desire for narrative speed which they ascribe to others.

Why this fear of skipping? It owes something to a nostalgia rather like Bowdler's for a slow, intensive, repetitive mode of reading apparently threatened by the proliferation of ephemerably fashionable novels. As Emma Clery has argued, "the ever-changing kaleidoscope of the [circulating] library that conceals a formulaic monotony is believed [by late-eighteenth-century critics] to encourage . . . a skimming and dipping technique which begins at the conclusion and allows a volume to be effectively gutted in minimum time, increasing the maximum rate of consumption."[82] But reviewers' hostility to skipping can be explained more narrowly by the conventions of their own genre, which (as I argue at the end of this book) alternates plot summary with synecdochal excerpts as systematically as the novels that they discuss sandwich prose narrative with verse fragment. In this context, the imaginary reader who skips the beauties becomes a parodic double for the reviewer who quotes

them. Parodic, but diametrically opposed, for the resistance of a hypothetical vulgar audience proves the seriousness of the inset poems – and
of the readers who enjoy them. The specter of an impatient public
differentiates Radcliffe from mere entertainers while distinguishing reviewers (and their audience) from the common reader. Reviews invite
each reader to identify with their author rather than with the audience
they describe: with the "few" who read against the plot instead of the
many who read for it.[83] The hybrid structure of the gothic allows
readers to define their own taste against the taste they impute to others.
Instead of branding their audience as passive consumers, Radcliffe's
novels present them with a choice of discourses. In turn, reviewers
project the divided structure of her texts onto her audience. Appreciation of style proves the self-control needed to resist "impatient" greed
for plot. The pace of reading becomes a test of taste.[84]

Speculations about what would be skipped were not unique to Radcliffe's reviewers. In a review of Byron's *Giaour*, Francis Jeffrey asserts that
the modern taste for the sublime makes every reader an amateur
anthologist: "after we once know what it contains, no long poem is ever
read, but in fragments; – and the connecting passages . . . are always
skipped after the first reading." In a different review, however, Jeffrey
warns that beauties can be recognized only against the background of
those apparently dispensable transitions. His critique of *Thalaba* urges
authors (and readers) not "to forget, that a whole poem cannot be made
up of striking passages; and that the sensations produced by sublimity,
are never so powerful and entire as when they are allowed to subside and
revive, in a slow and spontaneous succession."[85] Here, Jeffrey reconciles
local sublimity with organic structure not by proving the interest of dull
passages, but on the contrary by establishing the esthetic value of readers'
boredom. Yet where Jeffrey assumes readers' impulse to skip the "connecting passages" between the sublime moments, even at the cost of
weakening the effect of the whole, conversely Radcliffe's reviewers
expect "the common reader" (or all but "the few") to skip the lyric poems
in order to concentrate on the narrative that cements them. And while
Jeffrey includes himself among the "we" who skip, Radcliffe's reviewers
invoke the "impatient" or "common" reader not as an alter ego, but as a
straw man against whom their own audience can define itself.

Yet in social terms, oddly, Radcliffe's lyrics define her as a "common"
writer. The poet's delaying tactics bear an uncanny resemblance to the
language of those garrulous servants within her novels who irritate their
masters' curiosity by refusing to stick to the point of a story.[86] The same

anti-narrative irrelevance that Radcliffe uses to discourage vulgar readers is associated in the novels themselves with the lower classes, as if the poems and descriptions were as empty – or as intrusive – as the babble of servants. Indeed, the *British Critic*'s characterization of Radcliffe's verses as "impertinent" borrows a social vocabulary to describe the breakdown of generic subordination. Another review enjoins Radcliffe to "keep a stricter *rein* over her descriptive powers."[87] Where servants' ramblings betray their lack of verbal self-mastery, Radcliffe's self-indulgent digressions teach her readers to master their own narrative desires.

In that sense, the inscribed verse can be understood as a formal corollary to Radcliffe's rational supernatural. Since her own time, as is well-known, critics have consistently complained of Radcliffe's strategy of awakening readers' desire for horror only to disappoint it: as one reader testified in 1796, "her plan of writing . . . raises expectations, which it never gratifies."[88] The ostentatious intrusiveness of her quotations, inscribed poems, and descriptive set-pieces suggests that a second kind of bait-and-switch is equally characteristic: from the conventions of the novel to the structure of the anthology. The rational replaces the supernatural at the same time as narration gives way to a compilation designed not so much to entertain its audience as to improve their taste. Both strategies substitute edification for the pleasure that readers were tricked into expecting. Both replace immediate gratification by the discipline of delay.

Reviewers made sense of Radcliffe's peculiar interweaving of entertainment with disappointment by postulating a public hardly less divided than Shakespeare's. Since Radcliffe, novels have provided an occasion to differentiate lyric from narrative, style from plot, taste from curiosity – and oneself from other readers. Ironically, although nineteenth-century successors dismissed her novels as too easy to be improving, Radcliffe's technique of punctuating narrative with static landscape descriptions and tedious lyrics indirectly made possible the esthetic and moral ambitions of the Victorian novel. By polarizing two modes of novelistic discourse and two audiences for fiction, her career paved the way for George Eliot's interpolation of sententious, timeless truths guaranteed to bore the impatient common reader. In mimicking the anthology's modular form, Radcliffe's ostensibly immoral fiction also laid claim to its moral mission: not by inscribing sententious wisdom, as Richardson had done, but by forcing readers to forgo curiosity. The eighteenth-century novel took over more than the appeals of the anthology – what Barbara Benedict calls its "contemporaneity, variety, cultural instruction, and – of course – novelty."[89] By Radcliffe's time, the novel borrowed from the anthology not only its pleasures, but also, just as crucially, its pains.

The inscription of lyric allowed gothic novels, like contemporary anthologies, to counterbalance their own dependence on a passive middle-class market. Yet both ratified their own inferiority in the process of borrowing prestige from higher genres.[90] Conversely, the literariness of verse fragments became recognizable only by contrast with the prose that framed them: the biographies, introductions, and notes of anthologies, but also the novels that occasioned epigraphs and inset lyrics. Both reflected the widening division of labor separating decorative verse from informative prose. Radcliffe's reception renders that logic painfully clear: the fact that almost every reviewer denied beauty to her beauties – calling her verse prosaic and her prose poetic – made it all the more necessary for the structure of the novels to label them as such by emphasizing their lack of any function but an esthetic one.[91] Paradoxically, Radcliffe's inscription of verse forced readers to reinvent the same generic distinction that it appeared to challenge. By proving the power of low genres to establish a hierarchy of forms and audiences, the anthology shaped the production of new novels even more than the reproduction of the literary past.

CODA: FERRIER'S SECOND-HAND SENTIMENTS

Radcliffe's divided audience suggests that the campaign against narrative greed in which novelists deployed the anthology-piece remained at odds with the battle against solipsistic reading that they inherited more directly from the anthology. Where Radcliffe made textual discontinuity stand for the distinctions leavening what would otherwise become a mass market, in the next generation Susan Ferrier turned the excerpt to the opposite use, making textual collection the basis for a social cohesion that her fictions took it upon themselves to represent – if not always to create. Ferrier's three novels, *Marriage* (1818, 1841), *The Inheritance* (1824), and *Destiny* (1831), memorialize the common reading which *Mansfield Park* parodies and Bowdler's preface invokes. Forced as children to "cry [themselves] blind" memorizing anthology-pieces, her characters spend the rest of their lives showing just how "serviceable" to a heroine (in the words of *Northanger Abbey*) a well-stocked memory can prove.[92] They copy verses into friends' albums, select "beauties" to read aloud, cite poets to prove a point, juxtapose excerpts from different texts, "repeat" snatches of verse, apply French maxims to their acquaintances' behavior, embellish their speech with identified and unidentified literary allusions, and cement their friendships by exchanging hackneyed quotations.[93] Even when unable to attribute their platitudes to any specific source, they take care to disclaim originality. "Here is a sentiment to make amends," says one character. "I don't know whose it is, or whether I repeat it verbatim, but it is to this effect: 'Sorrow, like a stream, loses itself in many channels; and joy, like a sunbeam, reflects with greater force from the breast of a friend.'"[94] Writing in the wake of a ballad revival that collected popular speech in printed anthologies, Ferrier represented quotation instead as all that saved the middle-brow upper class from falling silent.

Like Henry Crawford or like the brother of the intended reader of the Lambs' *Tales*, the hero of *The Inheritance* courts the heroine by reciting poetry – or more precisely, by expurgating it. In congratulating his beloved on living in an age when "the dross of [Shakespeare's] compositions is daily draining off in improved editions, and even in theatrical representation, while the pure parts of his morality are not thought unworthy of being quoted from evangelical pulpits," the priggish hero provides product placement for what any nineteenth-century reader would have recognized as the *Family Shakespeare* whose first edition appeared in the same year as Ferrier's first novel. Even Byron's beauties, he adds more speculatively, will eventually be "culled by the lovers of virtue, as the bee gathers honey from even the noxious plant, and leaves the poison to perish with the stalk." His prediction proved true: arriving in Manchester a few years later, Friedrich Engels was struck by the ubiquity of "ruthlessly expurgated 'family' editions [of Byron] . . . prepared to suit the hypocritical moral standards of the bourgeoisie."[95] In a culture where love inspires young men to "cull" poems rather than to compose them, feeling becomes indissociable from reading – and reading, in turn, from quoting. The heroine of *Marriage* introduces a recitation by announcing that "my sentiments are all at second hand"; even the villain of the aptly titled *The Inheritance* makes it "an invariable rule to use other men's verse, as well as other men's prose, instead of his own."[96]

Ferrier follows that rule. Her words do little more than pad out the intervals between the epigraphs that pile up three to a chapter until the narrative nearly cracks under their weight. Quotation permeates not only characters' speech, but the narrator's representation of their consciousness. Conversely, those few characters who fail to quote become a blank in the text. In Ferrier's last novel, *Destiny*, as the two most vacuous characters sail across a loch, the narrator pauses to describe in detail

the varied beauties that skirted their shores; while, above all,
   "the gorgeous sphere
   Lit up the vales, flowers, mountains, leaves and streams,
   With a diviner day – the spirit of bright beams."
To the eye of taste and the feeling heart, there would have been rapture in every beam of light and breath of heaven, on such a day and amid such scenes. But Glenroy and Benbowie cared for none of these things. "As imagination bodies forth the form of things," so the two friends "turned them to shapes," and gave "to airy nothings a local habitation and a name." . . . Although they could not be said to find "sermons in stones, tongues in the trees, or books in the running brooks," [they] found much profitable matter of discourse in the various objects of nature that presented themselves. The crystal depths of the limpid waters over which the sun was shedding his noonday effulgence, suggested to their minds images of herrings, fat, fresh or salted.[97]

Ferrier measures the characters who appreciate the lake as a source of food against a hypothetical spectator whose enjoyment is purely esthetic and whose body remains metaphorical: "the eye of taste and the feeling heart." But the gluttons also stand opposite the narrator whose quotation makes the "varied beauties" of the landscape synonymous with the verbal "beauties" which evoke them. By going on to quote the same line that had earlier appeared as the epigraph to William Dodd's *Beauties of Shakespeare* – "to airy nothing a local habitation and a name" – the narrator underscores the characters' contrasting inability to "find" literature in landscape. Yet that failure can be conveyed, ironically, only by a second Shakespearean quotation: "they could not be said to find 'sermons in stones, tongues in the trees, or books in the running brooks'." The coincidence of the narrator's language with the epigraph to Dodd's *Beauties* defines "taste" less as the appreciation of landscape – or even of Shakespeare – than the appreciation of anthologists' front matter.

   This suggests, in turn, that Ferrier's quotations need to be read not only as allusions to Shakespeare (or Milton or Gray or Pope), but also as allusions to *The Beauties of Shakespeare* (or to Knox's *Elegant Extracts* or Enfield's *Speaker*). Ferrier is as eager as her heroine to acknowledge that her "sentiments are all at second hand" – or in this case, at third. Like Richardson's, Ferrier's quotations refer not so much to particular canonical texts as to the collections that have ensured them that status. Ironically, the strategic banality of those commonplaces helps explain

Ferrier's own exclusion from the same canon. Despite her usefulness in literary-historical narratives as a token of gender balance or national symmetry (the female Walter Scott, the Scottish Jane Austen), Ferrier's esthetic of the hackneyed has made her novels increasingly hard for even literary historians to read – or rather, frustratingly easy. Her epigraphs fail to repay or even allow the critical ingenuity and erudition which trace allusions back to their original context.[98] What she alludes to has neither context nor origin, for she quotes only the most familiar and fragmentary of anthology-pieces. Her pedantry repels not because the references are too difficult, but because their facility stops interpretation short. If reading Ferrier via the anthology opens up the possibility of interpreting her quotations as allusions to its project of drawing readers together by picking texts apart, then by the same token that interpretive strategy closes off the possibility of interpreting them as rich and complex allusions to an organic source. To trace her quotations to the anthology is not to add one more item to an infinitely expandable list of possible intertexts, but on the contrary to shut that process of expansion down. Ferrier's glib allusiveness poses the same question that Peter Murphy asks in a recent discussion of Samuel Rogers's repellently smooth "elegance": whether the revisionist project of recovering marginalized Romantics leaves any room for a reconstruction of "the ideologically and politically dominant culture that we often hope historical analysis can rescue us from."[99]

Within a hermeneutics of difficulty, commonplaces pose a dead end. Ferrier's novels deny their readers scope not only for interpretive but for psychological manipulation. Concerned less to express a subjectivity than to exercise readers' taste, they make no sense within the framework through which we usually read Romantic fiction. They become more legible once we situate them within the competing culture of the anthology, but only at an ideological price. Alan Richardson has recently adduced the centrality of the heroine's reading in *Marriage* to prove that in this period "psychic depth is increasingly established through reference to a character's literary experience."[100] The juxtaposition of quotations with Glenroy's and Benbowie's gluttony would seem to corroborate that claim, for the narrator's use of anthology-pieces to indicate what is *not* passing through the characters' heads makes interiority coextensive with the memorization of literature. Yet the absence of what Richardson calls "psychic depth" is easier for quotation to establish than its presence. The "second-handedness" of the characters' "sentiments" derives literary experience less from an

individual psyche than from communal exchanges: reciting, exchanging album verses, or – even when in private – reading the same few
fragments as the rest of the public. Indeed, the second (1841) edition of
Marriage, where Ferrier attributes a chapter and several interpolated
poems to her friend Charlotte Clavering, labels the novel itself a collab-
orative product of the same feminine literary sociability which it represents.[101] The "taste" that differentiates good from bad characters also
provides too much common ground for the former not to call the very
possibility of psychic depth into question. Quotation makes Ferrier's
readers just as interchangeable. In the process of constructing a
common literary culture, it forestalls any attempt by critics to penetrate
beyond or below what others perceive. The refusal of Ferrier's quotations to allude to anything more than their own canonicity locates
literary meaning on the shallowest collective surface rather than in the
individual "depth" that Richardson posits. Hence a second, more
specific, explanation for Ferrier's absence from recent projects to expand the canon. A fiction where parlor poets upstage madwomen in
the attic resists the esthetic of authenticity out of which so many
recuperations of women's writing have emerged. Literature allows Ferrier's characters – and readers – to ratify a consensus rather than
expressing themselves.

That curiously negative definition of taste can ultimately be traced to
the same anthologies from which Ferrier's individual quotations derive.
Ferrier's consensual ethos bears a striking resemblance not only to the
Elegant Extracts' subordination of "private" to "public judgment," but
also to Dodd's hope that reading the *Beauties of Shakespeare* will transmute
readers' individual identities into a "union of assent." Where Knox
prefaces excerpts with the assertion that people should read like each
other, and Bowdler with a memory that people did once read to each
other, Ferrier inscribes quotations within a description of characters
doing both. By staging (or rather fictionalizing) the footnote in which
Bowdler recalls a man reading aloud to women, *The Inheritance* turns
novelistic narrative to the use that editorial front matter had served in
earlier anthologies and expurgations. In both cases, literary appreciation depends not only on a suitor or a father to excerpt beauties, but
also on a third, extradiegetic reader – the narrator of *The Inheritance*, the
editor of *The Family Shakespeare* – to frame them by stories about literary
exchange. Knox, too, withdraws Shakespearean fragments from their
theatrical origins only to recontextualize them within scenes of common
reading. The more irreversibly each book replaces the audience

gathered together by theatrical performance with a virtual public of silent readers, the more lovingly each needs to describe (or prescribe) a live audience.

The anxious invocation of literary exchange that Ferrier's fiction shares with those editorial projects excludes her from a tradition of novels – gaining force throughout the nineteenth century – which represent reading instead as an escape from the collective loyalties of domestic life. A year before the first edition of *Destiny*, Stendhal's *Le rouge et le noir* opened with the hero being beaten by his father for his absorption in a book; six years after the second edition of *Marriage*, *Jane Eyre* began with a heroine reading, hidden from the adoptive family who punish her for touching their books; a few years later, David Copperfield would take refuge from a hostile step-family by isolating himself in a roomful of books "which no one else ever troubled."[102] The common reader began to look like an oxymoron. Those solipsistic scenes have become more familiar than Ferrier's representation of a literary community which links each reader not with an absent author, but with those others (present or absent) who have read the same text before. In the process of recognizing commonplaces, her readers learn to recognize themselves within a common culture. The place of quotation in Ferrier's novels reflects the power of anthology-pieces to interpellate the common reader for whom she writes, or against whom Radcliffe compiles. But their resistance to interpretation also challenges the language of criticism to theorize the ways of reading (easy, obvious, superficial) against which it defines itself.

CHAPTER 3

George Eliot and the production of consumers

In 1866, George Henry Lewes reflected that "it is a great pity that [*Felix Holt*] isn't quite ready for publication just in the thick of the great reform discussion so many good quotable 'bits' would be furnished to M.P.s."[1] The absence of those excerpts from the parliamentary record has been more than compensated since then by their ubiquity in other venues. Before her death, quotations from Eliot made their way not only into parliamentary debates, but into an anthology, onto a calendar, into four schoolbooks, onto an army officers' examination, into a sermon, into one reader's copy of the New Testament, and into various letters, and (as epigraphs) to the front of a socialist treatise and an abridgment of Boswell's *Life of Johnson*. In the years immediately following, her works were excerpted in a Zionist tract, provided chapter mottoes for at least one novel, and appeared in anthologies ranging from booklets for the pocket to albums for the sofa-table.[2]

Readers' fondness for quoting Eliot can ultimately be traced to the structure of her own narratives, punctuated with epigraphs and lapidary generalizations. It owes a more specific debt to Mrs. Poyser – in the words of another character in *Adam Bede*, "one of those untaught wits that help to stock a country with proverbs" – whose persona defined Eliot from the first as a source of quotable wit and wisdom. As a review of *Adam Bede* soon noticed, Mrs. Poyser's "wisdom is always coming out either spoken by herself, or quoted by somebody else . . . Adam Bede, finding his own language inadequate, is obliged to fall back on the expressions used by Mrs Poyser, whom accordingly he quotes."[3] Readers were quick to follow Adam's example. In fact, *Adam Bede* seems to have achieved almost immediately the parliamentary recognition that Lewes craved: according to an anecdote retailed by the erstwhile editor of an early-twentieth-century collection of *Stories from George Eliot* modeled after the Lambs' *Tales from Shakespeare*, "about six weeks after the publication of [*Adam Bede*], Mr. Charles Buxton remarked in a

speech made in the House of Commons, 'As the farmer's wife says in
Adam Bede, "It wants to be hatched over again and hatched different"'."[4]

The habit of quoting Eliot originated more directly, though, in the
publishing venture of one of her fans. In the year in which the first
bi-monthly parts of *Middlemarch* appeared, its publisher also brought out
a daintier volume of *Wise, Witty, and Tender Sayings in Prose and Verse
Selected from the Works of George Eliot*. Their editor, a sycophantic young
Scotsman named Alexander Main, succeeded neither in using the
anthology as a stepping-stone to a wider journalistic career, nor in his
equally unrealistic ambition of drowning with a copy of George Eliot's
works in his hands.[5] Instead, he lived to edit more anthologies. Three
more editions followed the *Sayings* over the next eight years, updated like
clockwork each time a new book by Eliot herself appeared. At the end of
1878, in time for Christmas presents, Main assembled an alternative
series of quotations for the *George Eliot Birthday Book*, a diary decorated
with a "thought" from George Eliot for every day of the year.[6] The fact
that every new book by Eliot prompted a new edition by Main suggests
that *Daniel Deronda* and the *Impressions of Theophrastus Such* were both
written in the expectation of being excerpted. And because buyers of the
Sayings and *Birthday Book* constituted only a fraction of the audience that
knew of their existence, Main's anthologies indirectly shaped the way
Eliot's work was perceived even by those who scorned to read her at less
than full length.

This chapter examines the effect of that awareness on George Eliot
– and on her readers. Anthologies redefined the genre of Eliot's
oeuvre and the gender of its author, in contradictory ways: they
canonized Eliot's novels by packaging her as a poet, and bracketed
her with male predecessors by marketing her to women. Nineteenth-
century reviews and twentieth-century criticism characterized Eliot's
work more explicitly as peculiarly quotable, even as – like Eliot herself
– they questioned the ethics of appropriating others' words. Their
distaste for Eliot's lapidary generalizations makes visible a shift away
from traditional assumptions about the relation of plot to pleasure,
but also a growing anxiety about the synecdochal conventions and
evidentiary standards of literary criticism. In the process, the figure of
the self-indulgent female reader about whom eighteenth-century
critics had worried gave way to a new specter of the self-important
female sage.

READING AGAINST THE PLOT

Ever since Radcliffe, the anthology had entered the novel; but only with Eliot did the novel enter the anthology. With the exception of Richardson's self-aggrandizing auto-anthologizing, anthologies before Main's remained largely the province of lyric, the essay, and Shakespeare. The few anthology-pieces that did come out of novels were precisely those passages that retarded or interrupted the narrative: sententious generalizations; landscape description; and snatches of lyric, like the mottoes from Scott's novels incorporated into collections of his poetry. In this context, to excerpt Eliot was to imply that the novels, or the best parts of the novels, were not narrative at all. Main's assertion that *Middlemarch* "is really a prose-poem much more than a novel in the ordinary sense of the word" says less about the form of *Middlemarch* than about the anthology-piece as a form.[7] The preface to the *Sayings* defines Eliot's achievement quite explicitly in terms of the relation between generic categories and individual careers:

What Shakespeare did for the Drama, George Eliot has been, and still is, doing for the Novel. By those who know her works really well, this branch of literature can never again be regarded as mere *story-telling* and the reading of it as only a pastime. George Eliot has magnified her office and made it honourable; she has for ever sanctified the Novel by making it the *vehicle* of the grandest and most uncompromising moral truth.[8]

Like Richardson, who prefaces his anthology of *Sentiments* with the assertion that "the *narrative* part of [*Clarissa*] was only meant as a vehicle for the *instructive*," Main reduces "story-telling" to the dispensable "vehicle" by which "truth" is conveyed.[9]

And he does dispense with it. Main's comparison of Eliot with Shakespeare invokes a dramatic model which the second edition of the *Sayings* borrows more obliquely. The latter not only adds several dialogues from *Middlemarch* but eliminates the narrator's voice by the double expedient of deleting speech tags and transposing the narrative into stage directions.[10] Thus, "Mr. Bulstrode, alone with his brother-in-law, poured himself out a glass of water, and opened a sandwich-box" becomes:

Mr. Bulstrode (pouring himself out a glass of water, and opening a sandwich box). – I cannot persuade you to adopt my regimen, Vincy?
Mr. Vincy. – No, no; I've no opinion of that system. Life wants padding.

When the narrative voice does appear outside of these parentheses, it is presented not as the narrator's but as the author's: each chapter begins with a section entitled "George Eliot (*in propria persona*)," truncated, in the 1878 *Birthday Book*, to "George Eliot." Main's insensitivity to free indirect discourse allows him to pad out these sections by misattributing to the '*propria persona*' statements that the novels themselves locate in the perspective of a character. Thus, Main's saying that "People *are* so ridiculous with their illusions, carrying their fool's caps unawares, thinking their own lies opaque while everybody else's *are* transparent" misquotes a passage that originally read:

[Mary] sat tonight revolving, as she was wont, the scenes of the day, her lips often curling with amusement at the oddities to which her fancy added fresh drollery: people *were* so ridiculous with their illusions, carrying their fool's caps unawares, thinking their own lies opaque while everybody else's *were* transparent.[11]

By transposing the past tense to the present, Main turns what the novel presents as Mary's thought into a general truth with no verbs marking when, or to whom, it occurs. Eliot's complaint about a different anthologizer could also be applied to Main: "You observe that he is so unreflecting as to take the words put dramatically into the mouths of my characters as the expression of my own sentiments."[12] By magnifying the narrator from a reporter of Mary's thoughts to a source of timeless wisdom, and by substituting parenthetical stage directions for the narratorial voice, Main crowds narrative out.[13]

More sweepingly, the *Sayings* leaves no room for the novel. The genre that made Eliot's name gives way to an over-representation of both her poems (one-seventh of the 1873 edition) and verse epigraphs taken from the novels (of which Main includes exactly half). Even within the chapter devoted to verse, Main reproduces a disproportionate number of the "songs" that punctuate the narrative of *The Spanish Gypsy* – songs which would later be excerpted, with musical settings, in yet another volume.[14] When a century later a U.S. Education Secretary included two quotations from Eliot poems in his *Book of Virtues* but none from her novels – implying that prose fictions have no place in an anthology even when they render an author too famous to exclude – he simply repeated the 1872 anthology's redefinition of Eliot as a poet.[15]

"Nor is it only as a novelist that George Eliot has claims upon our closest attention and our deepest regard," Main declares in the preface to his *Sayings*: "'The Legend of Jubal,' 'Armgart,' and 'The Spanish Gypsy,' so massive in structure, so lofty in tone, so rich in thought, fairly entitle their author to a foremost place among the ranks of British poets."[16] He dreamed of a second anthology which would place Eliot's work more literally within the poetic tradition. Two years after managing to sell the *Sayings* to a reluctant publisher, he wrote to John Blackwood again offering "to make a new selection of English lyrics, from Shakespeare and Spenser to Browning & George Eliot, under the title: '*The Spirit of British Poetry*'," which, he suggested, "might very easily, and I think, very properly, be made uniform with the first edition of the Sayings."[17] Although Blackwood understandably rejected the project, Main's proposal to make one anthology "uniform" with the other betrayed his ambition to erase all that differentiated the subject of one (a living female novelist) from the subjects of the other (dead male poets). Eliot herself went one better by asking for her *Sayings* to be republished in a form modeled after Matthew Arnold's Wordsworth anthology: "I have been examining the actual volume, and it seems to be capable of sufficient compression by substituting a thinner paper – still fine and tinted, but as thin, for example, as that of Matthew Arnold's Selections from Wordsworth." Like Main, Eliot used the anthology to inscribe herself within a poetic tradition.[18]

The more Main congratulated his idol for ennobling the novel, the more his own anthologies debased it. In a feat of literary-historical retrogression, the *Sayings* distanced Eliot from the novel as strenuously as the Lambs' *Tales* had novelized Shakespeare half a century earlier. Where the Lambs had used the conventions of the novel to reduce Shakespeare to a smaller, domestic, feminine scale, the dramatic form of the *Sayings* and Main's prefatory invocation of Shakespearean drama together "magnified" Eliot's "mere storytelling" into something more "grand." Where the Lambs redefined Shakespeare as a children's writer, Main helped to position *Middlemarch* as what Virginia Woolf would later call "one of the few English novels for grown-up people."[19] Where the Lambs had modernized Shakespeare by transposing his plots into a genre that postdated them, Main granted a living writer the status usually reserved for the dead.

Eliot acknowledged this when she asked Main to justify his plan for a *George Eliot Birthday Book* by showing her other anthologies devoted to writers still living: "Burns and Shakespeare books are no criterion for a living writer. The Tennyson book would be such."[20] Characteristically, the example with which Eliot chose to compare herself was not a novelist. The subordination of the living to the dead displaced the distinction between novelists and poets. Unlike Scott's, Eliot's poetic career came as an afterthought after five novels had already appeared; and unlike that of other ambitiously aphoristic novelists like Hardy or

Meredith, her verse never matched the success of her novels in her lifetime or after. One can wonder, then, how Main's *Sayings* – which, despite the overrepresentation of verse, was still dominated by extracts from Eliot's prose – managed to define her as a poet.

One explanation is that Main's anthologies do not so much substitute one genre for another as scramble generic signals to a point where "lyric" ceases to designate anything more specific than "anthology-piece." Main's unsuccessful plan to yoke Eliot with Shakespeare under the rubric of "British Poetry" makes clear that the novel is not the only genre that anthologies have the power to rename. His proposed "selection of English lyrics, from Shakespeare and Spenser to Browning & George Eliot" – which Main later revised to read simply *A Selection of British Lyrics from Shakespeare to George Eliot* – begins the history of "lyric" with a dramatist and ends it with a novelist.[21] The title makes no sense unless we remember that Main's overrepresentation of Eliot's poetry repeats earlier anthologies' redefinition of Shakespeare as a writer of lyrics. Thomas Percy's decision to excerpt only the songs from Shakespeare's plays in his *Reliques of Ancient Poetry* (1765) was repeated not only by later collections like Robert Bell's *Songs from the Dramatists* (1854), but by the overrepresentation of songs in the *Golden Treasury* edited by F. T. Palgrave a decade before the *Sayings*.[22] Songs provided ready-made the lyric fragments that other anthologies were forced to carve out of longer dramatic texts. While abridgments like the Lambs' turned Shakespeare into a novelist, and *Beauties* like Dodd's made him an essayist, Victorian editors obscured the dramatic status of the plays more obliquely by isolating Shakespeare from other dramatists at the same time as they quarantined touchstones from their dramatic context.

Put differently, Shakespeare provided Main with a precedent for excerpting works in a genre that anthologies routinely excluded. We saw in the previous chapter how Knox and Enfield established Shakespeare's uniqueness by placing him in a generic vacuum. Even more than a century later, in 1910, Henry Frowde's *Moments* series of pocket anthologies, which included no novelist but Eliot and Dickens, still excluded all dramatists except Shakespeare. Main's invocation of Shakespeare, too, sets off a chain of transformations in which narrative gets displaced by drama which in turn is redefined as lyric. In the preface to the *Sayings*, Shakespeare's name stands not only for Eliot's power to transcend genre, but for the power of anthologies to transform it. By transposing Shakespeare from the theater to the schoolroom, from acting to elocution, Dodd's *Beauties of Shakespeare* had erased the generic origins of its raw material. Main followed that example. The *Sayings* claimed for a single novelist the generic extraterritoriality that earlier anthologies had conferred upon a single playwright. In her case as in Shakespeare's, individual genius overruled the generic categories that normally govern admittance to anthologies – and to the canon. Name trumps genre. Main's *Sayings* and the anthologies that followed made Eliot's relation to other novelists as tenuous as her relation to other women. Like another admirer's description of Eliot as "the female Shakespeare, so to speak," their invocation of Shakespeare defined her as an anomaly.[23]

Yet ironically, by the end of the nineteenth century the tokenism which singled out a few novels by making them poems or tragedies or sermons *manqués* had become a defining feature of the genre itself. When Main classified Eliot's novels with prose poems, as when a review of *Felix Holt* asserted that "George Eliot's novels are not novels in the ordinary sense of the term – they are really dramas," or another of *The Mill on the Floss* praised the author for writing "not merely as a novelist, but, as a preacher" with the result that "the riddle of life, as it is here expounded, is more like a Greek tragedy than a modern novel," they simply recycled the same critical commonplace that prompted Carlyle to praise *Mary Barton* as deserving "to take its place far above the ordinary garbage of novels," or that led every novelist, as Bulwer-Lytton complained, to begin by declaring "I am not going to write a mere novel."[24] Main's defensive claim in the preface that by ranking Eliot with Shakespeare "I would not be supposed to undervalue the writings of other novelists" did nothing to answer his publisher's accusation that "in his preface he allows too little for all the good in Novels that have gone before."[25] The *Sayings* set into motion the substitution of individual genius for generic categories that made one review in the *Telegraph* a few months later pronounce it "almost profane to speak of ordinary novels in the same breath with George Eliot's."[26]

Yet although the review praised Eliot as incomparable, comparison and juxtaposition – "speaking in the same breath" – were precisely what allowed critics to dissociate Eliot from the novel in the decade leading up to her death. Eliot's name reappeared at the front of the next anthology that Main compiled, a collection of wit and wisdom of Samuel Johnson undertaken at G. H. Lewes's request. The surviving correspondence leads one to suspect that Lewes initiated the Johnson project as a way of distracting Main from Eliot, whom his attentions were beginning to embarrass. If so, the strategy backfired, for the

Johnson anthology ended up pairing Eliot's name with her former editor's. Main's *Conversations of Dr. Johnson (founded chiefly upon Boswell)* (1874) opens with a preface signed by Lewes – who by this point was lending Main his money as well as his name – followed by an epigraph taken from *The Spanish Gypsy*.[27] The double Lewes-Eliot signature retrospectively confirmed one reviewer's criticism of Main's *Sayings of George Eliot* as "unendurable Johnsonese."[28] Where the preface to the first edition of the *Sayings* had compared Eliot explicitly with Shakespeare, the publication of the second edition within weeks of Main's *Johnson* – which allowed the two volumes to be advertised together – gave her an even more respectable analogue. The parallel between Main's relation to Eliot and Boswell's to Johnson simply reinforced that analogy: young Scots adulators anthologizing older English sages. The company of a conservative male essayist erased not only Eliot's scandalous life, but her association with a frivolous genre.

The presence of an Eliot epigraph in a Johnson anthology betrays Main's inability to stop quoting Eliot even when commissioned to quote someone else. As he asked the Leweses, "what works of the imagination, for example (except hers) can one read who knows & loves & *worships* George Eliot as I do?" A quotation soon follows: "What a beautiful line that is, my dear Mrs. Lewes in a passage of the 'Spanish Gypsy' which I read yesterday: '*Friend more divine than all divinities*'." The fan mail from Main piled up in the Blackwood archives, beginning with a letter quoting yet a third line from *The Spanish Gypsy* and riddled throughout with apologies for "recalling one of Mrs. Lewes's 'wise and witty' [deliverances?]," forms as much of a cento as any published anthology.[29]

But Main's were not the only letters in which Eliot quotations appeared, nor his *Johnson* the only book for which Eliot provided an epigraph. An excerpt from a different poem appeared as a chapter motto in George Jacob Holyoake's *History of Co-operation in England* (1875–79), while a third reader inscribed quotations from Eliot's fiction at the front of a more sacred book: Lewes reported to Main "what I think will please you almost as much as it did me: Mrs. Cowper Temple told Mrs. Lewes that she had copied passages from 'Romola' into her New Testament."[30] Lewes had reason to think that the anecdote would excite Main, for the incorporation of Eliot's words into a devotional book repeated Main's own project of sacralizing Eliot through quotation. The gilt-edged pages of the *Sayings* and the red lettering of the *Birthday Book* help explain why a Swiss admirer proclaimed the *Sayings* his "breviary" and John Blackwood's wife (less flatteringly) pronounced it "undeniable Sunday reading."[31] (The "thinner paper" that Eliot described by analogy with Arnold's Wordsworth anthology was more commonly known as bible paper.) Not content to place an epigraph from Proverbs side by side with another from *The Spanish Gypsy*, Main reinforced the parallel between the wisdom books and the *Wit and Wisdom of George Eliot* (as the American abridgment of the *Sayings* was retitled) by including in the anthology itself one passage in which the narrator speaks for Solomon and another whose speaker presents his wisdom as a supplement to Solomon's:

If Solomon was as wise as he is reputed to be, I feel sure that when he compared a contentious woman to a continual dropping on a very rainy day, he had not a vixen in his eye – a fury with long nails, acrid and selfish. Depend upon it, he meant a good creature, who had no joy but in the happiness of the loved ones whom she contributed to make uncomfortable . . . Such a woman as Lisbeth for example.

Solomon's Proverbs, I think, have omitted to say, that as the sore palate findeth grit, so an uneasy consciousness heareth innuendoes.[32]

When Main consoled John Blackwood for a hostile review of *Middlemarch* with the speculation that "I have no doubt whatever that the fellow would write in precisely the same style and tone about the Sermon on the Mount,"[33] he projected onto the reviewer the "tone" in which he himself "plead[ed] guilty to being, not an admirer merely, but a *worshipper* of George Eliot."[34] Main might have been pleased to know that an imitation of his *Sayings* – *Moments with George Eliot* – would appear in 1913 in a series of miniature books between *The Sermon on the Mount* and *The Imitation of Christ*. Eliot herself did not shy from assigning quotations from her work a religious function. Writing to a friend shortly after Mazzini's death and Main's first edition, she eulogized the former:

Such a man leaves behind him a wider good than the loss of his personal presence can take away.
  "The greatest gift a hero leaves his race
  Is to have been a hero."
I must be excused for quoting my own words, because they are my *credo*.[35]

Main, too, used decontextualization to transpose Eliot's words from the most secular of nineteenth-century genres to the most sacred.

Yet Eliot's private letter and Mrs. Cowper Temple's manuscript inscriptions found even more public counterparts than the anthology. In a different letter to Main, Lewes boasted of hearing that "an orthodox West-End preacher" had quoted *Middlemarch* from the pulpit. (Eliot thus came to share Richardson's dubious distinction of being excerpted successively in a sermon and an anthology.)[36] He responded to Main's proposal of an anthology by describing another reader's larger-scale project: "Some years ago a lady suggested that 'texts' should be selected from [Eliot's] works to hang up in schoolrooms and railway waiting rooms in view of the banal and often preposterous bible texts, thus hung up and neglected. Your idea is a far more practical one."[37] Yet the first fantasy has not proved entirely impractical: in the year following the American broadcasting of *Middlemarch*, one college plastered the New York subway with advertisements reading "'It is never too late to be what you could have been.' George Eliot, *Middlemarch*." In the absence of Main's projected *Spirit of British Poetry*, it was left to the MTA to juxtapose Eliot belatedly with improving extracts of "Poetry in Motion."

Although the project of enlisting Eliot to decorate public transportation has only recently been realized, quotations from her novels entered the "schoolroom" well before her death. By 1879 she had given permission for her works to be extracted in four schoolbooks, defending "well-chosen extracts" as "really useful to the works from which they are taken."[38] In 1874, Main reported that a schoolmaster had agreed to buy multiple copies of the *Sayings*: "he means, of course, to use them for school prizes – not a bad way of circulating a book of the kind; for prizes are always *shown off*, you know."[39] And in the same year, an excerpt from *Middlemarch* which had already been quoted in the second edition of the *Sayings* reappeared on an examination for military officers, which required candidates to choose between "compar[ing] Cromwell and Napoleon, (1) as generals and (2) as statesmen" or discussing Will Ladislaw's assertion that "to be a poet is to have a soul *** in which knowledge passes instantaneously into feeling, and feeling flashes back as a new organ of knowledge."[40]

The examiner's strategy of substituting a quotation for a question can be traced to several sources. The contents of the test for young men bear a surprising resemblance to the contents of the birthday books that Main marketed to young women. Not only did the examination paper select a quotation included in Main, but its third essay topic – a platitude quoted from Henry Taylor, "The world knows nothing of its greatest men" – reappeared in a collection of *Birthday Greetings, . . . Poetical Extracts and Mottoes* published in the same year as Main's *George Eliot Birthday Book*.[41] The overlap of material betrays the congruence of method. The examination required of students what the anthology demanded from Main, and the sermon from its West End preacher: the ability to convert a piece of an old text into the starting-point for a new one.

That exercise was equally familiar to Marian Evans – not only as a reviewer, as I'll suggest at the end of this chapter, but also as a novelist. The question in the form of a quotation worked like an epigraph for the essays that glossed it. And by the 1870s, anachronism had made the epigraph Eliot's trademark. Although the convention of placing mottoes at the head of chapters had weakened in the quarter-century separating the death of the Author of Waverley from the birth of the author of *Scenes of Clerical Life*, George Eliot's career went on to overturn the historical trend. While *Adam Bede, The Mill on the Floss*, and *Silas Marner* each place an epigraph at the beginning of the book, the last three novels (*Felix Holt, Middlemarch*, and *Daniel Deronda*) put one or even two at the head of each chapter.[42] More strikingly, *The Lifted Veil*, published in 1859 without an epigraph, was reissued in 1878 with the addition of an unsigned epigraph composed (like many of her chapter mottoes) by Eliot herself. The fact that the two editions were separated by the revelation of George Eliot's identity in 1859, immediately after the appearance of her proleptically named story, suggests that the addition of an epigraph misrepresented as a quotation from a different author served to compensate for the belated attribution of the text itself to Marian Evans.[43] By turning literary history on its head, the revision of "The Lifted Veil" called attention to the epigraph. Similarly, the chapter mottoes of the last two novels were rendered all the more conspicuous by their rarity in most other English novels published within recent memory. By 1899, the younger novelist Mary Cholmondeley could signal her allegiance to Eliot by prefacing with epigraphs – several excerpted from the latter's work – each chapter of a novel set in "Middleshire," whose heroine writes long periodic sentences interspersed with epigrams and criticized by her brother, "who had the same opinion of George Eliot's works."[44] Cholmondeley inscribes Eliot doubly in *Red Pottage*: both by quoting her, and by quoting at all.

Eliot's mottoes turned her novels into anthologies to be mined for anthology-pieces in turn. Given how many of the epigraphs originated in working notebooks distinguished only in their professionalism from the private commonplace-books that Marian Evans kept separately, a hostile review of *The Mill on the Floss* was not entirely wrong to complain of passages of "didactic commonplace, which read like bits of private notebooks foisted into their present places," or a more favorable review to criticize the "long-winded reflections taken from the commonplace-book or the unpublished works of George Eliot."[45] Even after publication, Eliot copied her self-authored epigraphs into a notebook of her own, while encouraging Main to overrepresent the mottoes in his anthologies.[46] The only two quotations that she asked him to include in the *Birthday Book* were both epigraphs, and she pleaded even more explicitly for him to slant the collection away from prose narrative and toward "a good sprinkling of the best quotations from my Poems and poetical mottoes."[47]

Eliot's request may appear to anticipate William Bennett's assumption that poems constitute the most appropriate anthology fodder. Given how many of the chapter mottoes are in prose, however, Main's disproportionate representation of them cannot be explained on metrical grounds alone. A different explanation might be that the epigraphs looked quotable because they appeared to be quoted, even (or especially) when they were in fact composed by Eliot herself. Margreta de Grazia has argued that quotation marks originated as a way of signalling truths that can be generalized and passages that can be quoted, only later (in the eighteenth century) coming to mark text taken from another source.[48] The prominence of Eliot's epigraphs in Main's anthologies suggests that the confusion between quoted and quotable text persisted well into the nineteenth century, for the readers who excerpted Eliot responded to her own practice (and pretence) of quoting. When Main excerpted Eliot in the epigraph to his *Conversations of Dr. Johnson*, he mimicked her own use of the motto – just as the New Testament into which excerpts from Eliot were copied pastiched the commonplace-books out of which Eliot's own epigraphs came, just as Holyoake's use of a quotation from Eliot's verse to preface a chapter of his prose made *The History of Cooperation* resemble the chapters of *Felix Holt* that took their epigraphs from *The Spanish Gypsy*, and just as Mary Cholmondley's chapter mottoes copied not only Eliot's words but her practice of quoting others'. (Conversely, the passage from *The Spanish Gypsy* that provides an epigraph for the *Sayings* is itself labeled a quotation: the epigraph, which reads simply "Wise books / for half the truths they hold, are honoured tombs," is originally prefaced with "I say – nay, Ptolemy said it.") In one case, the epigraphs even reciprocate each other: Main's choice of a quotation from *The Spanish Gypsy* as an epigraph to the *Conversations of Johnson* not only copied Eliot's use of quotations from *The Spanish Gypsy* as epigraphs to chapters forty-four and forty-five of *Felix Holt*, but inverted Eliot's own use of a Johnson quotation as the epigraph to chapter sixty-one of *Middlemarch*. By calling readers' attention to the discontinuity of texts made up of different voices (even through ventriloquism, as in the self-authored mottoes), the epigraphs set the example that anthologists so enthusiastically followed.

Eliot's revival of Scott's chapter mottoes helps explain more specifically why Main excepted Scott from the refusal to "speak of Eliot in the same breath" with other novelists – or indeed why he included Scott in the list of poets among whom he hoped to rank her. Eliot's practice of clothing her own words as quotations made her heir to Scott's triple role as poet-novelist, literary collector, and ennobler of a low genre. Although the order in which Eliot's novels and poems appeared reverses the chronology of Scott's career, within the novels themselves the relation between verse epigraphs and prose narrative looks strikingly similar. Like Scott's, Eliot's pseudonymous epigraphs change the motto from a place where authorship shifts to a place where genre switches. Surprisingly, although Eliot often depicts characters reading Scott's novels and poetry – in *Middlemarch* alone, Mary Garth compares her life with his plots, Mr. Trumbull recites from *Anne of Geierstein*, Lydgate confesses that he "used to know Scott's poems by heart," and the Garths read *Ivanhoe* aloud – she never quotes either in a chapter motto (*Middlemarch*, 14.167, 32.346, 27.304, 57.617). Scott's absence from the epigraphs paradoxically confirms Eliot's debt to him: it would be redundant to quote him in mottoes whose form already alludes to his work.[49]

While Eliot borrowed Shakespearean stature by quoting Shakespeare directly, she became associated with Scott more obliquely, not by quoting him but by quoting like him – and by allowing Main to repackage her work in several of the forms that the Waverley Novels had already spawned. Writing to John Blackwood to propose an index to the characters in Eliot's novels (an idea eventually implemented by later critics) Main pleaded the precedent of Scott: "You will probably have seen the Index given at the end of each volume of one of the recent editions of Scott? Mine would be something of that sort."[50] While Eliot bracketed herself with Wordsworth by mimicking the design of Arnold's anthology, Main classed her with Scott by imitating the index to his works.

Main's proposal established a parallel not simply between Scott and Eliot, but between Scott's editors and Eliot's, including himself. Although he never invoked that precedent as explicitly as Shakespeare in his business correspondence about the anthologies, his obsession with

Scott can be gauged in other letters larded with quotations from the
Waverley novels and tedious jokes about *The Antiquary*, a novel that also
formed the subject of an essay submitted to *Blackwood's* with characteristically humiliating results. Main's idea of modeling an index to Eliot
after the index to Scott suggests that *The Genius and Wisdom of Sir Walter
Scott, Comprising Moral, Religious, Political, Literary, and Social Aphorisms,
Selected Carefully from his Various Writings: With a Memoir* (1839) could have
provided the model for the *Wise Sayings of George Eliot*.[51] By the same
token, one possible explanation for the disproportionate representation
of epigraphs in Main's anthology is the example set by the successors to
The Poetry contained in the Novels, Tales and Romances of the Author of Waverley
(1822) discussed in chapter one. Later editors would follow Main's
example: *A Souvenir of George Eliot: Scenes and Characters from the Works of
George Eliot: A Series of Illustrations by Eminent Artists* (1888) reproduces the
form of the *Galleries* and *Albums* which had earlier broken Scott's novels
into series of discontinuous scenes and portraits. In this context, Jane
Millgate's and Ian Duncan's argument that the form in which Scott
published and republished his novels fixed the shape in which novels
would be issued for the rest of the century could be extended to the
posthumous editing and repackaging of his fiction as well.[52]

The contrasting chronologies of Eliot's and Scott's careers, however,
forced Main to resort to editorial sleight of hand. Scott's poetry established his name before he began to publish novels and even longer
before he acknowledged them; in contrast, Eliot's first poem appeared
only after five novels and an equal number of stories. By bracketing her
with Scott, Main obscured the belatedness and insignificance of poetry
within Eliot's career. The generic hierarchy implied by Scott's initial
refusal to sign his novels legitimated Main's double ambition of redefining Eliot from novelist to poet and stripping her novels of their narrative
form. Yet as a novelist who granted new respectability to the genre,
Scott also provided a model for the project of "sanctifying the novel"
that Main undertook on Eliot's behalf. More specifically, Scott's attempt
to reclaim the genre from his feminine predecessors and contemporaries
supplied a precedent at once for Eliot's masculine persona and for
Main's eagerness to distance her fictions from what Marian Evans had
called "Silly Novels by Lady Novelists."[53]

In the context of so many strategic juxtapositions, one can understand Eliza Lynn Linton's longing for a time when people would finally
tire of "quot[ing] Kant and the author of 'Middlemarch'" in the same
breath.[54] By the last decade of her life, when an epigraph was appearing

in every chapter and an anthology every other year, Eliot was defined by the company she kept. Lewes's eagerness to circulate anecdotes about quotations in sermons and inscriptions in Bibles acknowledged the power of contextualization. Together with the question on the officers' exam, the examples in the schoolbooks, and the epigraphs to Johnson, *Red Pottage* and the *History of Co-operation in England*, these anecdotes made clear that novels could borrow seriousness not only from the texts that they quoted (like Eliot's epigraphs) but from the texts that quoted them. Eliot herself understood that authors' reputations were colored by the places in which excerpts from their work appeared: she expunged a Whitman epigraph from *Daniel Deronda* "not because the motto itself is objectionable to me – it was one of the finer things which had clung to me from among his writings – but because, since I quote so few poets, my selection of a motto from Walt Whitman might be taken as a sign of a special admiration which I am very far from feeling."[55] Eliot's peculiar vulnerability to intertextual appropriation is most strikingly concretized in the bookmark produced to commemorate the centenary of her birth with an embroidered quotation from *Scenes of Clerical Life*.[56] That object forms a material equivalent to the epigraphs in Main's *Johnson*, Cholmondley's *Red Pottage*, Holyoake's *History*, and Mrs. Cowper Temple's Bible – and indeed to the excerpts that make up Main's anthologies. Like all of them, it inserts Eliot's words into other books: not between the lines, but between the pages.

WOMEN OF MAXIMS

Eliot's hesitation to quote Whitman reflects an awareness that quotation can consecrate, but also a fear of guilt by association. The anthologization of her own work brought both possibilities home. Eliot's ambivalence about her complicity in that project was apparent from the moment when she authorized Main's *George Eliot Birthday Book* in terms as grudging as it would be possible to use without actually refusing. Her letter of consent to her publisher, John Blackwood, opens on a tone of distaste:

We have never seen or heard anything of the said "Birthday Books" – have you? They may be the vulgarest things in the book stalls for what we know. *Entre nous*, I am a little shocked at the tone of Mr. Main's letter . . . I can give no opinion about a "George Eliot Birthday Book" unless I saw the "Tennyson do" [Emily Shakespear's 1877 *Tennyson Birthday Book*] with which it is to follow suit. But in general suits are not what – I should be fond of following or having followed on my behalf.

Eliot's insistence on her ignorance allows her to keep a ginger distance
from the birthday book. So do the ironic quotation marks around
"Tennyson do." Yet the letter ends by hinting a willingness to be
overruled: "But I must refer the matter to your judgment . . . I believe
that you, as much as I, hate puffing, gaudy, claptrappy forms of publication, superfluous for all *good* ends. But anything graceful which you
consider an advantage to the circulation of my works we are not averse
to."[57] The coy double negative of the last sentence belies Eliot's earlier
refusal (via Lewes) to accept Blackwood's initial decision against publishing the *Sayings*.[58] Even in a letter to Main himself, Eliot refuses to
accept his gratitude for her consent: "I had already referred the decision
to Mr. Blackwood, Mr. Lewes and I having no acquaintance with this
new mode of serving up authors."[59] The modesty topos forces Eliot's
publisher to become her mouthpiece. The urge to displace responsibility
for the *Birthday Book* onto a vulgar compiler or mercenary publisher
betrays Eliot's embarrassment about her own role not only in authorizing the anthology, but in authoring its contents. Her private letters
repudiate the published anthology that sold on the strength of her name.

The correspondence that survives from the negotiations surrounding
the anthologies is riddled with misascriptions of Eliot's wishes to others:
to her partner, her publishers, her editor, her readers. That logic of
infinite regress seems to have infected even William Blackwood, who in
turn blames a different scapegoat for his own decisions about the form
of the *Birthday Book*: as he tells Eliot, "I quite join in your condemnation
of the binding but we had to consider a colonial class rather as likely to
be its largest buyers and cater to their taste accordingly."[60] Blackwood's characterization of that "class" translates into geographical
terms the contempt that Lewes had stated more bluntly: "The cover for
the Birthday Book *is* startling and ornate, but we suppose adapted to
the bookseller mind, and to the mind of the idiots who buy birthday
books!"[61] Responsibility for the *Birthday Book* is banished to the colonies,
far from the more civilized nation that Eliot invokes when she remarks
that "*entre nous*, I am a little shocked at the tone" or, in another letter,
"*entre nous*, I wish that the Preface [to Main's *Sayings*] had been touched
with a more fastidious finger, a more scrupulous regard to *mesure*."[62]

Lewes distinguished himself and Eliot even more sharply from Main's
anthology-reading audience when he conveyed her refusal to read
Main's *Conversations of Dr. Johnson*: "I can't promise to read your book for
some time yet . . . nor do I think Mrs. Lewes will be able to do so. But if
we thought it a masterpiece *that* wouldn't alter the fact – and if we

thought it rubbish hundreds of others might think it a masterpiece – and *they* are its real public.''[63] The letter defines his taste and Eliot's against the taste of the vulgar "hundreds" who read anthologies. Both partners remained as ambivalent about the *Birthday Book* which bears Eliot's name and Lewes's editorial input as about the *Conversations* to which Lewes had contributed a preface and Eliot an epigraph. Neither endorsed what their signatures were being used to market.

When Eliot wrote to Main to dismiss as "dolting and feeble" the *Tennyson Birthday Book* which provided his precedent, she added a pointed qualifier: "This is not the Poet's fault."[64] The corollary was presumably that the fault lay with the compiler – in this case with Emily Shakespear, but a reader as morbidly sensitive as Main would have been hard put not to apply the accusation to himself. In absolving Tennyson from blame for his birthday book, Eliot disclaimed responsibility for hers. Lewes used blunter weapons, ordering Main to delete from the *Sayings* a reference to Eliot's involvement in the selection of excerpts: "it would not do for the public to suppose she had had any share in the book, beyond that of giving permission to its being executed."[65] And time would prove him right. In a review of *Daniel Deronda* – a novel written in the wake of the first edition of Main's *Sayings* and immediately anthologized in the second – A. V. Dicey carps: "that Mr. Main should, *apparently with the author's sanction*, collect together 'wise, witty, and tender sayings' from George Eliot's writings may be open to remark."[66] Yet no remark is actually made, as if Eliot's involvement in an anthology of her own works was so obviously wrong that no explanation was needed.

Later critics have followed Dicey's assumption that Eliot's resistance is self-explanatory, her consent puzzling. Rosemary Ashton glosses Eliot's agreement as the triumph of personal vanity over esthetic principle: "though she was aware that such extracting would be damaging to the artistic structure of her works . . . her self-distrust and love of approbation induced her to permit it."[67] Yet the other side of Eliot's ambivalence requires just as much explanation: we need to understand not only why she authorized Main's anthologies, but why she disavowed them. The same "self-distrust" to which Ashton attributes Eliot's consent can be used to explain her embarrassment, for Main's anthologies drew the attention of readers (including Eliot herself) to three problems already latent in the novels themselves: the place of sententiousness within narrative, the boundary separating writer from reader, and the feasibility of addressing an audience without assigning it a gender.

Where Eliot craved a public, Main gave her a market.[68] The gilt-edged pages of the *Sayings* literalize Main's promise of the text's "rich worth," advertising its status at once as a material object and as a consumer good. Eliot's resentment of the vulgar audience who bought gaudily bound birthday books echoes her satire in *Middlemarch* of readers who judge books by their covers, like Mr. Trumbull, who boasts that he owns "no less than two hundred volumes in calf." As a consumer, Trumbull values books for their bindings; as an auctioneer, he prices a painting by its frame and a book by its lettering, "no less than five hundred [riddles] printed in a beautiful red."[69] While the form of the riddle-book anticipates the red-and-black lettering of the *Birthday Book*, its self-contained snippets of wit recall the contents of the *Sayings* – in later editions of which, ironically, the passage ridiculing the riddle-book would eventually be reproduced. Once recontextualized in the second edition of the *Sayings*, the passage draws attention to the materiality not only of the anthology, but of the novel.

Mr. Trumbull's description of the riddle collection as "an ornament for the table" and of his books as "calf" can serve as a reminder that *Middlemarch* itself is an object for sale. Yet his vulgarity immediately warns more tasteful readers to forget that fact. Eliot's distaste for the ostentatious binding of the *Birthday Book* needs to be set against her anxiety about her sensitivity to the physical materials of her own books. "I confess," she apologized to John Blackwood in a different context, "to the weakness of being affected by paper and type in something of the same subtle way as I am affected by the odour of a room."[70] In a culture where book was to text as body to mind, a novelist could downplay the materiality of her books only at the cost of lowering herself to notice such sensuous considerations as the obtrusiveness of the binding. The problem was not George Eliot's alone: as early as 1847, G. H. Lewes's novel *Ranthorpe* introduced its protagonist reading the wares of a book-stall without buying any of them, insisting that "he cared not for rare editions, large paper copies, or sumptuous bindings. His hunger was for knowledge; he had a passion for books – no matter what edition, what bindings; he cared not even whether they had covers at all."[71] Although the willful blindness to the cover which distinguishes Lewes's hero from Eliot's vulgar characters and "colonial" readers underscores the disjunction between reading and buying, the placement of this scene in the first chapter means that its readers may well have just purchased (or rented) *Ranthorpe* itself. In *Middlemarch*, too, the auctioneer's substitution of "volumes" for "books," like his specification of the binding and coloring, makes clear Eliot's worry about the crassly decorative uses to which books can be put – including her own.

Within Eliot's lifetime, the traditional fear of finding one's books recycled for trunk-linings or curl-papers gave way to a newer anxiety about finding oneself displayed on a coffee-table. It is appropriate that Trumbull commends *Anne of Geierstein* and *Ivanhoe* to Mary Garth, for *Middlemarch* is set at precisely the moment (1829–33) when Scott's Magnum Opus edition was redefining the novel from a dog-eared object read at the dressing-table to a luxury good displayed in aspirational drawing-rooms. The auctioning of the riddle-book literalizes the commodification of texts foreshadowed in the scene where Trumbull "read the title [of *Anne of Geierstein*] aloud as if he were offering it for sale." The slippage from reading Scott to selling Scott suggests that the audience of the Waverley Novels is no less tainted by commercialism than their author. Indeed, Eliot uses Scott as the prototype of a mercenary writer when, in an essay criticizing literature produced "under the pressure of money-need," she declares: "Still less is Scott to be taken as an example to be followed in this matter."[72] Yet the resemblance between the *Wit and Wisdom of George Eliot* and the *Wit and Wisdom of Sir Walter Scott*, or between the *Waverley Gallery* and the *Souvenir of George Eliot*, makes clear that her editors did in fact take his example. So does the parallel between Trumbull's taste and the "bookseller" esthetic of the *Birthday Book*.

"But Sir Walter Scott – I suppose Mr. Lydgate knows him," Ned Plymdale interrupts nervously when the other man mocks his gift to Rosamond Vincy, "the last *Keepsake*, the gorgeous watered-silk publication which marked modern progress at that time."[73] As the narrator's specification of the binding materials makes clear, Rosamond's gift book shares the "ornate cover" that attracted vulgar buyers to the *Birthday Book* – as well as its gilt-edged pages and engraved inscription plate. No less than the *Birthday Book* or Trumbull's library, annuals like the *Keepsake* subordinate contents to cover, text to book. A few Christmases after Rosamond receives her present, *Fraser's* – a monthly that could disclaim its own ephemerality only by distancing itself from annuals – already turned the beauty of those books against them, sneering that "the first and most important fact of the *Keepsake* is its binding."[74] Eliot's protest against the luxurious material form of the *Birthday Book* echoes the formulaic ambivalence of men who wrote for the annuals, from Wordsworth, who claimed that "it would disgrace any name to appear in an annual" but published in *Winter's Wreath*, to Tennyson, who claimed to "foreswear all annuals provincial or metropolitan" but continued to contribute to them, to Southey, who called annuals "picture-books for grown-up children" but sold work to several including the *Keepsake* itself.[75] ("There are a great many celebrated people writing in the *Keepsake*," Rosamond's suitor protests.) Rosamond's embarrassment about reading the *Keepsake* repeats theirs about writing for it: "Rosamond herself was not without relish for these writers, but she did not readily commit herself by admiration, and was alive to the slightest hint that anything was not, according to Lydgate, in the very highest taste."[76] At the same time, the character's reluctance to declare herself a *Keepsake* reader prefigures the author's reluctance to acknowledge her share in compiling the *Birthday Book*.

The narrator's reference to the annual "which marked modern progress *at that time*" emphasizes not only the ephemerality of gift books but the datedness of the *Keepsake*, begun in the year before *Middlemarch* is set and discontinued in the year when Eliot began to publish fiction. The phrase clinches a summary of Rosamond, earlier in the same chapter, as "that combination of correct sentiments, music, dancing, drawing, elegant note-writing, *private album for extracted verse*, and perfect blond loveliness, which made the irresistible woman for the doomed man *of that date*."[77] Eliot's insistence on "that date" and "that time" reinforces Rosamond's double personification of literary and sartorial fashion. Yet while the annual was long dead by the 1870s, the young lady's "album for extracted verse" was not. It survived in the blank pages of the *George Eliot Birthday Book*, used to collect autographs of celebrities or inscriptions from friends.[78]

Rosamond's specifically feminine vulgarity provides a clue to what worried Eliot about the *Birthday Book*. The shift from Eliot's enthusiasm for the *Sayings* to her embarrassment about the *Birthday Book* cannot be explained by the form of the two books alone. One might more logically expect the opposite reaction, since the *Birthday Book* lacks the gushing preface of the *Sayings* and, in its cloth-bound version, was actually cheaper than the *Sayings*.[79] What does explain that change, I think, is that the second anthology specifies the gender of its audience. Eliot's attempt to dissociate herself from the feminine forms of the annual, the album, and the gift book did not prevent *Middlemarch* itself from re-appearing in those settings – first in the *Birthday Book* and, ten years later, in *A Souvenir of George Eliot*, a gift book whose size and binding borrows the model of the annual, as does its subordination of text to engravings. This is not to say that the annuals were no different from anthologies such as Main's: on the contrary, in their means of production, the two formed mirror-images of each other, since the anthologies collected material earlier published in single-author volumes, while the poems originally published in annuals were often later collected into author-based editions. Yet both associate material ostentation and feminine readers with a loss of authorial integrity. Where the Bible, schoolbook, and sermon elevate the texts that they frame, the *Birthday Book* degrades them.

Main's second anthology genders its readers female in the process of reinforcing its author's masculine persona. By taking a Tennyson Birthday Book as his model, Main brackets Eliot with a male poet often criticized as "feminine" or "effeminate." And if Tennyson writes like the opposite sex, Main reads like them: he sets an example for his feminine audience by responding in ways that Eliot herself ascribes to women. Even before the appearance of the *Birthday Book*, the *Sayings* place Eliot's work in the category that she had begun her career by distancing herself from: "Silly Novels by Lady Novelists." The essay of that title, published in 1857, does not ridicule lady novelists alone. It also satirizes female readers who underline

moral comments, such as, for instance, that "It is a fact, no less true than melancholy, that all people, more or less, richer or poorer, are swayed by bad example"; that "Books, however trivial, contain some subjects from which useful information may be drawn"; that "Vice can too often borrow the language of virtue"; that "Merit and nobility of nature must exist, to be accepted, for clamour and pretension cannot impose upon those too well read in human nature to be easily deceived"; and that, "In order to forgive, we must have been injured." There is, doubtless, a class of readers to whom these remarks appear peculiarly pointed and pungent; for *we often find them doubly and trebly scored with the pencil, and delicate hands giving in their determined adhesion to these hardy novelties by a distinct* très vrai, *emphasized by many notes of exclamation.*[80]

Evans's ridicule of these "delicate hands" draws on a tradition that represents women leaving the impress of their bodies on books: from Lady Slattern in *The Rivals*, who "cherishes her nails for the purpose of making marginal notes" in library romances; to Dickens's sketch of girls' initials and underscorings in a circulating-library novel "whose pages, reduced to a condition very like curl-paper, are thickly studded with notes in pencil"; to Thackeray's reflection that

it is a wonder how fond ladies are of writing in books and signing their charming initials! Mrs. Berry's before-mentioned little gilt books are scored with little pencil-marks, or occasionally at the margin with a ! – note of interjection, or the words, "*Too true*, A.B." and so on. Much may be learned with regard to lovely woman by a look at the book she reads in.[81]

Marian Evans's satire points back to the pedantry of a Catherine Morland, but also forward to the model of feminine reading that the *Birthday Book* would later provoke. While "silly novels" invite marginal inscriptions beside the most platitudinous "moral comments," the *Birthday Book* places sententious passages opposite blank spaces where readers can write. Main himself drafted the *Sayings* and the *Birthday Book* by marking the "moral comments" in Eliot's novels; and his preface, which describes her sayings as "the grandest and most uncompromising moral truth," simply translates into English ladies' marginal comments of "très vrai." Main's anthologies make visible the same kind of abstraction that "Silly Novels by Lady Novelists" criticizes: "The most pitiable of all silly novels by lady novelists are what we may call the *oracular* species – novels intended to expound the writer's religious, philosophical, or moral theories." The oracular image that led John Morley to compare Eliot with "the inspired Pythia on the sublime tripod" owes as much to Main's taste for reading "moral comments" as to Eliot's for writing them.[82]

In a culture where (in the words of one 1893 article) women were expected to prefer "analysis" to "action" while men read for the plot and skipped "irrelevant chatter," Main read like the women for whom he wrote.[83] Eliot herself describes Main's response to her work in the same language that she had applied earlier to ladies' novels and lady readers. "Silly Novels" ridicules readers who "[under]score" "moral comments" and writers who rely on "the illustrative aid of italics and small caps," "the lucidity of italics and small caps," or "profuse italics." Those are precisely the forms of emphasis for which Eliot would later criticize Main, asking John Blackwood to "suggest to [Main] to avoid italics" in the second edition of the *Sayings*, and ordering G. H. Lewes to inform him that "your delight in italics and small caps is objectionable."[84] The male compiler's habit of underlining sententious passages brings together the private "underscoring" of lady readers with the "profuse italics" of published lady writers.

Instead of trying to exculpate women from the traditional accusation of reading with their bodies, the next generation of woman writers embraced it. The New Woman novelist Sarah Grand, for example, defends the morally serious books whose margins in library copies bear "the emphatic strokes of approval, the notes of admiration, the ohs of enthusiasm, the ahs of agreement." Grand's understanding of the forms in which readers can properly register their appreciation departs as sharply from George Eliot's as from Marian Evans's. Yet Arnold Bennett managed to turn even Eliot's scorn for feminine italics against her, calling her own use of emphasis "transparently feminine": "The average woman italicizes freely. George Eliot, of course, had trained herself too well to do that, at least formally; yet her constant, undue insistence springs from the same essential weakness, and amounts practically to the same expedient." His how-to manual *Journalism for Women* goes farther, warning aspiring lady journalists that only a course of "moral and intellectual calisthenics" can cure the typographical lapses that had betrayed George Eliot's sex.[85] Although Bennett's assertion that Eliot's masculine "training" hides a feminine "essence" is absurdly circular, he may not have been entirely wrong to hypothesize a conscious effort on Eliot's part to dissociate herself from the kinds of emphasis conventionally ascribed to women. In the same way that J. W. Cross's *Life* would later define Eliot as a masculine writer by assigning to her husband the memorializing role conventionally reserved for great men's widows, Eliot established her own good taste in contradistinction to the feminine vulgarity of her male editor and his female readers. The *Birthday Book* confirms its author's androgyny at the price of assigning its readers a gender. The "picture-books for grown-up children" read by the "infantine" Rosamond, like the birthday book embossed with an image of a baby, defines *Middlemarch* itself, by contrast, as "one of the few English novels for grown-up people." Long before Woolf, in fact, E. S. Dallas had already used young girls' putative lack of appreciation as evidence of Eliot's greatness: "We doubt, indeed, whether Miss Lydia Languish will care much for [*The Mill on the Floss*]."[86] The birthday book took over the girlish audience from which Eliot's own work had disencumbered the novel.

Yet the counterexample of Mr. Trumbull makes clear that misogyny alone does not explain Eliot's objection to being marketed to girls. The problem is less that the *Birthday Book* addresses women than that it reduces them to consumers – just as the "private album for extracted verse" and "watered-silk" annual form Rosamond Vincy into a pattern young woman whose only function is to buy fashionable things. The *Birthday Book* uses Eliot's words to cement girls' friendship, because its presentation plate labels it a gift and its blank spaces invite them to exchange signatures. It inscribes those friendships within the marketplace, however, by filling the facing pages with reminders of the dates on which birthday presents (or birthday books) need to be bought for friends in turn. In one sense, the monthly and daily dates invest Eliot's sayings with an almost religious perenniality, something like the Positivist calendar championed by her correspondent Frederic Harrison, who asserts that the greatest secular "books have a daily and perpetual value, such as the devout Christian finds in his morning and evening psalm."[87] But that schedule of reading is also a schedule of buying. The inscription plate at the front of the *Birthday Book* and the calendar pages facing the quotations implicate George Eliot in an endless cycle of gift-buying whose yearly rhythm repeats the planned obsolescence of the literary annuals that "marked modern progress at that time." Where Main's invocations of Shakespeare in the preface to the *Sayings* position Eliot as a classic for all time, the *Birthday Book* reshapes her for an age – and for a sex.[88]

David Carroll has argued persuasively that Eliot "wishes to define moral problems and assert certain values, but the forms of wisdom literature are no longer available."[89] But the problem could just as well be phrased in the opposite terms. The riddle-book in *Middlemarch*, the *Sayings*, and the *Birthday Book* suggest that the forms of wisdom literature were all too easily available as commodities – in other words, that their accessibility to vulgar, young, and feminine readers discredited any "wisdom" that they contained.

"OUTSIDE SAYINGS AND DOINGS"

Eliot's own epigraphs turn quotation to the opposite use: production instead of consumption, work rather than sociability. Amateurism alone distinguishes the album and the birthday book from her own working notebooks of sources. Yet that distinction is precisely what the traditional image of women leaving bodily traces on books undermines. Just as Dickens applies the language of masculine scholarship to female novel-readers who dispute each others' marginalia "like commentators in a more extensive way," Andrew Lang would later represent girls' mutilation of novels as a parody of scholarship like his own:

The thick double-columned volume in which I peruse the works of [Ann Radcliffe] belongs to a public library. It is quite the dirtiest, greasiest, most dog's-eared, and most bescribbled tome in the collection. Many of the books have remained, during the last hundred years, uncut, even to this day, and I have had to apply the paper knife to many an author, from Alciphron (1790) to

Mr. Max Muller, and Dr. Birkbeck Hill's edition of Bozzy's "Life of Dr. Johnson." But Mrs. Radcliffe has been read diligently, and copiously annotated.[90]

Despite Lang's contrast between trashy books covered in culinary grime and scholarly ones still uncut, his image of "annotation" suggests that gender alone differentiates the circulating library from the research library for which it provides a burlesque mirror-image. (In fact, even the most hostile representations of women defacing books cannot help contradicting the equally unflattering charge of feminine skimming: as one late-nineteenth-century narrator deadpans, "considering the speed with which [the hero's mother-in-law] read [a novel], it was constant food for astonishment that she could contrive to do a book so much damage.")[91] Thackeray could police that border only through the threat of male violence, attacking "the fashionable authoress" who

interlards her work with fearful quotations from the French, fiddle-faddle extracts from Italian operas, German phrases fiercely mutilated, and a scrap or two of bad Spanish; and upon the strength of these murders, she calls herself an authoress. To be sure there is no such word as authoress. If any young nobleman or gentleman of Eton College . . . should fondly imagine that he might apply to those fair creatures the title of *autrix* – I pity that young nobleman's or gentleman's case. Doctor Wordsworth and assistants would swish that error out of him in a way that need not here be mentioned.

All that distinguishes schoolboys' Latin tags from ladies' German quotations is the difference between literal and figurative punishment. While the former deserve the hypothetical schoolmaster's rod, the latter invite the lash of actual satirists like Thackeray, who laments, in yet another review of the annuals, that "the critical rod is, for the most part, thrown aside" in modern journalism.[92]

George Eliot's ambivalence about quotation reflects an equally fragile distinction between feminine pedantry (defacement) and masculine scholarship (annotation). While both of her criticisms of "italics and small caps" are paired with attacks on quotation – one mocking ladies' novels "seasoned with quotations from Scripture," the other protesting Main's "excessive use of quotation" – an earlier response to his *Conversations of Johnson* sounds less decisive:

As to quotations, please – please be very moderate, whether they come from Shakespeare or any other servant of the Muses. A quotation often makes a fine summit to a climax, especially when it comes from some elder author, or from the Bible, so that there is a certain remoteness in the English as if it came from

long departed prophets who lived as citizens of the ages that were future to
them and had our thoughts before we were born. But I hate a style speckled
with quotations.[93]

The immoderate presence of Shakespeare in Eliot's own epigraphs may
help explain why even within the letter, her warnings against quotation
are separated by a lyrical defense of the practice, whose wording echoes
the description early in *Middlemarch* of Dorothea's "plain garments,
which by the side of provincial fashion gave her the impressiveness of a
fine quotation from the Bible – or from one of our elder poets, – in a
paragraph of today's newspaper."[94] By contrasting old quotations with
ephemeral journalism (and thence with the fashionable clothes to which
newspapers are compared in turn), Eliot reverses the temporality of
Rosamond's quotations in the "private album for extracted verse"
designed to attract "the doomed man of that date." Where Main's
Birthday Book incorporates quotations into a calendar, *Middlemarch* opposes periodicals that date to quotations that endure.

The analogy depends on an unstated pun: Dorothea becomes recognizable as a beauty next to fashionable women, just as textual fragments
acquire the status of "beauties" only when inscribed within more
ephemeral modern texts. The comparison comments obliquely on the
epigraphs – quoted and pseudo-quoted, old and archaicized – whose
"impressiveness" depends on their placement "by the side of" less
dazzling prose. Yet if the relation between epigraph and chapter can be
figured by the relation between plain clothes and provincial fashion,
then it also needs to be compared with the contrast between Dorothea
and Rosamond that the novel goes on to express in terms of clothes: the
difference between Dorothea's "sleeves hanging all out of the fashion"
and Rosamond's "pale-blue dress of a fit and fashion so perfect that no
dressmaker could look at it without emotion," or between Dorothea's
marriage-proposal, which concludes "I shall want so little – no new
clothes" – and Mary's explanation that Rosamond cannot be married
until her linen is ready.[95] When Eliot compares the contrast between
quotations and their frame with the relation of Dorothea's clothes to
fashionable women's, therefore, we can see in retrospect that epigraphs
are to text as Dorothea's poetic subplot is to Rosamond's prosaic one.
The proleptic introduction of Dorothea "by the side of" provincial
fashion ten chapters before Rosamond's first appearance establishes not
only the interdependence of the two plots, but also the contrast between
epigraphs and text, from the very beginning.

Like the interplay among the subplots, however, the relation of mottoes to chapters forces readers to remain on the lookout simultaneously for similarity and for difference. Eliot complained to a friend of "the laudation of readers who cut [*Daniel Deronda*] into scraps and talk of nothing in it but Gwendolen. I meant everything in the book to be related to everything else there."[96] Main's enthusiasm, too, led him to cut the novels to pieces, sorting sententious passages from narrative ones and isolating the chapter mottoes in a separate section where they no longer stood "by the side of" the text. Eliot's protest against that fragmentation has often been quoted:

If [the preface to the second edition of the *Sayings*] were true, I should be quite stultified as an artist. Unless my readers are more moved towards the ends I seek by my works as wholes than by an assemblage of extracts, my writings are a mistake. I have always exercised a severe watch against anything that could be called preaching, and if I have ever allowed myself in dissertation or in dialogue [anything] which is not part of the *structure* of my books, I have there sinned against my own laws.

I am particularly susceptible on this point, because it touches deeply my conviction of what art should be, and because a great deal of foolish stuff has been written in this relation.

Unless I am condemned by my own principles, my books are not properly separable into "direct" and "indirect" teaching. My chief doubt as to the desirability of the "Sayings" has always turned on the possibility that the volume might encourage such a view of my writings.[97]

Although I have found no copy of the rejected preface to which this letter responds, by piecing together Main's extant writing with John Blackwood's responses one can begin to reconstruct the argument against which Eliot was reacting. In an earlier letter, Main told Blackwood that "as I have gone on noting passage after passage of richest and rarest worth, I have been simply astounded at the wealth thus brought to light – all of which riches are *as good as lost* if they are allowed to remain *only* in the body of the works themselves."[98] An epigraph to the first edition of the *Sayings* (taken from *The Spanish Gypsy*) hints more publicly that Eliot's work would be as good as dead without an intermediary like Main: "Wise books / For half the truths they hold are honoured tombs." Where Main's epigraph implies that Eliot's best passages were "lost" until they entered the *Sayings*, Eliot's letter complains that her work will be lost from that point onward.

Or rather, it acknowledges that her work is already lost. In stating that her novels *should* be organic wholes rather than accumulations of didactic parts, Eliot does not claim that they *are*. On the contrary, the statement that "I have always exercised a severe watch against anything that could be called preaching" presumes a danger that needs to be guarded against.[99] Although the passage begins in the conditional mode – "I *should* be quite stultified as an artist" – the indicative quickly takes over: "my writings are a mistake," "I have sinned," "I am condemned." The tone of all three confessions suggests that Eliot felt her readers' reactions to be (to paraphrase her characterization of the *Tennyson Birthday Book)* "the Writer's fault."

Put differently, Main's anthologies threatened Eliot less where they departed from her work than where they accentuated – almost parodically – those aspects of her own writing that worried her. The lament that "I have sinned against my own laws" and "I am condemned by my own principles" points to the gulf separating the esthetic theory formulated in her private letters from the impression made upon readers (including Main) by the published novels themselves. More immediately, in the confession of not practicing what she preaches, of divorcing the form of the novels from the content of her programmatic statements, Eliot reinscribes the very distinction between "indirect" and "direct" teaching that she set out to deny.[100]

Eliot's protests against the *Sayings* and the dismemberment of *Deronda* take the form of private letters. In her published work, however, her protests against sententiousness are undercut more subtly by their own sententious form. Main unwittingly exposed that contradiction when he incorporated them into the *Sayings*, excerpting from *Armgart* "Life is not rounded in an epigram" and "I hate your epigrams and pointed saws," selecting from *Felix Holt* "I think half these priggish maxims about human nature in the lump are no more to be relied upon than the universal remedies," reprinting from *Middlemarch* "there is no general doctrine which is not capable of eating out our morality if unchecked by the deep-seated habit of direct fellow-feeling with individual fellow-men," and quoting from *The Mill on the Floss* "the truth, that moral judgments must remain false and hollow, unless they are checked and enlightened by a perpetual reference to the special circumstances that mark the individual lot. All people of broad, strong sense have an instinctive repugnance to the men of maxims; because such people early discern that the mysterious complexity of our life is not to be embraced by maxims."

Donald Hawes has used the last two reflections to argue that Main's enterprise of isolating moral generalizations distorted the organic unity of Eliot's own work. Yet what makes these passages so quotable – for Main as for successive generations of critics from Q. D. Leavis to Hawes to me – is their own axiomatic self-containment. The first begins categorically "there is no . . . which is not . . ."; the second, "the truth, that . . . all people of broad, strong sense . . . discern that . . . ."[101] An anxiety about abstraction has long been built into the tradition of the maxim itself: Eliot's own most lapidary statement about the relation between the general and the particular, the epigraph that reads "Il est plus aisé de connoître l'homme en général que de connoître un homme en particulier," is quoted from the *Maximes* of La Rochefoucauld.[102] Conversely, in the same way that by classifying as "sayings" Eliot's cautions against generalization Main nullifies their contents, his anthologization of protests against quotation makes visible their own quotability. Sir Hugo Mallinger's remark that "Much quotation of any sort, even in English, is bad" gets quoted in the *Sayings*, as do two aphorisms from *Felix Holt* about the appropriation of wisdom: "Perhaps some of the most terrible irony of the human lot is this of a deep truth coming to be uttered by lips that have no right to it" and "There is hardly any mental misery worse than that of having our own serious phrases, our own rooted beliefs, caricatured by a charlatan or a hireling." The *Sayings* illustrate that "irony" as much as Eliot's protest against the preface expresses that "mental misery." Eliot's fear of recognizing one's own "serious phrases" in another's mouth, or "truths" emerging from the wrong lips, reveals an anxiety about the appropriation of words that her negotiations with Main would confirm a few years later.

Yet Eliot's letter does not attack Main so much as his readers, and hers. It begins with the polite qualifier that "Mr. Main himself, I have no doubt, is free from the misunderstanding which the clauses are likely to convey to others."[103] The letter accuses Main not of reading Eliot's novels as assemblages of extracts, but of "encouraging" his audience to do so. And Eliot herself should be numbered among that audience, for the letter makes clear that the *Sayings* changed her understanding of her own work. In the process of heightening the author's "severe watch" on her own sententiousness, Main paradoxically placed her in a position to experiment – more warily but also more self-consciously – with the aphoristic voice. Indeed, the generic departure of *The Impressions of Theophrastus Such* can be explained in part by Eliot's foreknowledge that future editions of the *Sayings* would excerpt it. When John Blackwood praises *Theophrastus Such* as "full of wit and wisdom," the echo of Main's title implies that the *Wise and Witty Sayings* are latent in *Theophrastus Such* from the very beginning. So does Main's own praise that "as for 'Sayings,' every page [of *Theophrastus Such*] bristles with them."[104] In moving from sententious novels to novelized essays, Eliot found a way at once to inhabit and to re-appropriate the persona to which Main had already lent her name.

Ruby Redinger has argued that Eliot's protest against the preface to the second edition refers to the audience that read the *Sayings* without reading the novels: "She remained uneasy because [Main] was necessarily breaking each novel down into segments of a few sentences which would stand alone, perhaps with misleading emphasis, *especially to one who had not read the whole story*."[105] However, given that the *Sayings* sold far fewer copies than any of the individual novels, it seems safe to assume that the primary audience for the anthology (unlike for Bowdler's or the Lambs' Shakespeare, or for the children's versions such as *Boys and Girls from George Eliot* and *Stories from George Eliot* that begin to appear after Eliot's death) consisted of Eliot's admirers, of re-readers rather than non-readers. Eliot's concern would then lie with people who had read both, or even with the much larger subset of people who had read the novels but only heard of the *Sayings*.[106] This suggests in turn that Eliot had no confidence that the reading of the novels themselves would suffice to counteract the anthology.

Eliot's letter accuses Main of widening the gap between the writer's intention and readers' responses which he had at first promised to close. At times she identifies Main as her ideal reader, telling him that "what you quote and emphasize is almost always what I most felt and believed when I wrote it," that "you know what I mean, and care the most for those elements in my writing which I myself care the most for," and even (according to Lewes's heavily edited report) remarking that "if I can only find one reader who understands me I shall be content," which Lewes glosses, for Main's benefit, to mean "that the works may be said to have been written for you!"[107] The excerpter who "know[s] what I mean" stands opposite the partial readers of *Deronda* who resist what "I meant." Eliot's letters to third parties, which praise just as fulsomely Main's "power of putting his finger on the right passages, and giving emphasis to the right idea (in relation to the author's feeling and purpose)," and call Main's collection "an indication that there exist careful readers, for whom no subtlest intention is lost," make clear that politeness alone does not explain her gratitude.[108] She responds to Main's letter quoting from *The Spanish Gypsy* with the assertion that "you have thoroughly understood me . . . In the passages which you quote from the Fifth Book, you have put your finger on the true key." Yet with characteristic ambivalence, she adds abruptly that "the lyrics were all written as the development of the drama required them, and are an organic part of the poem."[109] The explanation undermines her praise for Main's "understanding" by stripping of any legitimacy his decision to quote the "Songs" from *The Spanish Gypsy* while omitting their narrative context. Even the language that Eliot uses to evaluate Main's anthologies contradicts itself. Her attack on his "delight in italics" clashes with her earlier description of "looking through the 'Sayings' with that sort of delight which comes from seeing that another mind underlines the words one has most cared for in writing them."[110] Her praise of Main for "putting his finger on the right passages" and her reassurance that "you have put your finger on the true key," like her declaration that "I care for the finger pointing to the right passage more than for any superlative phrases, and your finger points well," belies her "wish that [Main's] Preface had been touched with a more fastidious finger."[111] In the decades separating the *Sayings* from "Silly Novels," Eliot had lost her old certainty about whether the reader's "delicate hand" embellished or defaced.

Eliot's ambivalence about the anthology can be explained in part by Main's resemblance to a series of literary doubles who appropriated her work throughout her career: readers who claimed to have written her work, or, conversely, who wrote sequels misrepresented by others as hers; readers who claimed to know (or to be) the originals of her characters; readers who adapted her novels for the stage; and, even more simply, readers who translated them. Over-authoritative fans haunted her from the beginning. In the first two years of "George Eliot's" existence, a fraud named Joseph Liggins took credit for the *Scenes of Clerical Life*, a busybody named Charles Bracebridge supported that claim before switching allegiance to identify various characters as Marian Evans's relatives, and two anonymous sequels to *Adam Bede* appeared, one marketed as George Eliot's own.[112] Eliot's letters to the editor disclaiming that sequel already anticipate the proprietary tone of her private letters repudiating Main's anthologies. In the same year, her reluctant authorization of the first French translation prefigured the grudging tone in which she would later consent to the *Birthday Book*: "Hitherto I have rejected propositions of translation, from the dread of having one's sentences metamorphosed into expressions of someone else's meaning instead of one's own."[113] Where anthologies widened

Eliot's audience at the cost of attaching Main's signature to her work, translations yoked her signature with others' writing.

In a letter summing up that eventful year, Eliot reiterated her fear of ceasing to "own" her words: "To part with the copyright of a book which sells 16000 in one year – to have a Liggins, a Bracebridge, and an unknown writer of one's 'sequel' to one's self – is excellent discipline."[114] Why the publishers to whom Eliot had voluntarily sold her copyright should be comparable to the impostors who claimed her work as theirs, or their work as hers, is not immediately clear. Yet Eliot links the two sets of events through more than a sense of financial injury. By juxtaposing them, she lends the term "copyright" its most literal force: the right to copy, whether by printing multiple copies from a single manuscript (as her publishers did), imitating characters (as did the sequels to *Adam Bede*) or copying a printed text in one's own handwriting (as Liggins did in a desperate attempt to authenticate his claim to be the author of the *Scenes*). Liggins's scribal ploy anticipated the practice of fans like Main and Mrs. Cowper Temple who would appropriate Eliot's work by copying it out. Reciprocally, Eliot's response to Main's anthologies crystallized an ambivalence about translation and even publication that was already latent at the beginning of her career. Indeed, Eliot identified misreading as part of the publishing process when she juxtaposed the "distortions" introduced by a proofreader with a fan letter pleading for a sequel to *Adam Bede* and compared both with Bracebridge's gossip, concluding: "I *do* feel more than I ought about such outside sayings and doings."[115] Like Bracebridge, the proofreader and the reader stood for a public that insisted on rewriting her work. Eliot's apology for the strength of her feelings betrayed the fear that readers' "sayings and doings" could not be kept safely "outside." No less than sequels, adaptations, translations, or anthologies, publication itself undermined the fragile distinction between the inside and the outside of the text.

Main's *Sayings* revived the problems of signature and appropriation that Marian Evans's acknowledgment of authorship had appeared to resolve a decade earlier. Like sequels and adaptations, the anthologies embarrassed Eliot by "encouraging a view of [her] writings" over which she had no control – but also, more positively, for which she bore no blame. If her private letters distancing herself from the *Birthday Book* repeated the terms of her published letters disclaiming the spurious sequel *Adam Bede, Junior*, it should also be said that George Eliot's eagerness to hide what Dicey called "the author's sanction" of the anthologies, like Lewes's decision that "it would not do for the public to suppose she had

had any share in the books," bears a more disquieting resemblance to Marian Evans's earlier policy of disavowing her (own) *Scenes of Clerical Life*. In 1859, the *Athenaeum* advanced the malicious theory that "Liggins" and "George Eliot" were both pseudonyms of a single author who played one alias against the other to gain media attention: "Long ago we hinted our impression that Mr. Liggins, with his poverty and his pretensions, was a mystification, got up by George Eliot, – as the showman in a country fair sets up a second learned pig to create a diversion among the penny paying rustics."[116] In the event, the accusation was easily disproved, but the theory of the second pig (which had the side-benefit of comparing the conspicuously learned author with a barnyard animal) predicted with uncanny prescience the series of doubles through whose mouths George Eliot would later speak: Lewes, John Blackwood, and above all Main. Like Liggins's name in the *Athenaeum*'s hypothesis, Main's editorial signature functioned as a screen that released the author from responsibility for marketing her work – at the same time as, like the real Liggins, Main took her image out of her power.

Where the *Athenaeum* claimed that Liggins was helping the career that he appeared to hurt, conversely the *Westminster Review* argued that Main was embarrassing the author he meant to promote: "Mr. Main . . . is one of those officious friends, who are always bringing you into trouble. He is what has been called 'your worst enemy – your worshiper'."[117] Eliot's disavowal of Main's anthologies repeated her avoidance of photographers (who, like Main, sought to reproduce her in miniature); of autograph-seekers (who, like Main, sold her name); of feminists who coaxed her to sign petitions supporting women's rights; and, intermittently, of individual fans like Edith Simcox or Elma Stuart whose admiration at once reassured and discomfited her. More loosely, as I shall argue at the end of this chapter, her own attitude toward the *Sayings* anticipated twentieth-century critics' embarrassment about her position as a moral teacher. But it also revived the tension between the desire to own her work and the reluctance to sign it that had shaped the beginning of Eliot's career – or, put differently, between the fear of having her work appropriated and the wish to have it read. In the end, her audience's insistence on quoting made one inseparable from the other.

THE ETHICS OF THE REVIEW

Eliot's early fear that translation might make an author's works "someone else's" persisted. When the editor of the *Revue des Deux Mondes* asked permission to abridge *Middlemarch*, Eliot consented for him to compile excerpts only on condition that they remain unmixed with summary: "he may do this in the form of articles containing simple extracts, not introducing into the text any matter of his own, seeing that I altogether abominate that *procédé* of M. Forgues and others who undertake to trim and abridge." By refusing to allow the synecdochal reproduction of her own words to be juxtaposed with a synthetic representation in someone else's, Eliot attempted to mark the limits of her own voice. Yet in the end, the *Revue* published a hybrid piece – review? translation? abridgment? anthology? – that interspersed "extracts" extending for two or three pages with shorter sections of summary and evaluation, switching from one to the other without quotation marks or even a full stop.[118]

The ill-defined generic status of the article on *Middlemarch* suggests how little separated reviews in the nineteenth century from other means of representing texts for a wider audience: translations, abridgments, anthologies. In sheer bulk, the number of Eliot quotations in Main's anthologies was dwarfed by the number that appeared in reviews. Nor was Eliot unusual in this respect, for many contemporary reviews excerpted so heavily as to borrow the fragmentary form of the anthology along with its evaluative function. All that distinguished the two genres was the proportion of excerpts to frame. Like post-1868 abridgers of Richardson, or like life-and-letters biographers, Victorian reviewers used plot summary in their own voice to connect excerpts in the author's. In sandwiching quotation with summary, reviews found a middle ground between the two book-length genres that competed to represent other texts in miniature: the anthology and the abridgment. Scott, for one, took the latter parallel for granted when he introduced a plot summary into a review as "the following abridgment."[119] What Hazlitt complained of the *Quarterly* in 1825 could be applied to almost any nineteenth-century periodical: "the poetical department is almost a sinecure, consisting of mere summary decisions and a list of quotations."[120]

Marian Evans's own journalistic career in the 1850s was no exception. The recurrence of the verb "extract" in her reviews for the *Leader* and the *Westminster* makes explicit how closely composing reviews resembles compiling commonplace-books. An article on Carlyle's *Selected Essays*, in which his words outnumber her own, begins by joking that her review will duplicate his anthology: "To make extracts from a book of extracts may at first seem easy."[121] Her review of Margaret Fuller's *Woman in the Nineteenth Century* describes its own composition in the language of the commonplace-book: "We had marked several other passages of Margaret Fuller's for extract."[122] A more hostile review of Dr. Cumming's work takes excerptability as a measure of worth: "Throughout nine volumes we have alighted on no passage which impressed us as worth extracting, and placing among the 'beauties' of evangelical writers."[123] The hypothetical anthology ("beauties") from which Evans excludes Cumming forms a mirror-image of the review in which she quotes his most glaring absurdities: one singles out the best passages, the other the worst. It would be too simple to claim that reviews canonize what they excerpt in the same way that anthologies do, for the pleasures of satiric quotation prevent the number of lines excerpted from standing in direct proportion to the reviewer's praise. Yet as Coleridge complained earlier in the century, even negative reviews ultimately propagate the texts – and the passages – that they excerpt: "if in a volume of poetry the critic should find a poem or passage which he deems more especially worthless, he is sure to select it and reprint it in the review; by which, on his own grounds, he wastes as much more paper than the author, as the copies of a fashionable review are more numerous than those of the original book."[124] In turn, advertisements eventually complete that cycle by excerpting praise from reviews as selectively as reviews excerpt from their subjects.

The conventions of the review shaped Victorian assumptions not only about how to read, but about the structure of literary texts. By alternating excerpts with plot summaries, they encouraged readers and writers alike to think of texts as accumulations of freestanding beauties strung together by longer stretches of narrative padding. Reviews defined style – for which only direct quotations could provide evidence – as more absolutely a form of personal property than plot, conventionally summarized in the reviewer's voice.[125] (Thus, Edmund Yates measured the lack of stylistic ambition in Wilkie Collins's supposedly overplotted novels against a hypothetical anthology: "Collins's style is not a thing of literary beauty like Mr Stevenson's, or a marvel of finish like Henry James's. It is jerky and absolutely unornamented. There are no elegant extracts to be got out of his stories; it would be no easy matter to compile beauties of Collins, and even birthday-book framers might be in difficulties.")[126] As a result, reviewers privileged the parts, which they were empowered to reproduce verbatim through sampling, over the whole, which they could represent only through their own inauthentic mediation. An early review of "Dickens's Fiction," for example, concluded its synopsis with an apology: "We have given the foregoing faint outline chiefly for the purpose of making our extracts more intelligible – but it can afford very little idea of the interest of a story of which the merit lies chiefly in the details."[127] At the same time as they trained readers to sift memorable generalizations from dispensable particulars, they also gave writers an incentive to produce self-contained passages that could be appreciated (or even, more simply, understood) outside of their narrative context. This held especially true for writers who began their own careers as reviewers – like Marian Evans. I suggested earlier that the aphoristic form of *The Impressions of Theophrastus Such* can be explained in part by Eliot's knowledge that future editions of the *Sayings* would excerpt it. A more basic version of the same consciousness came even earlier in her career: from the first, the experience of reviewing made her aware that her work would be transmitted through quotation.

The omnipresence of quotations in Victorian reviews means that reviewers' urge to excerpt Eliot holds no special significance in itself. While anthologies quoted Eliot more than any previous novelist, the reviews that did were simply following standard practice. What is unusual, however, is that both hostile and favorable reviews describe Eliot explicitly as a peculiarly quotable author – at the same time, paradoxically, as they question the adequacy of their own representational conventions. On the one hand, positive reviews began to describe Eliot's work as raw material for hypothetical anthologies long before Main's *Sayings* appeared. As early as 1866, a review by E. S. Dallas concluded an unbroken series of four chapter mottoes and two long quotations – a kind of miniature anthology that prefigured Main's overrepresentation of epigraphs – with the observation that "we might cull too from the talk of the characters to whom we are introduced a whole book of proverbs." Richard Simpson, too, praised Eliot for interspersing her "drama" with "a copious supply of maxims, ethical, psychological, and physiological, enough to furnish forth a 'just volume' of ana."[128] The "whole book" and the "just volume" form mirror-images for the equally hypothetical "Beauties" from which Marian Evans excludes Cumming. Like her, Simpson and Dallas take the number of potential anthology-pieces as a proof of literary value.

On the other hand, some reviewers raise the possibility of excerpting George Eliot only to reject it. Rather like the preface in which Samuel Johnson dampened readers' enjoyment of Shakespearean beauties a century earlier, John Chapman's review of *The Mill on the Floss* warns readers that their putative expectation of a miniature anthology will be disappointed:

Neither have we thought it desirable to give a collection of the quaint humor-isms that abound in the first two volumes, or to make a catena of the profound and far-reaching remarks which abound throughout the book; this would neither be fair to the author nor agreeable to our readers. These beauties are for the most part so organic, that to withdraw them from their context would be to dislocate them from that vital nexus which gives them their highest charm.

Chapman's refusal to make a "collection of quaint humorisms" repudi-ates not only the genre later exemplified by Main's *Witty Sayings*, but also the conventions of the review itself. Yet Chapman's model of quotation is less simple than his moralistic language of "fairness" would suggest. The review labels witty passages "beauties," even though it refuses "to withdraw them from their context"; conversely, it calls them "organic" even though it refers earlier to "the *separate* beauties" of *The Mill on The Floss*.[129]

In terming the beauties "organic" and the novel a "vital nexus," the review anticipates Eliot's own assertion that "forms of art can be called higher or lower only on the same principle as that on which we apply the words to organisms; viz., in proportion to the complexity of the parts bound up into one indissoluble whole."[130] An essay on Eliot published in the *Contemporary Review* by Edward Dowden in 1872 goes even further. Like Chapman, Dowden calls attention to the self-re-straint with which he resists the temptation to quote: "Many good things in particular passages of [Eliot's] writing are detachable; admir-able sayings can be cleared from their surroundings, and presented by themselves . . . But if we separate the moral soul of any complete work of hers from its artistic medium, if we murder to dissect, we lose far more than we gain."[131] Dowden's discussion of whether to quote makes the review an occasion to question the conventions of reviewing. But the wording of his statement that "admirable *sayings* can be cleared from their surroundings" can also be read more literally as a comment on the *Sayings* published by Main several months before. Just as Eliot's protest against Main's preface juxtaposes the assertion that "my books are not *properly* separable into 'direct' and 'indirect' teaching" with the acknowledgment that readers are dangerously skillful at separating the two, Dowden combines the claim that Eliot's sayings "can be" de-tached (by anthologists or reviewers) with the argument that they should not be. The ambivalence with which he weighs "loss" against "gain" is rendered all the more acute by his recourse to a Wordswor-thian tag: it takes a decontextualized quotation to defend the organic unity of the text.

Marian Evans's own reviews had already questioned the evidentiary value of quotation. Her review of *Men and Women* caps a quotation with the apology that "extracts cannot do justice to the fine dramatic touches by which Fra Lippo is made present to us, while he throws out this instinctive Art-criticism. And extracts from 'Bishop Blougram's Apology,' an equally remarkable poem of what we may call the dramatic-psychological kind, would be still more ineffective." After praising the latter as "masterly satire," Evans adds that "the poem is too strictly consecutive for any fragment of it to be a fair specimen."[132] Evans's denial that quotations provide a "fair" specimen or "do justice" to Browning anticipates Chapman's claim that to quote from *The Mill on the Floss* "would [not] be fair to the author" – or E. S. Dallas's remark in a review of the same novel that "if it were not rather a mean thing in a critic to pick out the plums from a first-rate novel, we could give many quotations from [the characters'] good sayings."[133] Where Dallas and Dowden question the fairness of quotation to readers, Evans and Chapman worry instead that it cheats authors. Yet all four define the excerpt as an ethical problem.

That uneasiness could threaten even the admissibility of quotations in court. In 1888, when Henry Vizetelly was tried for publishing a translation of Zola's *La Terre*, the prosecution felt the need to justify their use of excerpts from the novel as evidence. As the *Times* reports, the Solicitor-General

did not say that if they saw in a volume one isolated passage of an immoral tendency that that would be a sufficient justification for indicting the publisher of the book as being guilty of a misdemeanour. Undoubtedly there might be passages in works of a medical kind . . . which might not be subject to a prosecution, but if the passages were collected in a book and published for the purpose of ministering to the depraved taste of casual readers they would undoubtedly be subject to an indictment . . . It was not one, two, or three passages which had been chosen, but they had 21 passages, taken from different parts of the work in question.[134]

The Solicitor-General's insistence on sampling evenly "passages, taken from different parts of the work" responds to the fear that individual "passages" cannot be judged fairly unless the reader knows their proportion and position within a larger work. The same "isolated passages" which would be acceptable when framed by medical discourse take on a pornographic function once "collected" into the hypothetical pornographic anthology – or into the less hypothetical case for the prosecution. But the Solicitor-General was not the only party in the case to actualize that counterfactual collection. After pleading guilty, the defendant struck back by compiling a parodic anthology of *Extracts Principally from English Classics* to show that juxtaposition could render passages from even the most canonical works obscene.[135] The *Times* itself was hard put to avoid compiling a third such anthology: in an earlier obscenity case, as the report of Vizetelly's trial recalled, "it had been held that if any one published a report of the case containing the passages complained of they would be liable to be proceeded against." Like Coleridge's fear that hostile reviews could double as reprints, the *Times*'s warning acknowledged the difficulty of representing a text without reproducing it. Juries and reviewers both judged on the basis of representative passages; but both also worried, as had Marian Evans, about the power of parts to misrepresent a whole.

Evans's anxiety about judging Browning's work through "fragment" and "specimens" reappears at the end of *Middlemarch* in Eliot's insistence on distinguishing "fragments" from "samples": "The *fragment* of a life, however typical, is not the *sample* of an even web."[136] By extending her doubts about exemplarity from the author's work to the characters' lives, Eliot repudiates the metaphor of the textual web which *Middlemarch* so repetitiously invokes to hold its multiple plots and modes of discourse together. Yet R. H. Hutton rejects that logic when he labels a quotation from *Middlemarch* itself "a sharp saying and a *sample* of many another with which every chapter of *Middlemarch* is plentifully strewn."[137] Similarly, Dinah Mulock reverses Evans's claim that no excerpt constitutes a "fair specimen" of "Bishop Blougram's Apology" in a review that labels a quotation from *The Mill on the Floss* "a mere chance specimen of [Eliot's] care over small things."[138] Evans's denial that fragments count as "specimens," and Eliot's that fragments constitute "samples," clash with Hutton's definition of textual fragments as "samples," and Mulock's as "specimens." Indeed, Henry James, who compares *Daniel Deronda* with "a group of little uneven ponds," faults Eliot precisely for not producing an even web: for a "disproportion between the meagre effect of the whole and the vigorous character of the different parts." A. V. Dicey, too, complains in his review of *Middlemarch* that "the parts are more striking than the whole."[139] Yet Dicey's and James's reviews necessarily substitute the former for the latter.

Nineteenth-century reviewers' apologies for quoting too little or too much, or for quoting at all, can be explained only in part by a gradual historical shift away from quotation. My survey of the main periodicals suggests that the average length of excerpts decreased toward the end of the nineteenth century, but such trends are difficult to measure or to date. Edwin Eigner and George Worth offer no evidence for their heavily teleological assertion that "book reviews . . . beginning in the late 1840s were becoming self-conscious about the time-honoured practice of filling out the bulk of the articles with passages extracted from the novels under discussion. By the late 1850s most reviewers had enough respect for the integrity of the work of fiction to resist representing it through snippets."[140] I would date that self-consciousness further back, to the origins of the modern periodical press itself. The *Monthly Review* declared six months after its inception in 1749 that "a short extract may, perhaps, enable the reader to conclude with tolerable certainty" about the quality of the work from which it is taken. Later journals duplicated that self-consciousness without the corresponding self-confidence. Less than a year after the founding of *Blackwood's Edinburgh Magazine* in 1817, a review in it already ended a quotation with the apology that

these specimens may suffice to show the peculiarities of Mr Lamb's genius and manner; but the charm of his Poetry pervades the whole bulk of the volume, and it is as impossible fully to comprehend that charm from a few partial passages, as it would be from a few casual smiles to understand the full expression of an intellectual and moral countenance.[141]

Three years earlier, Francis Jeffrey's review of *The Excursion* in the *Edinburgh* blamed the poet for the reviewer's need to quote what he called "extracts": "while we collect the fragments, it is impossible not to lament the ruins from which we are condemned to pick them." Conversely, another reviewer adduced the difficulty of excerpting Wordsworth as evidence of his talent: "It is almost impossible to select any passage without injury to its effect, owing to a want of that interest which the context supplies. We shall, however, venture to cite the following tender touches."[142] Reviewers' attacks on books for either resisting or requiring quotation reinforce their formulaic apologies for their own representational conventions. Both betray the tension between an organicist theory and a synecdochal practice.

Anthologies made painfully visible the challenge facing Victorian reviewers: on what grounds could a short text claim to stand for a long one? Twentieth-century criticism has inherited that dilemma along with a canon of familiar quotations from Eliot's work which bears a striking resemblance to Main's. As Barbara Johnson observes, "the question of how to present to the reader a text too extensive to quote in its entirety has long been one of the underlying problems of literary criticism."[143] Like nineteenth-century book reviews, current academic criticism necessarily continues to represent the whole by its parts: no study of *Middlemarch* can offer more than fragmentary evidence. Yet no less than the reception of Richardson, Radcliffe, and Scott, readers' appropriations of George Eliot suggest that the most quotable moments of a novel are the least narrative, and therefore the least representative of the genre.

Reviewers' uncertainty about the structure of the novel reveals more intimate doubts about their own function. The technical question of how to represent another text in miniature is easier to face than the problem of whether a profession devoted to representing other texts can claim an independent voice. It may appear ironic that late-twentieth-century anthologies of readerly responses such as the *Critical Heritage* series, which excises plot summary as systematically as illustrative quotation, have occluded the review's own double function of anthologizing and abridging. Yet publishers' reluctance to engage in second-degree anthologizing (by quoting quoted material) betrays an anxiety about the secondary status of criticism which from the beginning has dogged not only anthologies but reviews and biographies. Hazlitt's fear that the reproduction of "extracts" might reduce reviewing to a mechanical activity echoes Boswell's speculation in the *Life of Johnson* that reviewers paid by the sheet could fairly be docked for "extracts, made from the book reviewed." By challenging the value of the reviewer's labor, Boswell implicitly renounces his own moral right to the full profits from a *Life* which sandwiches Johnsonian quotations with Boswellian narrative as regularly as contemporary reviews embedded quotations in plot summary.[144] In acknowledging their kinship with anthologists, reviewers and biographers questioned their own claim to be producers of new texts rather than reproducers of others. The anthologist has always been the critic's double.

By faulting George Eliot for authorizing Main's anthology (as did A. V. Dicey's review of *Deronda*) or by disclaiming the desire to quote her (as did Chapman and Dowden), Victorian reviewers distanced themselves from a genre that might otherwise have appeared uncomfortably similar. Contemporary reviewers shared Main's reflex to distinguish sententious or lyrical passages that could be appreciated out of context from narrative passages that could not. Yet while Main dismisses the latter as a "vehicle" for the former, reviewers criticize the former as intrusions upon the latter. In an earlier review, Dicey posits an inverse proportion between the quantity of "sayings" and the quality of narrative: "As the number of George Eliot's 'wise, witty, and tender' sayings increase, the directness with which she paints living persons diminishes." By appropriating the title of the anthology, he turns Eliot's organicist model of art against her. For Dowden's reluctance to "detach" beauties and Chapman's refusal to "withdraw them from their context," Dicey substitutes the accusation that the beauty of the sayings deprives *Middlemarch* itself of unity:

The parts are more striking than the whole . . . No one who admires beautiful writing or who can appreciate striking and original thoughts can fail to feel that the chorus or reflective portion of the book is full of beauty and power. To a large class of persons it forms probably the great charm of *Middlemarch* . . . But a critic, even while he admires the reflections themselves . . . can hardly deny that the part taken by George Eliot as the moralizer over her own handiwork, if it gives her novel a peculiar character, also damages its whole effect . . . The very brilliancy of the epigrams, . . . the elaborate care given to the separate parts, leaves in the mind a sense of something like strain, and makes it hard to look at the work as a whole.[145]

As "a critic," Dicey excludes himself from the "large class of persons" embodied by Main and Main's readers. Henry James, too, argues that the better the individual sayings are, the worse the overall narrative must be. In his "*Daniel Deronda*: A Conversation," one character complains that the novel is "broken" between competing plots and marred by the "importunity of the moral reflections":

What can be drearier than a novel where the function of the hero – young, handsome, and brilliant – is to give didactic advice, in a proverbial form, to the young, beautiful, and brilliant heroine? . . . I never read a story with less current. It is not a river; it is a series of lakes. I once read of a group of little uneven ponds resembling, from a bird's-eye view, a looking-glass which had fallen upon the floor and broken, and was lying in fragments. That is what *Daniel Deronda* would look like.

James's image of "broken looking-glass" rewrites Eliot's often-quoted "parable" in *Middlemarch* of the "pier-glass" on which, when a candle is held up to any one point, "the scratches will seem to arrange themselves in a fine series of concentric circles around that little sun."[146] For Eliot's image of the mirror as a system of infinite connections, James substitutes the mirror as a pile of pieces.

James's accusation that *Daniel Deronda* lacks "current" repeats not only George Saintsbury's complaint that the narrator rambles on "while

the action stands still" but Dicey's charge that self-contained "reflections" impede "movement": "The reflections, if they somewhat injure
the movements of the drama, are in themselves so beautiful that we
should scarcely care to have them omitted." More positively, E. S.
Dallas defends the lack of "movement" in *Adam Bede* as the corollary to
its wealth of "sayings": the characters "are so full of strange humors and
funny pretty sayings that we entirely overlook the want of movement in
the story. Besides which, when the dialogue ceases, the author's reflections are so pointed, and his descriptions are so vivid, that we naturally
think more of what we have than of what we have not."[147] Main's
project of separating the sayings from "storytelling" simply took to its
logical conclusion the tradeoff between the whole and the parts that
reviewers (from the most flattering to the most savage) uniformly took
for granted. His anthologies acted on Dicey's observation that "the very
brilliancy of the epigrams . . . makes it hard to look at the work as a
whole." James's and Dicey's characterization of *Daniel Deronda* as a series
of didactic "fragments" differs from Main's procedure in nothing but
tone. The same could be said of W. C. Brownell's charge that Eliot's
sententiousness disunifies her novels: "Every sentence stands by itself; by
its sententious self."[148] Even a laudatory account of *Scenes of Clerical Life*
in the *Saturday Review* accuses Eliot of sacrificing connection to beauties:
"Almost every sentence seems finished into an epigram or an aphorism.
The pudding is often too profuse in plums – too scanty in connective
dough."[149] Where Main's preface praises Eliot's aphorisms as "riches,"
the review calls them too rich to be digestible.

The plum pudding soon became a stock image among Eliot's reviewers. The metaphor of aphoristic "plums" in narrative "dough"
anticipates not only Dallas's confession of being tempted to "pick out
the plums," but Dowden's language in an article entitled "The Interpretation of Literature" which generalizes the contrast between organicist
theory and reviewers' practice that his essay on George Eliot earlier
posited. Dowden attacks Leigh Hunt's "admirable" reviews for what his
Eliot article had dubbed "murdering to dissect": Hunt "point[s] out the
'beauties' of each author" until "the parts become more important than
the whole" and "we forget that fine lines and phrases must grow out of
the heart of the subject, if they are not to wither like the rootless
blossoms stuck in a child's flower-bed." But from cut flowers the reviewer's quotations soon metamorphose into plums: "His pleasure in
dainty phrases and exquisite lines was so quick and so fine, that he could
not let them remain quietly in their right places, but in his eager and

almost sensuous delight he must put in his thumb, and pick out his poetical plums, exclaiming, 'What a good critic am I!'" The reviewer becomes Jack Horner – a fate that anthologists feared as well. Soon after the *Sayings of George Eliot* appeared, the only contemporary novelist to rival Eliot's ambivalent engagement with the aphorism was anthologized in *The Pilgrim's Scrip: or, Wit and Wisdom of George Meredith* (1888, soon followed by a *George Meredith Birthday Book*). Brought out by the publisher of *Wit and Wisdom of George Eliot*, the Meredith anthology is prefaced by the apology that "Every author suffers more or less from being mutilated, and from having his thoughts considered apart from their organic relations. George Meredith himself says that 'A gathering of all plums is not digestible.'"[150] Like Eliot's, Meredith's aphorism against aphorism absolved him of responsibility for the anthology that bore his name.

Culinary metaphors have a long history in literary criticism, and to compare reading to eating – or even, more specifically, to compare the novel to a sweet – is in itself too hackneyed to be worth noticing. What is surprising about these late-nineteenth-century metaphors, however, is the specific sweet involved: pudding, not candy or pastry. When Trollope acknowledged more conventionally that people read novels "as men eat pastry after dinner, – not without some inward conviction that the taste is vain if not vicious," or that novels should be "used sparingly as sweetmeats, and not as though they were sufficient to supply the bread and meat of our daily lives," he named confectioneries more sugary than the economical, nutritious, and quintessentially British family pudding.[151] ("There was a comfortable, good-humored feeling abroad," as Henry James complained, "that a novel is a novel, as a pudding is a pudding, and that our only business with it could be to swallow it.")[152] In objecting to the plums which relieve the doughy stodginess of puddings, Eliot's reviewers reversed the age-old comparison of fiction with sweetmeats and instruction with plain food. Earlier critics of the novel assumed (as one reviewer summed up tritely in 1812) that "books, merely entertaining, produce the same effect upon the mental faculties, which a luxurious diet does upon the corporeal frame: they render it incapable of relishing those pure instructive writings, which possess all the intrinsic qualities of wholesome, unseasoned food."[153] The review of *Scenes of Clerical Life* – like Dowden's essay and like the preface to *Wit and Wisdom of George Meredith* – suggests just the opposite. The *Saturday Review* compares fictional narrative with bland "connective dough" and moral wisdom with tempting but unhealthy "plums"; Dowden, too, makes stylistic beauties the object of "sensuous" hunger. What had been the sugar became the pill. In the process, the anthologies intended to prove Eliot's moral and artistic rigor became instead the sign of vanity and vulgarity.

A hostile review of *The Mill on the Floss* inverts the terms of the culinary metaphor even more radically, contrasting nutritious plot with dilute preaching: "We ask for meat, and she gives us pap – for a history, and she gives us sermons."[154] The reviewer's religious metaphor lends a satirical inflection to the language later appropriated by Main, who credits Eliot with "sanctifying the novel"; by Eliot herself, who describes the quotation from *The Spanish Gypsy* as her "credo"; by the reviewer who praises *Middlemarch* as "a homily against ill-assorted marriages"; and by John Blackwood, who characterizes the same novel (read on a Sunday while his family was at church) as "better than any sermon that was ever preached by man." Blackwood's description of *Middlemarch* as a substitute for church extends to Eliot's original work his wife's ambiguous characterization of the *Sayings* as "Sunday reading." So does his report that one of his copyeditors has declared: "George Eliot's I don't rank as Novels but as second Bibles . . . Such books are worth nine tenths of the Sermons ever preached or published." Yet like the hostile reviewer, Blackwood elsewhere uses "sermon" as an insult, denying strenuously that "the teaching of [Eliot], the most condensed and *unsermonising* of Writers, could be best and most easily approached from a Volume of Extracts such as [Main's]."[155] The awkwardness of Blackwood's coinage, "unsermonising," reveals his uneasiness about the place of moral teaching in the novel.

CONCLUSION: "THE BUSINESS OF THE NOVEL"

By the end of her career, Eliot's work came to function as a test case for that issue. Hostile reviewers of Hardy, for example, routinely invoked her as a benchmark against which to measure the younger man's sententiousness. A review of *Desperate Remedies* places the new novelist by bracketing him with Eliot: "Like George Eliot the author delights in running off to *sententiae*, in generalizing abstractions out of the special point in hand. He inclines to this intellectual pastime a little too often, and with a little too much of laboured epigram." A review of *Far from the Madding Crowd* criticizes both novelists' use of abstraction in more narrowly social terms: "George Eliot . . . has drawn specimens of the illiterate class who talk theology like the Bench of Bishops – except that they are all Dissenters . . . But neither [Shakespeare's] clowns, nor George Eliot's rustics, nor Scott's peasants, rise to anything like the flights of abstract reasoning with which Mr Hardy credits his cider-drinking boors." Writing in the *Academy*, Andrew Lang blamed the didacticism of *Far from the Madding Crowd* on Eliot's example, faulting Hardy's "patronizing voice, in which there are echoes, now of George Eliot, and now of George Meredith." Havelock Ellis's review of *Jude the Obscure*, too, digresses to criticize Eliot for forgetting that "the permanent vitality of sermons is considerably less than that of art."[156] Reviewers were not the only ones to read Hardy as George Eliot's successor; the *George Eliot Birthday Book* may have provided a model for Cecil Palmer's *Thomas Hardy Calendar: a quotation from the works of Thomas Hardy for every day in the year* (1921). But the frequency with which Eliot's name spills into reviews of another novelist suggests just how synonymous she had become with the sententiousness that worried the late-Victorian reviewing profession.

In 1870, a more general article discussing the relation of "fiction" to "maxims" chose Eliot as its central example. The essay begins by echoing Main's metaphor of the novel as a "vehicle" for "conveying" maxims, but ends by accusing the latter of defacing the former:

There is no vehicle so useful as the novel for conveying odds and ends of knowledge . . . If this is done with skill and grace, these chance embellishments greatly increase the pleasure one finds in reading the book. In the works of George Eliot, for example, we meet with simple phrases or sentences that are suggestive, and frequently more satisfactory than a ponderous volume . . . But everything depends on the manner in which the novelist introduces these glimpses of thought, or erudition, or wit. They must not be obtruded, or the illusion of the story is destroyed. Mrs. Poyser must find a fitting occasion for her sarcasms . . . If a man uses a story for the purpose of stringing together maxims or reflections, then let him say so; and we accept as a graceful sort of foil – as in the case of *Sartor Resartus*, or *Companions of my Solitude*, or *Henry Holbeach* – the connecting link of narrative. The first and chief business of the novel, however, is to give us authentic descriptions of this or that section of the world; and we cannot have the face of the picture disfigured by prominent aphorisms.[157]

This argument turns the language of the "beauty" against itself: the sayings that "embellish" at the beginning of the paragraph "disfigure the face" by the end of it. Yet even the initial praise defines maxims as ornamental, not functional. Rather than representing plot as the means to sweeten or disguise a moral, it represents narrative as the end which moralizing decorates (at best) or obstructs.

The charge that maxims interrupt the "business of the novel" restates David Masson's argument – in a more ambivalent discussion of "the interfusion of exposition with fiction" published eleven years earlier – that "the proper limits within which a poet or other artist may seek to inculcate doctrine" depend on whether one accepts the consensus that "the representation of social reality is, on the whole, the proper business of the novel."[158] But it echoes even more closely the language of a contemporary reviewer who asserts that "a novel ceases to be a novel when it aims at philosophical teaching. It is not the vehicle for conveying knowledge. Its business is to amuse."[159] "The Uses of Fiction" eliminates the chiasmus equating writers' "business" with readers' "amusement": its concession that sayings give "pleasure" confirms its charge that they disrupt "business." Digression becomes the textual equivalent of loitering. Like Mrs. Humphry Ward's argument that a nineteenth-century work ethic makes Richardson unreadable until the narration is pruned of sententious digressions, these articles equate narrative particulars with efficiency, and abstract speculation with authorial self-indulgence. (James's metaphor of the broken mirror concretizes the relation of self-contained fragments to self-centered narcissism.) Where eighteenth-century critics had accused fiction of taking readers away from their business, and plot of distracting them from morals, Eliot's reviewers worried instead that moral discourse distracted her from the business – and the responsibility – of fiction.

The pivot demarcating the culture that disciplined the readers of *Clarissa* from the esthetic that condemned the author of *Deronda* can be found in the reviews of Ann Radcliffe discussed in the previous chapter, for critics managed to attack her audience for skipping non-narrative digressions while simultaneously faulting Radcliffe for inserting them in the first place. Readers' alleged inability to restrain the pace of their reading – to resist the "tempt[ation] to pass over any of [the embellishments] for the sake of proceeding more rapidly with the story" – inverts the lack of self-restraint that prevents Radcliffe herself from "keep[ing] a stricter rein over her descriptive powers."[160] The *Dublin University Magazine* enjoins Eliot, in even more morally loaded terms, to "*learn* the difference . . . between careful selection and careless accumulation of small details, between that larger insight and *sterner self-control*, which go to the making of a first-rate novel, and the microscopic cleverness that evolves a series of faithful but disjointed sketches." That conjunction of pedagogy with moralism returns as late as 1965 in Walter Allen's account of the evolution through which Eliot's "digressions were much more curbed . . . once she had *learned* how to *control* them."[161] Over the course of the past two centuries, narratorial generalizations have meta-morphosed from a test of readers' obedience to a lapse in authors' self-discipline.

As we saw earlier, "Silly Novels by Lady Novelists" characterized women readers and women novelists by a common taste for self-contained platitudes. Evans's gendering of the maxim appears surprising at first, for it clashes with an older (though equally misogynistic) belief that women read frivolously for the plot, men seriously for ideas. That contradiction can be explained in part by the Victorian assumption that men, reading more widely, could get their ideas directly from nonfictional genres. (As Eliot's friend Edith Simcox observed, critics of the novel with a purpose "complain of the mixture of powder and jam, and pretend that they would rather take their morals and economics unsweetened in church or lecture-rooms. Of course we know better.")[162] But the contradiction points as well, I think, to a historical shift in assumptions about the place of plot in fiction – or indeed about the structure of works of art in general – which culminated in reviewers' refusal to quote George Eliot. Richardson's disapproval of "young People; who are apt to read rapidly wth. a View only to *Story*," and Lockhart's distaste for the "class of readers" who wanted the *Memoirs of Scott* reduced to plot summary, eventually gave way to complaints about the vulgarity of the opposite "class": in Dicey's review, the "large class of persons" who care more for individual maxims than for the continuity of the whole; in William Blackwood's letter, the "colonial class of readers" who buy anthologies of sayings rather than the novels from which they are taken; and in "Silly Novels by Lady Novelists," the feminine "class of readers to whom [platitudinous] remarks appear peculiarly pointed and pungent." The silly ladies of Marian Evans's essay underline the same "digressions, . . . fine sentiments and judicious remarks" which Haywood shows Miss Loyter skipping. Where Clara Reeve and Samuel Johnson attacked the audience that "read Richardson for the story," a hundred years later the reviewer who stated in the first person that "we ask for story" included himself among it.[163] And once Victorian critics had reversed the older hierarchy that subordinated narrative to sententiousness, it was only a matter of time before the respective genders of the two discourses changed places to match.

Put differently, Gaye Tuchman's argument that the growing prestige of the novel in the second half of the century drove women out of the field holds true less for the genre itself than for the place of plot within it.[164] What became less feminine in the course of becoming more serious was not the novel, but narrative discourse. The fiction of the 1890s eventually clinched that shift by associating didactic digressions not simply with female writers ranging ideologically from Sarah Grand to Marie Corelli, but with a feminine moralism opposed at once to the narrative pleasure of masculine romance like Stevenson's or Kipling's and to the avant-garde doctrine of art for art's sake.[165] Eliot's career paved the way for both by replacing the figure of the self-indulgent female reader with the specter of the self-important female sage.

The consequences of that reversal remain with us. Reviewers' moralistic denunciation of explicit moralizing survived the growth of professional literary criticism in the next century, when esthetic ambitiousness replaced moral seriousness as that to which vulgar narrative pleasure was opposed. A hundred years after "The Uses of Fiction" decreed that moral generalizations "must not be obtruded," we still find Graham Martin comparing the narrator of *The Mill on the Floss* with an Intourist guide, or W. J. Harvey urging readers to ignore Eliot's "authorial intrusions" and "moral comments": "These comments are a means to an end; they are one of the bridges between our world and the world of the novel. They are not ends in themselves, not the proper objects of our contemplation. And we are meant to pass easily and quickly over these comments."[166] Where Main calls the narrative a vehicle for the sayings, Harvey reduces the sayings themselves to a bridge. Harvey's invitation to "pass quickly over" the moral comments all but licenses readers to ignore them – a possibility already acknowledged by the character in James's "*Daniel Deronda:* a Conversation" who confesses that the didactic passages induce "an occasional temptation to skip." His claim that the moral comments are "not the proper objects of our contemplation" revives the tone of ginger distaste that critics in Eliot's own lifetime used to describe her union with Lewes. By 1989, when Dorothea Barrett celebrated Eliot's "rebelliousness and eroticism" while calling her sibylline image "unfortunate," sententiousness finally replaced sex as the scandal that admirers needed to explain away.[167]

Harvey presents skipping not only as the ideal but as an unavoidable norm. He clinches the apologetic claim that "the number and length of such [moral] comments is not as great as some critics assume" with the assertion that "the great majority of intrusive comments last for only two or three sentences and with rare exceptions are surely passed over by the impetus of any non-analytical reading."[168] The fact that such "intrusions" are more frequently reproduced than any other part of George

Eliot's work – in anthologies, in reviews, and in critical studies including Harvey's own – does not in itself disprove this last argument, since quotation is always a product of analysis in the most literal sense. Yet no positive evidence can be imagined either, since what Harvey calls "non-analytical reading" leaves no trace to prove what it skips and where it lingers.

More fundamentally, the invitation to quicken our pace takes for granted that any reader can recognize those moments when the text shifts from narrative to saying. This would suggest in turn that "non-analytical" readers identify sententious passages as systematically as do critics who adduce them as evidence, reviewers who excerpt them as specimens, and editors who collect them into anthologies: the only difference is that each group ignores what the other prizes. While some readers' fondness for quoting Eliot's wisdom suggests that her work invites analysis, so does other readers' distaste for the sayings. Both inscribe the contrast between the general and the particular within the same series of binary oppositions that (as David Carroll has shown) leads critics to distinguish the "Jewish element" of *Daniel Deronda* from the English marriage-plot and the immoral "third book" of *The Mill on the Floss* from the first two.[169] As we saw in chapter one, Richardson's project of collecting precisely those passages which "young People" would otherwise be tempted to skip presumed that even the youngest and laziest readers were qualified to distinguish sententious from narrative discourse. Conversely, Eliot herself worried that even the silliest lady readers unerringly recognized hackneyed platitudes to mark in the margin. The reception of Eliot's work makes "non-analytical reading" an oxymoron. Readers "cut the book into scraps" whether they search for the sayings or read for the plot. As Stanley Fish has argued in a different context, "critical controversies become disguised reports of what readers uniformly do."[170]

Yet Harvey's contrast between the critics who linger on the maxims and the amateur readers who skip them altogether does suggest one answer to the puzzle of exactly how George Eliot managed, in Main's words, to "sanctify the novel." The form of Eliot's novels does not in itself account for her power (or her editors') to change the hierarchy of genres. But the realignment of audiences that her career brought about contributed more obliquely to that shift. Where earlier the difference between novel and lyric had been interchangeable with the opposition between those who read for the plot and those who read for the beauties, Eliot's sententiousness projected that split into the novel-reading public itself. The novel's difference from other genres gave way to a divide within its own audience: on the one hand, the "frivolous readers who care only for story" whom Lewes identified among the buyers of *Felix Holt*; on the other, the inner circle of commonplacers whose hand-written marginalia and fan mail warded off the threat of the anonymous, inarticulate mass market that Wilkie Collins called "the unknown public."[171] Like Radcliffe's inscribed poetry, Main's anthologies forced readers to ratify the same generic hierarchy that his project promised to challenge. Both internalized the traditional inferiority of the novel to other genres by subordinating narrative to other modes of novelistic discourse – stylistic beauties in one case, moral truths in the other – and some novel-readers to others. Where Radcliffe's reviewers distanced themselves and their audience from the hypothetical "common reader" who skipped the poems that slowed the narrative, Eliot's editors strategically bored the "frivolous reader" by interrupting the plot with equally static and self-contained maxims. Both used pace to define their audience in contradistinction to a larger, hypothetical public.

Textual discriminations bring professional distinctions. Over the past two centuries, the task of identifying reusable quotations has helped to demarcate a class of readers for hire – editors, reviewers, teachers, critics, producers and consumers of academic books like this – from the larger audience for which some claim to speak (like Harvey) but against which all define themselves. In the *Family Shakespeare*, Bowdler's assumption that reading requires the real or imagined presence of the opposite sex suggests that the awareness of other audiences which "embarrasses" readers also underpins their identity. Yet the parallel that Dickens draws between annotated editions and defaced circulating-library novels, or that Eliot tried to prevent readers from drawing between her commonplace-books and Main's gift books, calls that distinction into question. While the preference for beauties or for plot has continued to differentiate one class of novel-readers from another, the shift from a culture in which critics enjoy beauties while ladies devour stories to one where the vulgar appreciate stylistic ornament and the elite demands organic unity makes clear how arbitrary those markers of difference are. The common reflex to sift the whole from the detail unites the very audiences that it serves to distinguish. It also erases the difference between nineteenth-century reviewers offering bookbuyers representative samples and twentieth-century critics reading against the grain. More recently, the critical profession has begun to swing back from the nineteenth-century preference for the whole to the eighteenth-century preference for the parts: an interpretation of a buried footnote now proclaims symptomatic ingenuity as surely as the highlighted introductory synopses that one finds in second-hand textbooks betray the earnest dullard. The choice between summary and synecdoche remains a test of allegiance.

It might seem apposite to quote Paul de Man quoting Pascal: "'*quand on lit trop vite ou trop doucement, on n'entend rien.*'"[172] But the demand for anthologies suggests that the pace of reading has never posed hermeneutic problems so urgently as moral and even social dilemmas. The divergence of mass culture from high art set into motion during Eliot's lifetime lent new weight to the disjunctions between appreciation and impatience which Richardson's novels established and his editors widened. Far from reducing its readers to passive consumers, as opponents of fiction traditionally accused, the novel has relentlessly forced them to choose which audience to identify themselves with, and which rhythm of reading. In that context, its rise appears less a populist challenge to social and sexual hierarchies – as its defenders claimed, and its attackers accused, in the two centuries leading up to Ian Watt's *Rise of the Novel* – than, on the contrary, a means to stratify anew an expanding public.[173] As how one reads became more important than what, the conservative hierarchy of genres gave way to a reactionary hierarchy of readers. One belated product of that shift is the academic criticism of the novel made possible by careers like Eliot's, made systematic by work like Watt's. An exploration of the place of the novel within twentieth-century literary theory might provide an opportunity to reconsider the role that scale and pace play in reading, or what alternatives to the slow-motion interpretation of lyric-sized excerpts the discipline might develop. But it would also allow the critical profession to think about what language, if any, professional readers can invent to talk about the experience of those who consume texts without producing others.

Notes

INTRODUCTION

1 "De bons esprits ont tiré la substance de mille volumes in-folio, qu'ils ont
fait passer toute entière dans un petit in-douze; à-peu-près comme ces
habiles chymistes, qui expriment la vertu des plantes, la concentrent dans
une phiole, & jettent le marc grossier. Nous avons fait des abregés de tout ce
qu'il y avoit de plus important; on a réimprimé le meilleur: le tout a été
corrigé d'après les vrais principes de la morale. Nos compilateurs sont des
gens estimables & chers à la nation" (Louis-Sebastien Mercier, *L'an deux
mille quatre cent quarante. Rêve s'il en fût jamais* [1771; Londres, 1785], 187–88;
Memoirs of the Year Two Thousand Five Hundred, trans. W. Hooper, 2 vols.
[London: G. Robinson, 1772], 2.6–7; I have substituted "compiler" for
"composer" as the translation of *compilateur*). Fifty years later, Sir Walter
Scott situated the same operation firmly in the present, dismissing "those
ponderous folios so dear to the seventeenth century, from which, under
favour be it spoken, we have distilled matter for our quartos and octavos,
and which, once more subjected to the alembic, may, should our sons be yet
more frivolous than ourselves, be still further reduced into duodecimos and
pamphlets" (*Rob Roy*, ed. Eric Anderson [1817; New York: Knopf, 1995],
10.95). On Mercier's library, see Roger Chartier, *The Order of Books*, trans.
Lydia Cochrane (Stanford: Stanford University Press, 1994), 69.
2 Samuel Taylor Coleridge, *Biographia Literaria*, ed. James Engell and
W. Jackson Bate (1817; Princeton: Princeton University Press, 1983),
1.3.49.
3 Hannah More, *Strictures on the modern system of female education*, 2 vols. (London:
T. Cadell, 1799), 1.7.174–75, 2.26–27; Friedrich Engels, *The Condition of the
Working Class in England* (1845), trans. W. O. Henderson and W. H.
Chaloner (Stanford: Stanford University Press, 1968), 273; Marjorie Perloff,
"The Future of an Illusion: Why Anthologies Make Bad 'Textbooks',"
MLA Convention, 29 December 1998. Antin's remark is quoted in Douglas
Messerli, ed., *"Language" Poetries: An Anthology* (New York: New Directions,
1987), and repeated in Messerli's anthology *From the Other Side of the Century: A
New American Poetry* (Los Angeles: Sun and Moon Press, 1994); thanks to Dan
O'Neill for finding this passage.

4 Roland Barthes, *S/Z*, trans. Richard Miller (Oxford: Blackwell, 1990), 4. See also Barthes's axiom that "a text's unity lies not in its origin but in its destination" ("The Death of the Author," *Image-Music-Text*, trans. Stephen Heath [New York: Hill and Wang, 1977], 142), and Michel de Certeau's comparison of readers with "poachers" or "travelers" *(The Practice of Everyday Life*, trans. Stephen F. Rendall [Berkeley: University of California Press, 1984], 184). Both metaphors of course draw on the same image of the "commonplace" that manuscript anthologies invoke.

5 Not surprisingly, the anthology has attracted more attention from scholars of earlier periods: see, e.g., Ann Moss, *Printed Commonplace-Books and the Structuring of Renaissance Thought* (Oxford: Clarendon Press, 1996); Arthur Marotti, *Manuscript, Print, and the English Renaissance Lyric* (Ithaca: Cornell University Press, 1995); Mary Thomas Crane, *Framing Authority: Sayings, Self, and Society in Sixteenth-Century England* (Princeton: Princeton University Press, 1993); Margaret Ezell, *Writing Women's Literary History* (Baltimore: Johns Hopkins University Press, 1993); Richard Halpern, *The Poetics of Primitive Accumulation: English Renaissance Culture and the Genealogy of Capital* (Ithaca: Cornell University Press, 1991), 47–49; Walter Ong, SJ, *Interfaces of the Word* (Ithaca: Cornell University Press 1977), 147–88; and Max W. Thomas, "Reading and Writing the Renaissance Commonplace Book: A Question of Authorship?" in Martha Woodmansee and Peter Jaszi, eds., *The Construction of Authorship: Textual Appropriation in Law and Literature* (Durham: Duke University Press, 1994), 401–16, 281–302.

6 For a trenchant critique of this model of canon-formation, to which I am indebted throughout, see John Guillory, *Cultural Capital: The Problem of Literary Canon Formation* (Chicago: University of Chicago Press, 1993), 3–55; but for a defense of it, Carey Kaplan and Ellen Cronan Rose, *The Canon and the Common Reader* (Knoxville: University of Tennessee Press, 1990), and Paul Lauter, *Canons and Contexts* (New York: Oxford University Press, 1991).

7 Robert Crawford, *Devolving English Literature* (Oxford: Clarendon Press, 1992); Barbara Benedict, *Making the Modern Reader: Cultural Mediation in Early Modern Anthologies* (Princeton: Princeton University Press, 1996), 221. Given the importance of compilation in electronic media, it may not be surprising that some of the most exciting recent work on the anthology has taken the form of websites, such as the *Romantic Circles* anthologies page (<http://humanitas/ucsb.edu/liu/canonweb.html>) and the "Anthologies and Miscellanies" page edited by Harriet Linkin, Laura Mandell, and Rita Raley (<http://www.muohio.edu/anthologies/>), or at least has been electronically published, like the special issue of *Romanticism on the Net* devoted to anthologies (7 [August 1997], ed. Laura Mandell). Anthologies have recently come to provide another forum for reflections on the history of anthologizing: see, for example, Roger Lonsdale's introduction to his *New Oxford Book of Eighteenth-Century Verse* (1984) and Jerome McGann's "Rethinking Romanticism," *ELH* 59 (1992): 725–54, which forms a companion-piece to his *New Oxford Book of Romantic Period Verse* (1993).

8 Vicesimus Knox, *Winter Evenings, or, Lucubrations on Life and Letters*, 2 vols. (London: Charles Dilly, 1790), 2.10; F. T. Palgrave, "On Readers in 1760 and 1860," *Macmillan's* 1 (April 1860), reprinted in Christopher Ricks, ed., *The Golden Treasury of the Best Songs and Poems in the English Language, Selected and Arranged with Notes by Francis Turner Palgrave* (1861; Harmondsworth: Penguin, 1991), 451–54 (453). Similarly, Robert deMaria has argued that Locke's "New Method of a Common-Place Book" (1706) enlists the commonplace-book to turn back the clock on extensive reading ("Samuel Johnson and the Reading Revolution," *Eighteenth-Century Life* 16 [1992]: 86–102).

9 Rolf Engelsing, "Die Perioden der Lesergeschichte in der Neuzeit," *Archiv für geschichte des Buchwesens* 10 (1970): 945–1002; see also Martha Woodmansee, *The Author, Art, and the Market* (New York: Columbia University Press, 1994), 90–100. For a counterargument to Engelsing, however, see Robert Darnton, *The Great Cat Massacre* (New York: Vintage, 1985), 249–52. Benedict's argument that, despite their "brevity and mnemonic literary devices," anthologies "promote 'extensive' reading by promising many pieces, not great ones; nonce, not timeless texts; the latest, not the best" ceases to apply, I think, after 1774 (*Making the Modern Reader*, 18). Similarly, Friedrich Kittler argues that in late-eighteenth-century Germany anthologies responded to elites' anxiety about the perceived explosion of reading: the anthology replaced the Bible as the book that unified a culture (Friedrich A. Kittler, *Discourse Networks 1800/1900* [1985], trans. Michael Metteer [Stanford: Stanford University Press, 1990], 144, 149).

10 James Buzard, *The Beaten Track: European Tourism, Literature, and the Ways of Culture, 1800–1918* (Oxford: Clarendon Press, 1993), 122–27.

11 See Gillian Beer's observation that "as critics . . . we remember (or pretend to remember) the totality of a narrative and so misread its passing . . . But a long narrative must either accept or combat the reader's constant forgetting" ("Origins and Oblivion in Victorian Narrative," in *Sex, Politics, and Science in the Nineteenth-Century Novel*, ed. Ruth Bernard Yeazell [Baltimore: Johns Hopkins University Press, 1986], 63–87; 64).

12 M. H. Abrams, ed., *The Norton Anthology of English Literature*, 6th edn. (New York: Norton, 1993), xxxi.

13 *The Thomas Hardy Calendar: a quotation from the works of Thomas Hardy for every day in the year*, compiled by C[ecil] P[almer] (London: C. Palmer, [1921]); Virginia Woolf, review of *A Treasury of English Prose*, ed. Logan Pearsall Smith, in *Athenaeum*, 30 January 1920, reprinted in *The Essays of Virginia Woolf*, ed. Andrew McNeillie (London: Hogarth Press, 1988), 3.171–76 (174). Thanks to Steve Monte for calling Woolf's essay to my attention.

14 *The Life of Sir Walter Scott, Bart*, abridged from the larger work by J. G. Lockhart (1848; Edinburgh: Adam & Charles Black, 1871), ix.

15 This view of the novel – most compellingly argued in Watt's *The Rise of the Novel. Studies in Defoe, Richardson, and Fielding* (Berkeley: University of California Press, 1957) – has more recently fueled the ethical ambitions of Doody's

The True Story of the Novel (London: HarperCollins, 1997). For a more skeptical analysis of the novel's role in the construction of class and gender, see Nancy Armstrong's polemical *Desire and Domestic Fiction: A Political History of the Novel* (Oxford: Oxford University Press, 1987).

16 The term is Hans Robert Jauss's, in *Toward an Aesthetic of Reception*, trans. Timothy Bahti (Minneapolis: University of Minnesota Press, 1982), 25. My thinking here is indebted to Jerome J. McGann, *A Critique of Modern Textual Criticism* (Chicago: University of Chicago Press, 1983) and "The Monks and the Giants: Textual and Bibliographical Studies and the Interpretation of Literary Works," in McGann, ed., *Textual Criticism and Literary Interpretation* (Chicago: University of Chicago Press, 1985), 180–200 (198), as well as to John Sutherland, "Publishing History: A Hole at the Center of Literary Sociology," in *Literature and Social Practice*, ed. Philippe Desan et al. (Chicago: University of Chicago Press, 1989), 267–82 (277).

17 Pierre Bourdieu, *The Field of Cultural Production: Essays on Art and Literature* (New York: Columbia University Press, 1994), 36. See also Terry Eagleton's argument that literary critics need to consider not only "the ideological use of particular literary works" but "the ideological significance of the cultural and academic institutionalization as such" (*Criticism and Ideology* [London: NLB, 1975], 56–57); Timothy Reiss's warning that "not only do we need to know what any given culture does, or would understand as 'art,' but we also need to know what particular sociocultural role is played by *that* discourse among all the others surrounding it" (*The Meaning of Literature* [Ithaca: Cornell University Press, 1992], 3); and, for the social function of literature in this period, Clifford Siskin, *The Work of Writing: Literature and Social Change in Britain, 1700–1830* (Baltimore: Johns Hopkins University Press, 1998).

18 For a theory of these paratextual moments, see Gérard Genette, *Seuils* (Paris: Seuil, 1987).

19 Peter Widdowson, *Hardy in History: A Study in Literary Sociology* (London: Routledge, 1989), 12. More recent case studies like Patsy Stoneman's *Brontë Transformations* (London: Harvester, 1996) confirm Widdowson's argument that reception history must encompass not only "reviewing, literary criticism, publishing" but "education, the advertising and tourist industries, adaptation into other media" (*Hardy*, 15).

20 The same could be said of a third school which uses omniscient narration to report the responses of a reader who personifies the critic *à clef*; compare Garett Stewart's argument against "the homogenized and depleted reader [who] stalks its occasioning texts as the personification of meaning per se" (*Dear Reader: The Conscripted Audience in Nineteenth-Century British Fiction* [Baltimore: Johns Hopkins University Press, 1996], 10). See also John Guillory's argument that institutional acts rather than opinions alone cause works to become part of the canon ("Canon," in *Critical Terms for Literary Study*, ed. Frank Lentricchia and Thomas McLaughlin [University of Chicago Press, 1990], 233–49 [237]).

1 RICHARDSON'S ECONOMIES OF SCALE

1 Cleanth Brooks, "The Heresy of Paraphrase" (1947), in *Critical Theory Since Plato*, ed. Hazard Adams (New York: Harcourt Brace Jovanovich, 1971), 1033–41. Brooks is typical of most twentieth-century critics in treating summary as a competitor to criticism rather than its object of study; exceptions include Barbara Herrnstein Smith, "Narrative Versions, Narrative Theories," in *On Narrative*, ed. W. J. T. Mitchell (Chicago: University of Chicago Press, 1981), 209–39 (213); Robert Mayo's survey of the "epitome" in eighteenth-century magazines and miscellanies *(The English Novel in the Magazines, 1740–1815* [Evanston: Northwestern University Press, 1962], 237); and Pat Rogers's analysis of Swift's and Defoe's abridgers ("Classics and Chapbooks," in *Books and their Readers in Eighteenth-Century England*, ed. Isabel Rivers [New York: St Martin's Press, 1982], 27–45).

2 To Aaron Hill, 12 July 1749, in Samuel Richardson, *Selected Letters of Samuel Richardson*, ed. John Carroll (Oxford: Clarendon Press, 1964), 126.

3 To Johannes Stinstra, 2 June 1753, Richardson *Letters*, 230.

4 [Samuel Richardson], *PAMELA: OR, VIRTUE Rewarded*, 6th edn., 4 vols. (London: S. Richardson, 1742), 3.30.239. Except where otherwise noted, references to *Pamela* give volume, number, and page in this edition.

5 Samuel Richardson, *The History of Sir Charles Grandison*, ed. Jocelyn Harris (London: Oxford University Press, 1972), 2.10.309.

6 The commonplace book is first mentioned in the third edition: Samuel Richardson, *Clarissa*, ed. Florian Stuber, 8 vols. (1751; New York: AMS, 1990), 8.49.214.

7 Samuel Richardson, *Clarissa*, ed. Angus Ross (Harmondsworth: Penguin, 1985), 133.480, 17.95. Except where specified, further references to *Clarissa* give letter and page numbers from this modernized reprint of the first (1747–48) edition.

8 On narrative distance, see Gérard Genette, *Figures* 3 (Paris: Seuil, 1972), 184–86, 252–56; and, for impersonality, Emile Benveniste's argument that the third person is a "non-person" (*Problèmes de linguistique générale* [Paris: Gallimard, 1966], 265). Summary is not, of course, the only strategy used to shorten Richardson: *Pamela*, more compact and less polyvocal than the later novels, has traditionally been cut down not only by transposing letters into narrative, but by omitting the second half altogether.

9 To Tobias Smollett, 13 August 1756, Richardson, *Letters*, 328; preface to Richardson, *Grandison*, 3. A similar division of labor differentiates abridgements of *Robinson Crusoe* from Defoe's own anti-narrative *Serious Reflections during the Life and Surprising Adventures of Robinson Crusoe* (1720).

10 Franklin's debt to Richardson is established by Robert Newcomb, "Franklin and Richardson," *Journal of English and Germanic Philology* 57 (1958): 27–35; however, Newcomb tends to overstate this debt by assuming that a parallel between Richardson's and Franklin's maxims shows influence rather than the dependence of both on a common stock of commonplaces.

See also John Dussinger's discussion of the tension between Richardson's
narrative immediacy and atemporal generalizations ("Truth and Storytelling in *Clarissa*," in *Samuel Richardson: Tercentenary Essays*, ed. Margaret Anne
Doody and Peter Sabor [Cambridge: Cambridge University Press, 1989],
40–50).

11 Samuel Richardson, *Clarissa*, 7 vols. (London: Samuel Richardson, 1749),
1.iii; T. C. Duncan Eaves and Ben D. Kimpel, *Samuel Richardson: A Biography*
(Oxford: Clarendon Press, 1971), 489.

12 To Benjamin Kennicott, 26 November 1754, quoted in Eaves and Kimpel,
Samuel Richardson, 420.

13 If "sentiments" and "maxims" are as closely related as the title of the
Collection suggests, then Charlotte's claim makes sense in the context of the
French tradition of *moralistes*, and of the incorporation of sententious elements into the French novel itself: see Geoffrey Bennington, *Sententiousness
and the Novel: Laying Down the Law in Eighteenth-Century French Fiction* (Cambridge: Cambridge University Press, 1985). The fallibility of this national
stereotype is made clear, however, by the desire of Richardson's French
translator/abridger, Prévost, to substitute pure "histoire" for the superfluous "réflexions" of the "éditeur anglois": see Thomas Beebee, *Clarissa on the
Continent: Translation and Seduction* (University Park: Penn State University
Press, 1990), 66.

14 James Boswell, *The Life of Samuel Johnson*, ed. R. W. Chapman (Oxford:
Oxford University Press, 1980), 480. On the place of sententiousness in
Clarissa, see also Kevin L. Cope, "Richardson the Advisor," in *New Essays on
Samuel Richardson*, ed. Albert J. Rivero (New York: St Martin's Press, 1996),
17–34.

15 C[lara] R[eeve], *The Progress of Romance*, 2 vols. (Colchester: W. Keymer,
1785), 1.137.

16 To Aaron Hill, 29 October 1746; to Edward Moore, 1748; Richardson,
Letters, 70, 118.

17 Samuel Richardson, *Letters and Passages Restored from the Original Manuscripts of
the History of CLARISSA. To which is subjoined, A Collection of such of the Moral and
Instructive SENTIMENTS, CAUTIONS, APHORISMS, REFLECTIONS and
OBSERVATIONS contained in the History, as are presumed to be of general Use and
Service* (London: S. Richardson, 1751), ix.

18 Elizabeth Griffith, *The Morality of Shakespeare's Drama Illustrated* (London: T.
Cadell, 1775), xii; Walter Scott, *The Genius and Wisdom of Sir Walter Scott,
Comprising Moral, Religious, Political, Literary, and Social Aphorisms, Selected Carefully from his Various Writings: With a Memoir* (London: W. S. Orr, 1839), x. See
also Michael McKeon's argument that the cult of sensibility raised worries
that "the circuit between . . . example and precept . . . could be shorted out
by the very textual pleasures that were supposed to complete it" ("Prose
Fiction: Great Britain," *The Cambridge History of Literary Criticism. Vol. 4: The
Eighteenth Century*, ed. H. B. Nisbet and Claude Rawson [Cambridge: Cambridge University Press, 1997], 238–63 [257]).

19 Linda K. Hughes and Michael Lund, *The Victorian Serial* (Charlottesville: University of Virginia Press, 1991), 283; see Alan D. McKillop, "Wedding Bells for Pamela," *Philological Quarterly* 28 (1949): 323–25.

20 E.g., Robert Darnton, "Readers Respond to Rousseau," in *The Great Cat Massacre and Other Episodes in French Cultural History* (London: Allen Lane, 1984), 215–56; *The Literary Underground of the Old Regime* (Cambridge: Harvard University Press, 1982).

21 Patricia Meyer Spacks, *Boredom: The Literary History of a State of Mind* (Chicago: University of Chicago Press, 1995), 163. Spacks works backward from modern boredom to initial interest: "In order to suggest what may have made these outmoded novels 'interesting' to their first readers, I hope simultaneously to discover why later audiences should dismiss them as 'boring'" (131).

22 "Exploralibus" [Eliza Haywood], *The Invisible Spy*, 2 vols. (Dublin: Robert Main, 1755), 2.162.

23 To Thomas Edwards, 1 August 1755, quoted in Eaves and Kimpel, *Samuel Richardson*, 421.

24 E. S. Dallas, ed. [and abridger], *Clarissa* (London: Tinsley, 1868), xvii.

25 *Meditations from the Sacred Books . . . mentioned in the HISTORY OF CLARISSA as drawn up by her for her own use. To each of which is prefixed, A Short Historical Account, Connecting it with the Story* (London: J. Osborn, 1750), 3. This claim is somewhat disingenuous, however, since Richardson limited the circulation of the *Meditations* to personal friends and admirers of the novel. For the publication history of the *Meditations*, as well as a sensitive interpretation of them, see Tom Keymer, "Richardson's *Meditations*: Clarissa's *Clarissa*," in *Samuel Richardson: Tercentenary Essays*, ed. Margaret Anne Doody and Peter Sabor (Cambridge: Cambridge University Press, 1989), 89–109; 104.

26 Mark Kinkead-Weekes, "*Clarissa* Restored?," *Review of English Studies*, n.s. 10 (May 1959): 156–71 (156–57).

27 In that sense, the table of contents simply makes visible the work of ordering on which the novel itself depends: as Rosemarie Bodenheimer notes in another context, the plot of any correspondence is constructed not by the letter-writers, but by their editor (*The Real Life of Mary Ann Evans: George Eliot, her Letters and Fiction* [Cornell: Cornell University Press, 1994], 18–19).

28 Compare Thomas Beebee's argument that "the editorial voice presents *Clarissa* . . . as its own scholarly edition" (*Clarissa on the Continent*, 60), and Mark Kinkead-Weekes' observation that the first half of *Grandison* is "structured in alternating slabs of 'present tense' epistolary writing and retrospective narrative" (*Samuel Richardson: Dramatic Novelist* [Ithaca: Cornell University Press, 1973], 288); see also, more generally, Elizabeth Heckendorn Cook's discussion of the "figure of the author-editor who appropriates, fragments, and disseminates private letters as a branch of public morality" (*Epistolary Bodies: Gender and Genre in the Eighteenth-Century Republic of Letters* [Stanford: Stanford University Press, 1996], 28).

29 See Kinkead-Weekes, *"Clarissa* Restored?"; Tom Keymer, *Richardson's "Clarissa" and the Eighteenth-Century Reader* (Cambridge: Cambridge University Press, 1992), 246–49; and William Beatty Warner, *Reading Clarissa: The Struggles of Interpretation* (New Haven: Yale University Press, 1979), 182–209. Glen M. Johnson counts 104 footnotes added to the third edition: "Richardson's 'Editor' in *Clarissa*," *Journal of Narrative Technique* 10 (1980): 99–114 (100).

30 Richardson, *Clarissa* (1751), 8.49.215.

31 On the substitution of fragments for narrative after the rape, see Keymer, "Richardson's *Meditations*," 91–92, and Terry Castle, *Clarissa's Ciphers: Meaning and Disruption in Richardson's "Clarissa"* (Ithaca: Cornell University Press, 1982), 36.

32 On the "blackening" of Lovelace in each successive edition, see Kinkead-Weekes, *"Clarissa* Restored," 157–59, 164, and Warner, *Reading Clarissa*, 182–209.

33 *Clarissa on the Continent*, 45. See also Howard W. Weinbrot, *"Clarissa*, Elias Brand and Death by Parentheses," in *New Essays on Samuel Richardson*, ed. Albert J. Rivero (New York: St Martin's Press, 1996), 117–40, which interprets Brand as a double for both Lovelace and Richardson.

34 Richardson, *Clarissa* (1751), 7.100.394.

35 Richardson, *Clarissa* (1751), 8.49.202.

36 Richardson, *Clarissa* (151), 7.100.397.

37 To Lady Echlin, 7 July 1755; Richardson describes the *Collection* as "pith and marrow" again to Thomas Edwards, 1 August 1755; both quoted in Eaves and Kimpel, *Samuel Richardson*, 421.

38 Richardson, *Clarissa* (1751), 7.100.386.

39 On the increase in italicization, see John Carroll, "Richardson at Work: Revisions, Allusions, and Quotations in *Clarissa*," in *Studies in the Eighteenth Century II*, ed. R. F. Brissenden (Canberra: Australian National University Press, 1973), 53–72.

40 For the interpretive closure of the third edition, see Keymer, *Richardson's "Clarissa*," 246 49, and Warner, *Reading Clarissa*, 182–209.

41 To Thomas Edwards, 16 July 1753, Richardson, *Letters*, 238–39.

42 To Patrick Delany, 22 December 1753, Richardson, *Letters*, 260.

43 For the origin of this phrase, see Harris's annotation (*Grandison* 3.480).

44 Richardson, *Clarissa* (1751), 7.99.382.

45 Clarissa, too, shows Anna only part of the complete collection of letters that she sends Mrs. Norton, suppressing the letters that reflect badly on the Harlowes (*Clarissa* 409.1199).

46 See Terry Castle's argument that "given the unconstrained cutting and excerpting of documents going on elsewhere in *Clarissa*, Clarissa's own activity of selective extraction, which unwittingly violates the integrity of the scriptural text, is a troubling one" (*Clarissa's Ciphers*, 131).

47 Richardson, *Clarissa* (1751), 7.99.382–83.

48 On Richardson and authorial disavowal, see Lennard Davis, *Factual Fic-*

tions: The Origins of the English Novel (New York: Columbia University Press, 1983), 174–92.

49 Richardson to James Leake, August 1741, Richardson, *Letters*, 45. On continuations of *Pamela*, see James Turner, "Novel Panic: Picture and Performance in the Reception of *Pamela*," *Representations* 48 (Fall 1994): 70–96.

50 To William Warburton, 19 April 1748, Richardson, *Letters*, 85. On this contradiction, see also Davis, *Factual Fictions*, 175.

51 Samuel Richardson, "Address to the Public," *History of Sir Charles Grandison* (London: Samuel Richardson, 1754), 7.442; Samuel Richardson, *The Case of Samuel Richardson . . . with Regard to the Invasion of his Property in The History of Sir Charles Grandison* (London: S. Richardson, 1753), 2. In the argument that follows I am indebted to Mark Rose's incisive analysis of the piracy of *Grandison*, which he takes to typify Richardson's role as an "emblem of the link between the book trade, concerned with property, and the discourse of originality" (*Authors and Owners: The Invention of Copyright* [Cambridge: Harvard University Press, 1993], 117).

52 To Anne Dewes, 15 December 1756, Richardson, *Letters*, 331, my emphasis.

53 Lady Elizabeth Echlin, *An Alternative Ending to Richardson's Clarissa*, ed. Dimiter Daphinoff (Bern: Francke, 1982). For Hill, see Richardson, *Letters*, 75–77. Richardson writes that Solomon Lowe "amused himself with collecting many of the moral Sentiments scatter'd thro' the Volumes [of *Clarissa*], of which he was so good as to make me a Present" (to David Graham, 3 May 1750, *Letters*, 158). For a sophisticated analysis of the kinds of readerly participation that the first edition of *Clarissa* demands, see Keymer, *Richardson's Clarissa*, 65–84.

54 To Lady Bradshaigh, 30 May 1754, quoted in Eaves and Kimpel, *Samuel Richardson*, 412.

55 Harris, "Introduction," in Richardson, *Grandison*, xxviii. See also Harris, "Learning and Genius in *Sir Charles Grandison*," in *Studies in the Eighteenth Century IV*, ed. R. F. Brissenden and J. C. Eade (Canberra: Australian National University Press, 1979), 167–91.

56 See Richardson, *Grandison* 3.484.

57 Michael E. Connaughton, "Richardson's Familiar Quotations: *Clarissa* and Bysshe's *Art of English Poetry*," *Philological Quarterly* 60 (1981): 183–95; A. Dwight Culler, "Edward Bysshe and the Poet's Handbook," *PMLA* 63 (1948): 865–85; Alan Dugald McKillop, *Samuel Richardson: Printer and Novelist* (Chapel Hill: University of North Carolina Press, 1936), 141. John Carroll makes a useful distinction between Richardson's allusions, which tend to refer to an entire work, and direct quotations, which do not ("Richardson at Work," 70).

58 Jocelyn Harris, "Richardson: Original or Learned Genius?" in *Samuel Richardson: Tercentenary Essays*, ed. Doody and Sabor, 188–202 (188–89).

59 Harris, "Richardson: Original or Learned Genius?," 188; Richardson, *Clarissa* (1751), 7.100.386.

60 Edward Bysshe, ed., *The Art of English Poetry*, 3rd edn. (London: Samuel Buckley, 1708), sig. 3.

61 Connaughton, "Richardson's Familiar Quotations," 189, 194.

62 Harris, "Richardson: Original or Learned Genius?," 202, 190. Connaughton's argument that the subject headings under which Bysshe classifies each quotation provide evidence about their function in Richardson's text suggests another way in which the *Art* can usefully be studied as a source.

63 On drama, see Margaret Anne Doody, *A Natural Passion: A Study of the Novels of Samuel Richardson* (Oxford: Clarendon Press, 1974), 107–27, and Kinkead-Weekes, *Samuel Richardson*. I am arguing not *against* the claim that Richardson's quotations sometimes allude to an entire context – as a range of studies have shown, from Gillian Beer's on Milton ("Richardson, Milton, and the Status of Evil," *Review of English Studies* n.s. 19 [1968]: 261–70) to Janet Aikins's on *Venice Preserv'd* ("A Plot Discover'd," *University of Toronto Quarterly* 55 [Spring 1986]: 219–34) – but rather *for* the inclusion of Bysshe's *Art* among the contexts being alluded to.

64 Culler, "Edward Bysshe," 867; Connaughton, "Richardson's Familiar Quotations," 194.

65 To Johannes Stinstra, 2 June 1753, Richardson, *Letters*, 229. Harris adduces this anecdote to prove the extent of Richardson's reading: "Richardson's muse was nourished by works translated from English, and by the English Moderns. As an apprentice, Richardson bought his own candles to read into the night" (Harris, "Richardson: Original or Learned Genius?," 189).

66 I discuss a rather different function of executorship in *Grandison* – as a legal expression of bonds between men – in "*Sir Charles Grandison* and the Executor's Hand," *Eighteenth-Century Fiction* 8 (April 1996): 329–42.

67 On this passage, see also Castle, *Clarissa's Ciphers*, 132.

68 Compare Leopold Damrosch's discussion of Richardson's "*narrator absconditus* miming the hidden God who presides over the sublunary world but never shows his hand directly" (*God's Plot and Man's Stories: Studies in the Fictional Imagination from Milton to Fielding* [Chicago: University of Chicago Press, 1985], 258).

69 John Kelly, *Pamela's Conduct in High Life* (London: Ward and Chandler, 1741), iii–iv.

70 Henry Fielding, *Tom Jones*, ed. R. P. C. Mutter (Harmondsworth: Penguin, 1966), 12.1.552.

71 Samuel Formey, *L'esprit de Julie, ou Extrait de la Nouvelle Héloïse. Ouvrage utile à la société, et particulièrement à la jeunesse* (Berlin: Jean Jasperd, 1763).

72 *Les Pensées de J.-J. Rousseau, citoyen de Genève* (Paris: Prault, 1763); *Esprit, Maximes et Principes de Monsieur Jean-Jacques Rousseau* (Neuchâtel, 1764); for the many imitators, see Jean Sénelier, *Bibliographie générale des oeuvres de J.-J. Rousseau* (Paris: Presses Universitaires de France, 1950), 195–211 and

Théophile Dufour, *Recherches bibliographiques sur les oeuvres imprimées de J.-J. Rousseau* (Paris: Giraudin-Badin 1925), 225. For a different case, see Jean-Jacques Tatin, "La dissemination du texte Rousseau: Le 'Contrat-social' dans les recueils de 'Pensées de J.-J. Rousseau'," *Littérature* 69 (1988): 19–27.

73 "Je ne m'attachai pas a éplucher ça et là quelques phrases éparses et séparées . . . Je résolus de relire ses écrits avec plus de suite et d'attention que je n'avois fait jusqu'alors . . . Je n'en avois pas saisi l'ensemble assez pour juger solidement d'un système si nouveau pour moi. Ces livres-là ne sont pas, comme ceux d'aujourd'hui des aggrégations de pensées détachées" (Jean-Jacques Rousseau, *Rousseau juge de Jean-Jacques*, in *Confessions, autres textes autobiographiques*, ed. Bernard Gagnebin [Paris: Gallimard, 1959], 657–992; 930–32).

74 "On blâme en general cette maniére d'isoler et défigurer les passages d'un Auteur pour les interpreter au gré de la passion d'un censeur injuste" (Rousseau, *Rousseau juge de Jean-Jacques*, 695). One of Rousseau's early anthologists appropriates the analogy more positively: the *Analyse des ouvrages de Jean-Jacques Rousseau, de Geneve, et de M. Court de Gebelin, Auteur du Monde primitif, par un solitaire* (Genève: B. Chirol, 1785) begins: "L'analyse est un portrait en miniature; il doit être si ressemblant, que quiconque a connu l'original, puisse s'écrier: *Le voilà, c'est lui-même.*"

75 See Rousseau's handwritten statement that "il déclare tous les livres anciens et nouveaux, qu'on imprime et qu'on imprimera désomais sous son nom, en quelque lieu que ce soit, ou faux ou alterés, mutilés et falsifiés avec la plus grande malignité, et les desavoue . . . L'impuissance où il est de faire arriver ses plaintes aux oreilles du public, lui fait tenter pour dernière ressource de remettre à diverses personnes des copies de cette déclaration, écrites et signées de sa main" ("Déclaration relative à différentes réimpressions de ses ouvrages," in Rousseau, *Confessions*, 1186–87 [1187]).

76 *Julie ou La Nouvelle Héloïse. Lettres de deux amants habitants d'une petite ville au pied des Alpes*, recueillies et publiées par Jean-Jacques Rousseau (1761; Paris: Garnier-Flammarion, 1967), 3, 583.

77 On the disappearance of epistolary fiction in early-nineteenth-century Britain, see Nicola J. Watson, *Revolution and the Form of the British Novel 1790–1825: Intercepted Letters, Interrupted Seductions* (Oxford: Clarendon Press, 1994); Elizabeth Heckendorn Cook, *Epistolary Bodies: Gender and Genre in the Eighteenth-Century Republic of Letters* (Stanford: Stanford University Press, 1996), 173–83; Mary Favret, *Romantic Correspondence: Women, Politics, and the Fiction of Letters* (Cambridge: Cambridge University Press, 1993), 197–213; on Austen's anti-epistolarity, April Alliston, *Virtue's Faults: Correspondences in Eighteenth-Century British and French Women's Fiction* (Stanford: Stanford University Press, 1996), 232–36; and, for France, Janet Gurkin Altman, *Epistolarity: Approaches to a Form* (Columbus: Ohio State University Press, 1982), 31–34, and Laurent Versini, *Le roman épistolaire* (Paris: Presses Universitaires de France, 1979), 168–215. Watson's brilliant explanation of this decline in

terms of the political implications of correspondence is limited only by its failure to take into account the nineteenth-century survival (and indeed growth) of non-fictional epistolary genres such as the published correspondence and the life-and-letters biography. As I shall suggest, what fell from favor was not the letter itself so much as its alliance with the novel.

78 Philip Stevick's abridgment of *Clarissa* (San Francisco: Rinehart, 1971) uses third-person present-tense summaries to connect excerpts from the prefaces and postscript, though not in the body of the text itself. The one exception that I have found among post-1868 abridgments is Mary Howitt's version of *Grandison* (London: Routledge, 1873), which does not interpose editorial summaries at all.

79 Frederic Harrison, "The Life of George Eliot," in *The Choice of Books and Other Literary Pieces* (London: Macmillan, 1886), 204.

80 J. G. Lockhart, *Memoirs of the Life of Sir Walter Scott*, condensed and revised by the editor of "The Chandos Classics" (1869; London: Frederick Warne, n.d.), vi.

81 J. G. Lockhart, *The Life of Sir Walter Scott, Bart*, abridged from the larger work by J. G. Lockhart (1848; Edinburgh: Adam & Charles Black, 1871), ix.

82 Lockhart, "Preface," *Life of Scott* (1871). See also Francis Hart's argument that Romantic biography is torn between "the distrust of literally reported discourse" and "the shift of attention away from epistolary or conversational substance to the indirect personal revelation of style, tone, 'spirit'" (*Lockhart as Romantic Biographer* [Edinburgh: Edinburgh University Press, 1971], 39).

83 To Tobias Smollett, 13 August 1756, in Richardson, *Letters*, 328.

84 To Thomas Edwards, 1 August 1755, quoted in Eaves and Kimpel, *Samuel Richardson*, 421.

85 J. G. Lockhart, *Memoirs of the Life of Sir Walter Scott, Bart.*, 7 vols. (Philadelphia: Carey, Lea, Blanchard, 1838), 6.100. I discuss biographers' display of their own self-restraint more fully in "The *Life of Charlotte Brontë* and the Death of Miss Eyre," *Studies in English Literature* 35 (1995): 757–68.

86 Sir Walter Scott, *Waverley; or, 'Tis Sixty Years Since*, ed. Andrew Hook (1814; Harmondsworth: Penguin, 1972), 493; see also the 1829 "General Preface" to the Waverley Novels, in *Waverley*, 519–34 (525).

87 I introduce Genette's cumbersome term "extradiegetic" because the narrator of the *Life* is neither uniformly third-person not uniformly heterodiegetic: he periodically speaks in the first person and occasionally represents his own actions (either as a character interacting with Scott in the past or as a biographer taking editorial decisions in the present), but his voice functions primarily to frame and summarize other narratives (like Scott's "autobiographical fragment").

88 Sir Walter Scott, *Redgauntlet* (1824, 1832; ed. Kathryn Sutherland, Oxford: Oxford University Press, 1985), 226.

89 For the political implications of this shift, see Watson, *Revolution and the Form of the British Novel*, 149–53.

90 See also Homer Obed Brown's analysis of the incest themes that the Waverley Novels share with *Tom Jones: Institutions of the English Novel from Defoe to Scott* (Philadelphia: University of Pennsylvania Press, 1997), 157.

91 Alexander Welsh, *The Hero of the Waverley Novels* (New Haven: Yale University Press, 1963), 30–57.

92 Fielding, *Tom Jones*, 11.6.526–19.

93 Ward, *Clarissa*, iv.

94 Two analyses of what abridgers leave out can be found in Margaret Anne Doody's and Florian Stuber's devastating critique of Sherburn's abridgment (*"Clarissa* Censored," *Modern Language Studies* 18 [Winter 1988]: 74–88) and in Jay Fliegelman's *Prodigals and Pilgrims: The American Revolution against Patriarchal Authority, 1750–1800* (Cambridge: Cambridge University Press, 1982), whose suggestive comparison of the British first edition of *Clarissa* with American abridgments is weakened by his failure to factor in a third term: the British abridgments produced for young people as early as 1756 (not, as he speculates, in the late 1760s) (286).

95 See also David Richter's argument that in the 1790s attacks on novels for representing bad behavior gave way to accusations that novel-reading encouraged escapism; he explains this change by "an upward valuation of sloth relative to lust as a deadly sin" (*The Progress of Romance: Literary Historiography and the Gothic Novel* [Columbus: Ohio State University Press, 1996], 121).

96 [R. H. Hutton,] "Clarissa," *Spectator* (September 1865), reprinted in R. H. Hutton, *A Victorian Spectator: Uncollected Writings of R. H. Hutton,* ed. Robert Tener and Malcolm Woodfield (Bristol: Bristol Press, 1991), 99–106 (100).

97 On this collection (1821–24), see Brown, *Institutions,* 181–85, and Jane Millgate, *Scott's Last Edition: A Study in Publishing History* (Edinburgh: Edinburgh University Press, 1987), 99–104.

98 Sir Walter Scott, "Samuel Richardson," in *Biographical Memoirs of Eminent Novelists,* 2 vols. (1834; Freeport: Essay Index, 1972), 2.1–76 (69).

99 Sir Walter Scott, *Ivanhoe,* ed. A. N. Wilson (1819; Harmondsworth: Penguin, 1984), 530.

100 Joseph Ritson, *Scottish Songs* (London: J. Johnson, 1794), cxi, lxix.

101 On the logic of the poetic "relique" more generally, see Katie Trumpener, *Bardic Nationalism: The Romantic Novel and the British Empire* (Princeton: Princeton University Press, 1997), 28.

102 See Sir Walter Scott, ed., *Minstrelsy of the Scottish Border,* ed. Thomas Henderson, 4 vols. (Edinburgh: Blackwood, 1902), 3.335.

103 Robert Crawford, *Devolving English Literature* (Oxford: Clarendon Press, 1992), 125, 123–24. On the tension between composition and compilation in Scott, see also Peter T. Murphy, *Poetry as an Occupation and an Art in Britain 1760–1830* (Cambridge: Cambridge University Press, 1993), 142–48, and Fiona Robertson, *Legitimate Histories: Scott, the Gothic, and the Authorities of Fiction* (Oxford: Clarendon Press, 1994), 145.

104 Scott, *Minstrelsy,* 1.4.

105 Lockhart, *Life*, 4.1.10. Compare Scott's own proposal in 1822 that his collected epigraphs be prefaced by a confession that "the Author of Waverley finding it inconvenient to toss over books for a motto generally made one" (*Letters*, ed. Herbert Grierson, 12 vols. [London, 1932–37], 7.103–4, quoted in Susan Manning's notes to *Quentin Durward* [Oxford: Oxford University Press, 1992], 539). However, *The Poetry contained in the Novels, Tales and Romances of the Author of Waverley* (Edinburgh: Constable, 1822) substitutes a rather different prefatory statement about authorship: "we believe by far the greater part of the Poetry interspersed through these Novels to be original compositions by the author. At the same time the reader will find passages which are quoted from other authors ... indeed it is our opinion that some of the following poetry is neither entirely original, nor altogether borrowed; but consists in some instances of passages from other writers, which the Author has not hesitated to alter considerably, either to supply defects of his own memory, or to adapt the quotation more explicitly and aptly to the matter at hand."

106 William Hazlitt, *The Spirit of the Age* (1825; Plymouth: Northcote, 1991), 48. Although Hazlitt names only "the Scotch novels," his later attack on their "editor"'s anonymity makes clear whose are meant.

107 Walter Bagehot, "The Waverley Novels" (1858), in *Literary Studies*, ed. Richard Holt Hutton, 3 vols. (London: Longmans, Green, 1902), 85–126 (124–5); Thomas Carlyle, "Memoirs of the Life of Sir Walter Scott," *London and Westminster Review* 12 (1838): 293–345, reprinted in *Critical and Miscellaneous Essays*, 6 vols. (London: Chapman and Hall, 1888), 6.21–80 (33). Compare the pedantic Dr Folliott in *Crotchet Castle*: "My quarrel with [the Enchanter] is, that his works contain nothing worth quoting; and a book that furnishes no quotations is, *me judice*, no book" (Thomas Love Peacock, *Crotchet Castle*, ed. Raymond Wright [Harmondsworth: Penguin, 1969], 204).

108 *The Genius and Wisdom of Sir Walter Scott, Comprising Moral, Religious, Political, Literary, and Social Aphorisms, Selected Carefully from his Various Writings: With a Memoir* (London: W. S. Orr, 1839), *Beauties of Sir Walter Scott, Bart.: being a selection from his writings and life: comprising historical, descriptive, and moral pieces, lyrical and miscellaneous poetry*, 2nd edn. (Edinburgh: Cadell, 1849), *The Abbottsford Miscellany: A Series of Selections from the Works of Sir Walter Scott* (Edinburgh: Adam and Charles Black, 1855). For albums that use fragments of Scott's prose or verse as captions for engravings, see *Portraits of the Principal Female Characters in the Waverley Novels; to which are added, Landscape Illustrations* (London: Charles Tilt, 1833), *The Waverley Gallery of the Principal Female Characters in Sir Walter Scott's Romances. From Original Paintings by Eminent Artists. Engraved under the Superintendence of Charles Heath* (London, 1841), *Cabinet of Poetry and Romance: Female Portraits from the Writings of Byron and Scott, with poetical illustrations* (London: David Bogue, 1845), and *The Waverley Keepsake: Seventy Engravings from Real Scenes Described in the Novels* (London: David Bogue, 1853); and *The Waverley Poetical Birthday Book*

(London: Eyre and Spottiswoode, 1883), followed by *The Scott Birthday Record, containing extracts for every day in the year*, ed. Douglas R. Campbell (London: Henry Drane, 1897), *The Waverley Proverbial Birthday Book: being a collection of the Proverbs and other Wise Sayings to be Found in the Waverley Novels* (London: Remington, 1890), and *Birthday Chimes: selections from the Poems and Tales of Sir Walter Scott*, ed. W[illiam] T. D[obson] (Edinburgh: Nimmo, 1891). The static images of the albums take to its logical conclusion the use of landscape description to interrupt the plot that Ian Duncan shows at work in *Waverley* itself: *Modern Romance and Transformations of the Novel: The Gothic, Scott, Dickens* (Cambridge: Cambridge University Press, 1992), 87.

109 On the gender of the Waverley novels, see Ina Ferris, *The Achievement of Literary Authority: Gender, History, and the Waverley Novels* (Ithaca: Cornell University Press, 1991).

2 CULTURES OF THE COMMONPLACE

1 Barbara Benedict, *Making the Modern Reader: Cultural Mediation in Early Modern Anthologies* (Princeton: Princeton University Press, 1996), 6, 157–60; Trevor Ross, "Copyright and the Invention of Tradition," *Eighteenth-Century Studies* 25 (1992): 1–27; see also Douglas Lane Patey, "The Eighteenth Century Invents the Canon," *Modern Language Studies* 18 (Winter 1988):17–37, and Julia Wright, "'The Order of Time': Nationalism and Literary Anthologies, 1774–1831," *Papers on Language and Literature* 33 (Fall 1997): 339–65. But Richard Terry warns against overstating the novelty of literary-historical self-consciousness in this period ("The Eighteenth-Century Invention of English Literature: A Truism Revisited," *British Journal for Eighteenth-Century Studies* 19 [Spring 1996]: 47–62), while Marilyn Butler dates the process instead to the 1820s ("Revising the Canon," *Times Literary Supplement* [4 December 1987], 1349). I'm indebted as well to William St. Clair's unpublished lectures on the parameters of the post-1774 canon ("The Reading Nation in the Romantic Period," University of Cambridge, 1999); to John Brewer's analysis of cultural retrospection in *The Pleasures of the Imagination: English Culture in the Eighteenth Century* (London: HarperCollins, 1997), 427–92; and to Peter Uwe Hohendahl's exploration of an analogous case in *Building a National Literature: The Case of Germany, 1830–1870* (Ithaca: Cornell University Press, 1989).

2 Lonsdale argues that Robert Anderson's *Works of the British Poets* (13 vols., 1792–95) and Alexander Chalmers's *Works of the English Poets* (21 vols., 1810) established the principle of excluding anonymous texts as well as the work of living and female poets ("Introduction," *New Oxford Book of Eighteenth-Century Verse*, ed. Roger Lonsdale [Oxford: Oxford University Press, 1984], xxxvi). Andrew Ashfield suggests that the canonization of a generation of recently-deceased poets in the 1770s set a precedent for excluding living poets ("Introduction," *Romantic Women Poets 1770–1838: An Anthology*, ed.

Andrew Ashfield [Manchester: Manchester University Press, 1995], xi). As early as 1784, Vicesimus Knox felt the need to defend his departure from the practice of excluding living poets: see his *Elegant Extracts: or useful and entertaining Passages in Prose Selected for the Improvement of Scholars in Classical and other Schools* (London: Charles Dilly, 1784), v–vi. On the exclusion of the living in later anthologies, see Sabine Haas, "Victorian Poetry Anthologies," *Publishing History* 17 (1985): 51–64 (59).

3   Vicesimus Knox, ed., *Elegant Extracts in Prose, Selected for the Improvement of Young Persons*, 10th edn. (London, 1816).

4   Vicesimus Knox, *Elegant Extracts: or Useful and Entertaining Pieces of Poetry, Selected for the Improvement of Youth in Speaking, Reading, Thinking, Composing; and in the Conduct of Life* (London: C. Dilly, 1784), iv–v. On the subordination of individual taste to the public voice, see also John Barrell, *The Political Theory of Painting from Reynolds to Hazlitt* (New Haven: Yale University Press, 1986), 4, 82, and Leo Damrosch, "Generality and Particularity," in *The Cambridge History of Literary Criticism. Vol. 4: The Eighteenth Century*, ed. H. B. Nisbet and Claude Rawson (Cambridge: Cambridge University Press, 1997), 381–93 (390).

5   Samuel Johnson, "Gray," in *Lives of the Poets*, ed. Arthur Waugh (Oxford: Oxford University Press, 1975), 463. On the relation of this passage to Gray's *Elegy*, see also John Guillory, *Cultural Capital: The Problem of Literary Canon Formation* (Chicago: University of Chicago Press, 1993), 90–91; and, on the origins of Johnson's term, Trevor Ross, "Just When *Did* 'British Bards Begin t'Immortalize?,'" *SECC* 19 (1989): 383–98 (389).

6   Knox, *Extracts . . . Poetry* (1784), vi. The quotation is from *Essais*, 3.12.

7   See also Jonathan Brody Kramnick's argument that Johnson's common reader "is common not in his or her social status but in his or her lack of particular traits (of class, region, gender, and so on)" ("The Making of the English Canon," *PMLA* 112 [October 1997]: 1087–1101 [1098]).

8   Knox, *Extracts . . . Poetry* (1784), v.

9   Knox, *Extracts in Prose* (1816), ii.

10 William Hazlitt, *Select British Poets, or New Elegant Extracts from Chaucer to the Present Time* (London: Wm. C. Hall, 1824), ii, xi. Thanks to Jeffrey Robinson for pointing out the contradiction in the frontispiece; on Hazlitt's model of allusion more generally, see David Bromwich, *Hazlitt: The Mind of a Critic* (New York: Oxford University Press, 1983), 275–88.

11 *The Beauties of Shakespeare, selected from his plays and poems* (London: G. Kearsley, 1783), i; Francis Turner Palgrave, ed., *The Golden Treasury of the Best Songs and Poems in the English Language*, ed. Christopher Ricks (Harmondsworth: Penguin, 1991), 5; Cleanth Brooks and Robert Penn Warren, eds., *Understanding Fiction* (New York: F. S. Crofts, 1943), xiii; William Bennett, ed., *The Book of Virtues* (New York: Simon and Schuster, 1993), 11.

12 "Preface," in Frank Kermode and John Hollander, eds., *Oxford Anthology of English Literature* (New York: Oxford University Press, 1973). See also Guillory's argument that "by suppressing the context of a cultural work's

production and consumption, the school produces the illusion that 'our' culture (or the culture of the 'other') is transmitted simply by contact with the works themselves. But a text tradition is not sufficient in itself either to constitute or to transmit a culture" (*Cultural Capital*, 43).

13 Knox, *Extracts in Prose* (1816), iii. In an earlier preface, Knox bids more explicitly for the widest possible market: "The title-page describes it as compiled for the use of boys. It is very certain that it is not exclusively adapted to boys . . . Such Books as this are calculated to become the companions of all, without distinction of sex, who are in the course of a polite and comprehensive education" (Knox, *Extracts in Prose* [1783], iv).

14 Knox, *Extracts . . . Poetry* (1784), v.

15 William Enfield, ed., *The Speaker: or Miscellaneous Pieces, Selected from the Best English Writers, and disposed under proper heads, with a view to facilitate the improvement of youth in reading and speaking* (London: Joseph Johnson, 1774), xxxii. The patriotic pedantry of the *Speaker* replaced what Enfield later calls "the affectation of introducing foreign words and phrases" (*The Speaker* [London: Joseph Johnson, 1803], xliii). On Enfield's pedagogical career, see P. O'Brien, *Warrington Academy, 1757–86* (Wigan: Owl Books, 1989), 71–72; and for Barbauld's relation to both the Academy and to Enfield's *Speaker*, Guillory, *Cultural Capital*, 101–7.

16 Anna Laetitia Barbauld, *The Female Speaker; or, Miscellaneous Pieces in Prose and Verse . . . Adapted to the Use of Young Women* (London: Joseph Johnson, 1811), iv. Barbauld's subsequent recommendation of Boileau over Virgil makes clear that she is distinguishing not so much English from foreign languages as modern languages from ancient ones. I draw here on Nancy Armstrong's argument that "modern educational institutions continued the project of feminizing the subject as they made what had been a specifically female body of knowledge into a standard for literacy in general" (*Desire and Domestic Fiction: A Political History of the Novel* [New York: Oxford University Press, 1987], 103), as well as Walter Ong's analysis of the relation between classical education and masculinity ("Latin Language Study as a Renaissance Puberty Rite," *Rhetoric, Romance and Technology* [Ithaca: Cornell University Press, 1971]) . On collections of women's poetry in this period, see Greg Kucich, "Gendering the Canons of Romanticism: Past and Present," *Wordsworth Circle* 27 (Spring 1996): 95–102 (which draws a useful distinction between the representation of women in anthologies and miscellanies), and Elizabeth Eger, "Fashioning a Female Canon: Eighteenth-Century Women Poets and the Politics of the Anthology," in *Women's Poetry in the Enlightenment: The Making of a Canon, 1730–1820*, ed. Isobel Armstrong and Virginia Blain (Basingstoke: Macmillan, 1999), 201–15.

17 Vicesimus Knox, ed., *Elegant Epistles: Being a Copious Collection of Familiar and Amusing Letters, Selected for the Improvement of Young Persons, and for General Entertainment* (London: Longman, 1795), iii.

18 Knox, *Extracts in Prose* (1816), iii.

19 See also Trevor Ross's argument that the late-eighteenth-century debate over literary property reflects the conflict described by Pocock between an older conception of civic virtue founded on private possession and an emerging idea of civilization as the result of economic exchange ("Copyright and the Invention of Tradition," 8).

20 Vicesimus Knox, *Winter Evenings, or, Lucubrations on Life and Letters*, 2 vols. (London: Charles Dilly, 1790), 1.7–9. Knox's association of the modern canon with geopolitical expansion already suggests an awareness of the relation between colonialism and canon formation that Gauri Viswanathan has argued in *Masks of Conquest: Literary Study and British Rule in India* (New York: Columbia University Press, 1989).

21 For Knox's biography, see Robert W. Uphaus, "Vicesimus Knox and the Canon of Eighteenth-Century Literature," *The Age of Johnson* 4 (1991): 345–61. It may be worth noting that Enfield's *Speaker* was published by the radical Joseph Johnson.

22 Hannah More, *Coelebs in Search of a Wife*, 2 vols. (London: Cadell, 1808), 1.186.

23 Hannah More, *Strictures on the Modern System of Female Education*, 2 vols. (London: T. Cadell, 1799), 1.7.174–75, 2.26–27; More, *Florio: A Tale, for Fine Gentlemen and Fine Ladies* (London: T. Cadell, 1786). Thanks to Elizabeth Eger for the second reference. On the gender of the detail, see also Naomi Schor, *Reading in Detail: Aesthetics and the Feminine* (New York: Methuen, 1987).

24 C[lara] R[eeve], *The Progress of Romance*, 2 vols. (Colchester: W. Keymer, 1785), 2.98. On the apiary topos, see Ann Moss, *Printed Commonplace-Books and the Structuring of Renaissance Thought* (Oxford: Clarendon Press, 1996), 12–14.

25 Quoted in Allen T. Hazen, "The *Beauties of Johnson*," *Modern Philology* 35 (February 1938): 289–95 (290).

26 Jane Austen, *Northanger Abbey*, in *Complete Novels* (Oxford: Oxford University Press, 1994), 1.5.1086. Barbara Benedict argues that this passage ascribes to miscellanies the improbability and coarseness for which romance is traditionally faulted (*Making the Modern Reader*, 215).

27 Compare Walter Ong's argument that originality could become the highest literary value only once Enlightenment encyclopedism had rendered the commonplace redundant (*Rhetoric, Romance, and Technology*, 255–83). Ann Moss explains the decline of the commonplace over the course of the seventeenth century in rather more nuanced terms by "a growing sense that evidence was empirically and scientifically measurable across a spectrum of probability" as well as "a social code of polite behavior and a consensual aesthetic of good taste which was inimical to its primary qualities of abundance and display" (*Printed Commonplace-Books*, 275–76).

28 Laura Riding and Robert Graves, *A Pamphlet Against Anthologies* (London: Jonathan Cape, 1927), 185.

29 Margaret Ezell, *Writing Women's Literary History* (Baltimore: Johns Hopkins University Press, 1993), 164; that Ezell's plea for teachers to replace the

anthology by the database comes at the end of a richly nuanced analysis of seventeenth- and eighteenth-century anthologies lends it extra poignancy. See, however, Marjorie Perloff's argument that a canon which professes to expand continually strips canonicity of any meaning ("Why Big Anthologies Make Bad Textbooks," *Chronicle of Higher Education* 45 [16 April 1999]: B6–B7 [B6]).

30 See Thomas Bonnell, "Bookselling and Canon-Making: The Trade Rivalry over the English Poets, 1776–1783," *Studies in Eighteenth-Century Culture* 19 (1989): 53–89, and "John Bell's Poets of Great Britain," *Modern Philology* 85 (November 1987): 128–52; Trevor Ross, "The Emergence of 'Literature': Making and Reading the English Canon in the Eighteenth Century," *ELH* 63 (1996): 397–422; and, on the relation between exhaustive series and selective anthologies, Roger Chartier, *The Order of Books*, trans. Lydia Cochrane (Stanford: Stanford University Press, 1994), 68–69.

31 Paul Duguid, "Material Matters: The Past and Futurology of the Book," in *The Future of the Book*, ed. Geoffrey Nunberg (Berkeley: University of California Press, 1996), 63–102 (66).

32 The following pages draw heavily on Gary Taylor, *Reinventing Shakespeare: A Cultural History from the Restoration to the Present* (New York: Weidenfeld and Nicolson, 1989), Jonathan Bate, *Shakespearean Constitutions: Politics, Theatre, Criticism 1730–1830* (Oxford: Clarendon Press, 1989), 183–201, and Michael Dobson, *The Making of the National Poet: Shakespeare, Adaptation and Authorship, 1660–1769* (Oxford: Clarendon Press, 1992); on Margreta de Grazia's argument that over the course of the eighteenth century Shakespearean anthologies changed from a fund of rhetorical commonplaces to "a register of Shakespeare's singular utterances" ("Shakespeare in Quotation Marks," in *The Appropriation of Shakespeare*, ed. Jean I. Marsden [New York: Harvester Wheatsheaf, 1991], 57–72); and, for contemporary Shakespeare editing more generally, on her *Shakespeare Verbatim: The Reproduction of Authenticity and the 1790 Apparatus* (Oxford: Clarendon Press, 1991).

33 Samuel Johnson, "Preface to Shakespeare" (1765), in *Shakespeare Criticism: A Selection*, ed. D. Nichol Smith (London: Oxford University Press, 1949), 77–124 (80).

34 Charles Lamb, "On the Tragedies of Shakespeare, considered with reference to their fitness for Stage Representation" (1811), reprinted in *Shakespeare Criticism*, ed. Smith, 190–212 (193).

35 Jane Austen, *Mansfield Park*, in *Complete Novels*, 3.3.682.

36 *Ibid.*, 1.1.1072–73.

37 *Ibid.*, 1.13.552; see also Gary Kelly, "Reading Aloud in *Mansfield Park*," *Nineteenth-Century Fiction* 37 (1982): 29–49 (42–43).

38 George Eliot, *The Mill on the Floss* (1860; Harmondsworth: Penguin, 1979), 2.1.201, 2.3.236.

39 *A Drunk Man Looks at the Thistle*, in Hugh MacDiarmid, *Selected Poems*, ed. Alan Riach and Michael Grieve (Harmondsworth: Penguin, 1994), 97.

40 Austen, *Mansfield Park*, 1.15.564.

41 Charles, Prince of Wales, *The Prince's Choice: A Personal Selection from Shake-speare* (London: Hodder and Stoughton, 1995); Charles Cowden Clarke, *Tales from Chaucer in Prose, Designed Chiefly for the Use of Young Persons* (London, 1833); Sir Edward Sullivan, *Tales from Scott* (London: Elliot Stock, 1894).

42 Alexander Pope to Jacob Tonson, in *Correspondence of Alexander Pope*, ed. George Sherburn (Oxford: Clarendon Press, 1956), 2.213.

43 Taylor, *Reinventing Shakespeare*, 137; Terence Hawkes, *That Shakespeherian Rag* (London: Methuen, 1986), 77, 86.

44 Elizabeth Macauley, *Tales of the Drama* (Chiswick: C. Whittingham, 1822), vi. See also Julie Stone Peters' argument that the canonization of Renais-sance soliloquies in the eighteenth century reflects their resemblance to novelistic representations of interiority (*Congreve, the Drama and the Printed Word* [Stanford: Stanford University Press, 1990]).

45 "Preface," in Charles [and Mary] Lamb, *Tales from Shakespeare, Designed for the Use of Young Persons*, 2nd edn. (London: M. J. Godwin, 1809), v–xi.

46 Knox, *Winter Evenings*, 2.377.

47 Margaret Anne Doody argues, more specifically, that Lennox inscribes Shakespeare in a female tradition of romance: see "Shakespeare's Novels: Charlotte Lennox Illustrated," *Studies in the Novel* 19 (Fall 1987): 296–307.

48 Thomas Bowdler, ed., *The Family Shakespeare, in which nothing is added to the original text; but those words and expressions are omitted which cannot with propriety be read aloud in a family* (London, 1818), x.

49 Thomas Bowdler, "A Letter to the Editor of the British Critic" (London: Longman, 1823), 16.

50 Thomas Bowdler, ed., *The Family Shakespeare* (London: Longman, 1863), vii.

51 Austen, *Mansfield Park*, 1.15.561, 1.17.571.

52 *Ibid.*, 1.13.552; Knox, *Winter Evenings*, 1.203–5, 1.3.

53 Bowdler, *Family Shakespeare* (1818), x.

54 "Extract from a critique by Lord Jeffrey, in the Edinburgh Review, LXXI," inserted in Thomas Bowdler, ed., *The Dramatic Works of William Shakespeare: Adapted for Family Reading* (London: Griffin, 1861).

55 Marianne Farningham, *Girlhood* (1869), quoted in Kate Flint, *The Woman Reader, 1837–1914* (Oxford: Clarendon Press, 1993), 89.

56 This sexual self-consciousness provides a corollary to Jon Klancher's argu-ment about class-consciousness among turn-of-the-century readers: "His-torically, readers acquired the reading habit by acquiring self-consciousness as members of a particular audience, and after 1790 in England that knowledge could only come from the pressure of adjacent social audiences" (*The Making of English Reading Audiences, 1790–1832* [Madison: University of Wisconsin Press, 1987], 44).

57 Walter Bagehot, "The First Edinburgh Reviewers" (1855), in *Literary Studies*, ed. Richard Holt Hutton, 3 vols. (London: Longmans, Green, 1902), 1.144–87 (175); Thomas Carlyle, *Reminiscences*, ed. J. A. Froude (New York: Scrib-ner's, 1881), 319.

58 William Dodd, *The Beauties of Shakespear: regularly selected from each play. With a general index digesting them under proper heads. Illustrated with explanatory notes, and similar passages from ancient and modern authors* (London, 1752), xvii.

59 Bowdler, "Letter," 32. "Blushes on the cheek of modesty" are, of course, conventionally ascribed to women rather than men; for the trope of the modest girl's cheek, see Ruth Bernard Yeazell, "Podsnappery, Sexuality and the English Novel," *Critical Inquiry* 9 (December 1982): 339–57 (339–43).

60 Bowdler defends this cut (one of the few scenes to be excised in its entirety) on the excuse of narrative unity, but strategically exaggerates Katherine's embarrassment in the process ("Letter," 25).

61 "Preface," in Lamb, *Tales* (1809), ix–x.

62 Ian Michael argues that eighteenth-century anthologists deliberately withheld information about their projected audience: see *The Teaching of English from the Sixteenth Century to 1870* (Cambridge: Cambridge University Press, 1987), 179.

63 On the practice of family reading, see Naomi Tadmor, "'In the even my wife read to me': Women, Reading, and Household Life in the Eighteenth Century," in *The Practice and Representation of Reading in England*, ed. James Raven, Helen Small, and Naomi Tadmor (Cambridge: Cambridge University Press, 1996), 162–74.

64 Vicesimus Knox, "On Novel Reading," *Essays Moral and Literary*, 2 vols. (1778; Dublin: R. Marchbank, 1783), 1.70. See also Peter de Bolla's argument that eighteenth-century theorists associate the virtues of reading aloud with masculinity and the vices of private reading with the feminine (*The Discourse of the Sublime* [Oxford: Basil Blackwell, 1989], 237).

65 Bowdler, *Family Shakespeare* (1861), 37.

66 Beatrice's tomboy antics in Cowden Clarke's leadup to *Much Ado About Nothing* present a more comic view of cross-gendered childhoods, but Cowden Clarke goes so far as to invent a "half-girl" boy cousin for Beatrice in order to redress the balance.

67 In that sense, each reader is made aware of his or her own position on the continuum that Max Horkheimer and Theodor Adorno call "a hierarchical range of mass-produced products of varying quality" (*Dialectic of Enlightenment*, trans. John Cumming [New York: Continuum, 1994], 123).

68 For these terms, see Katie Trumpener's incisive analysis of the tension between the national tale (the work of early-nineteenth-century writers, usually female, usually Irish, who "map developmental stages topographically, as adjacent worlds in which characters move and then choose between") and the more male-dominated historical novel which grows out of it in Scotland, stressing the inevitability of historical change and replacing "the stability of culture in place" by "the fragility of culture over time" (*Bardic Nationalism: The Romantic Novel and the British Empire* [Princeton: Princeton University Press, 1997], 141–42).

69 Austen, *Northanger Abbey*, 1.1.1072–73, and *Emma*, 1.4.784; on the latter

passage, see also Benedict, *Making the Modern Reader*, 218, and Adela Pinch, *Strange Fits of Passion: Epistemologies of Emotion, Hume to Austen* (Stanford: Stanford University Press, 1996), 161. At the other end of Austen's career, *Sanditon* makes Sir Edward into a kind of walking anthology, ridiculous not for his own words but for his use of others'.

70 Ann Radcliffe, *The Mysteries of Udolpho*, ed. Bonamy Dobrée (1794; Oxford: Oxford University Press, 1970), 184, my emphasis; Ann Radcliffe, *The Romance of the Forest*, ed. Chloe Chard (1791; Oxford: Oxford University Press, 1986), 172, my emphasis.

71 See, e.g., chapter 5 of *The Mysteries of Udolpho*, where Radcliffe transposes a singular to a plural in a quotation from Thomson's *Seasons*: "Seating themselves on the short dry turf, they opened the basket of provisions, while / by breezy murmurs cool'd, / Broad o'er *their* heads the verdant cedar waves" (*Udolpho*, 54).

72 On the much rarer converse – quoting prose in poetry – see William Flesch, "Quoting Poetry," *Critical Inquiry* 18 (1991): 42–63.

73 George Moir, from *Treatises on Poetry, Modern Romance, and Rhetoric . . . Contributed to the Encyclopedia Britannica* (Edinburgh: Adam and Charles Black, 1839), excerpted in *The Critical Response to Ann Radcliffe*, ed. Deborah Rogers (Westport: Greenwood, 1994), 135. Put differently, Radcliffe's work makes visible the novel's function as a container for other genres which Bakhtin has argued: see M. M. Bakhtin, "Epic and Novel," in *The Dialogic Imagination*, trans. Michael Holquist and Caryl Emerson (Austin: University of Texas Press, 1981), 3–40 (5). One reviewer compares the intrusiveness of Radcliffe's inscribed poems with that of the landscape descriptions, complaining of

> overcharged descriptions of the beauties of nature, which, however interesting either the scenes themselves, or a delineation of them in descriptive poetry, may be, are impertinent in a work of narration, inasmuch as they call off the reader's attention from the principal objects, and interrupt the emotions which the work is calculated to produce . . . The same observation is strictly applicable to another prevailing defect of many of our modern novelists; a defect into which our fair author has occasionally fallen; we mean the insertion of sonnets and other poetic effusions into the body of the work: these, like the former, either interrupt unnecessarily the progress of the narration, or, what is as bad for the author as the other for the reader, are entirely overlooked; while the same effusions, if published separately, might have added to the writer's profit and fame. (*Monthly Mirror* 3 [March 1797]:155–58, excerpted in Rogers, *Response*, 52–53.)

74 "The mainspring of narrative is precisely the confusion of consecution and consequence, what comes *after* being read in narrative as what is *caused by*; in which case narrative would be a systematic application of the logical fallacy denounced by Scholasticism in the formula of *post hoc, propter hoc*" (Roland Barthes, "Introduction to the Structural Analysis of Narratives" [1966], in Susan Sontag, ed., *A Barthes Reader* [New York: Hill and Wang, 1982], 251–95 [266]).

75 William Enfield, review of *The Mysteries of Udolpho*, *Monthly Review* 15 (November 1794), reprinted in *Novel and Romance, 1700–1800. A Documentary Record*, ed. Ioan Williams (London: Routledge and Kegan Paul, 1970), 395.

76 Anna Laetitia Barbauld, "Mrs. Radcliffe," in *The British Novelists*, 50 vols. (London, 1810), 43.viii. Given Scott's debt to Radcliffe's invention of the inset poem, it comes as no surprise that he leaves ambiguous whether that precedent is expected to please readers or to irritate them: after observing that "songs, sonnets, and pieces of fugitive verse, amuse and relieve the reader in the course of [Radcliffe's] volumes," Scott immediately quotes Mrs. Barbauld's assertion that "the true lovers of poetry are almost apt to regret its being brought in as an accompaniment to narrative" (Sir Walter Scott, *Biographical Memoirs of Eminent Novelists, and other Distinguished Persons*, 2 vols. [1834; Freeport: Essay Index, 1972], 2.384–85).

77 [Thomas Noon Talfourd], "Memoir of the Life and Writings of Mrs. Radcliffe," in *Gaston de Blondeville . . . to which is prefixed a memoir of the author*, 2 vols. (London: Henry Colburn, 1826), 1.1–132 (131).

78 Review of *The Mysteries of Udolpho*, *British Critic* 4 (August 1794): 110–21 (120).

79 [S. T. Coleridge,] review of *The Mysteries of Udolpho*, *Critical Review* 2nd ser. 11 (August 1794): 361–72 (369).

80 Ann Radcliffe, *The Italian* (Oxford: Oxford University Press, 1968), 1.3.37.

81 James Buzard, *The Beaten Track: European Tourism, Literature, and the Ways of Culture, 1800–1918* (Oxford: Clarendon Press, 1993), 125.

82 E. J. Clery, *The Rise of Supernatural Fiction, 1762–1800* (Cambridge: Cambridge University Press, 1995), 97.

83 I borrow the phrase from Peter Brooks, *Reading for the Plot: Design and Intention in Narrative* (New York: Knopf, 1984). See also William B. Warner's argument that the "haunting" of the "legitimate" novel by subgenres like the gothic interminably defers "the consolidation of 'the' novel's institution" (*Licensing Entertainment: The Elevation of Novel Reading in Britain, 1684–1750* [Berkeley: University of California Press, 1998], 292), and Patrick Brantlinger's analysis of the novel's position on the border between high and low culture (*The Reading Lesson: The Threat of Mass Literacy in Nineteenth-Century Britain* [Bloomington: University of Indiana Press, 1998], 14).

84 See Jon Klancher's argument that "the intense cultural politics of the Romantic period obliged writers not only to distinguish among conflicting audiences, but to do so by elaborating new relations *between* the individual reader and the collective audience" (*Making of English*, 11); and, on deferred pleasure as a marker of esthetic legitimacy more generally, Pierre Bourdieu, *Distinction: A Social Critique of the Judgement of Taste*, trans. Richard Nice (Cambridge: Harvard University Press, 1984), 486.

85 Francis Jeffrey, review of *The Giaour*, *Edinburgh Review* 21 (July 1813), reprinted in *The Romantics Reviewed: Byron*, ed. Donald Reiman, 2 vols. (New York: Garland, 1972), 2.842–47 (842); review of *Thalaba*, *Edinburgh Review* 1 (October 1802), 63–83 (70).

86 On servants' garrulity in Radcliffe, see Claudia L. Johnson, *Equivocal Beings: Politics, Gender, and Sentimentality in the 1790s* (Chicago: University of Chicago Press, 1995), 109.

87 The reviewer praises the omission of inset poems from Radcliffe's last novel (also lacking chapter mottoes), where she

> rejected the light poetry with which its predecessors had been so freely interspersed; and she, moreover, kept a stricter rein over her descriptive powers than she ever had done before . . . To the romance, a series of good poems is appended; and there can be few persons of good taste, who will not rejoice at this innovation, on the author's former mode of publishing her poetic effusions. As they are, they are most beautiful; but introduced in a tale, even though forcibly connected with it, they would have been ill-placed, and therefore ill-esteemed; which could not have occurred, without the greatest injustice having been done by some party or other, to their very superior merit. (Review of *Gaston de Blondeville, Scots Magazine* n.s. 18 [1826]:703–4, excerpted in Rogers, *Response*, 71–72 [72])

Here again, the hypothetical "injustice" done by "some party or other" stands opposite the reviewer's own judgment, making it necessary to quarantine the poems from the prose.

88 Elihu Hubbard Smith, letter of 28 June 1796, in *The Diary of Elihu Hubbard Smith*, ed. James J. Cronin (Philadelphia: American Philosophical Society, 1973), 181–82, excerpted in Rogers, *Response*, 26. Disappointment has remained a commonplace of Radcliffe criticism, from Scott's complaint that "Mrs Radcliffe. a mistress of the art of exciting curiosity, has not been uniformly fortunate in the mode of gratifying it" ("Mrs Radcliffe," 376) to George Saintsbury's that "the hair is invited to stand on end only that it may find it as well to settle down again" ("Introduction," *Tales of Mystery* [New York: Macmillan, 1891], xiv–xvii, in Rogers, *Response*, 168).

89 Benedict, *Making the Modern Reader*, 176.

90 See Douglas Lane Patey's argument that the post-Romantic perception of the eighteenth century as a low point in the history of lyric has blinded critics to the fact that this period was the first to define lyric as more poetical than dramatic, epic, or didactic poetry ("Aesthetics and the Rise of the Lyric in the Eighteenth Century," *SEL* 33 [1993]: 587–608 ([593–95]). See also Clery's suggestion that quotations in the gothic allow "high culture authors [to be] invited like fairy godmothers to the christening of this popular culture form" (*Rise of Supernatural Fiction*, 113).

91 One reviewer classes Radcliffe among writers "who are poets in prose, but whose poetry forsakes them the moment they attempt to embody their ideas in verse" (review of *The Poetical Works of Ann Radcliffe, Edinburgh Review* 59 [1834]: 327–41 [337]). George Moir repeats the chiasmus that "she always shews more of the spirit of poetry in her prose" (Moir, *Treatises*, 134). Later, William Dean Howells observes sardonically that Radcliffe's novels "abound in a poetry which makes itself felt nearly everywhere, except in the verse which they also abound in" (*Heroines of Fiction*, 2 vols. [New York: Harper, 1901], 1.83).

92 Susan Ferrier, *Marriage* (1818; ed. Herbert Foltinek, Oxford: Oxford University Press, 1986), 3.18.423; see also Susan Ferrier, *The Inheritance*, 3 vols. (1824; London: Richard Bentley, 1882), 1.27.241.

93 Ferrier, *Marriage*, 1.7.35, 1.10.50, 3.2.321, 3.18.415–23, 3.16.401, 3.16.401, 125.221, 1.27.229, 1.48.426; Susan Ferrier, *Destiny*, 3 vols. (Philadelphia: Carey and Lea, 1831), 2.41.214.

94 Susan Ferrier, *Marriage*, ed. Rosemary Ashton (1841; London: Virago, 1986), 63.287.

95 Ferrier, *Inheritance*, 1.45.391; Friedrich Engels, *The Condition of the Working Class in England* (1845), trans. W. O. Henderson and W. H. Chaloner (Stanford: Stanford University Press, 1968), 273.

96 Ferrier, *Marriage*, 3.2.321; Ferrier, *Inheritance*, 2.15.131. See also Pinch's acute analysis of quotation as a marker of "the tendency of affective life to get located among rather than within people" (*Strange Fits*, 166).

97 Ferrier, *Destiny*, 1.8.26.

98 Compare Roger Lonsdale's argument that "assumptions proper for the reading of [*The Waste Land*] do not necessarily apply to eighteenth-century poetry: that, for example, brief allusions are intended to bring huge cultural perspectives to bear on a poem, or to import entire literary contexts into it, or to achieve complex ironic or atmospheric effects" ("Gray and 'Allusion': The Poet as Debtor," in *Studies in the Eighteenth Century* IV, ed. R. F. Brissenden and J. C. Eade [Canberra: Australian National University Press, 1979], 31–56 [54]). Both of Ferrier's twentieth-century editors complain of the quotations: Rosemary Ashton apologizes for Ferrier's habit of "quoting from contemporary authors rather too often," while Herbert Foltinek dissociates Ferrier's "trite phrases" from her "lively commentary," dismissing the former as "aberrations from her true forte" (Rosemary Ashton, introduction to Ferrier, *Marriage* [1841; London: Virago, 1986], vi, xi; Herbert Foltinek, introduction to Ferrier, *Marriage*, xiv).

99 Peter T. Murphy, "Climbing Parnassus, and Falling Off," in *At the Limits of Romanticism: Essays in Cultural, Feminist, and Materialist Criticism*, ed. Mary A. Favret and Nicola J. Watson (Bloomington: Indiana University Press, 1994), 40–58 (55).

100 Alan Richardson, *Literature, Education, and Romanticism: Reading as Social Practice, 1780–1832* (Cambridge: Cambridge University Press, 1994), 202.

101 The 1841 edition of *Marriage* adds Clavering's initial to two of the poems quoted or read by characters, though not to the inset "History of Mrs Douglas" in 1.14 (2.8.197, 3.18.422).

102 Charles Dickens, *David Copperfield*, ed. Trevor Blount (Harmondsworth: Penguin, 1966), 105. On the growing synonymy of reading with privacy in the nineteenth century, see also Patricia Meyer Spacks, "The Privacy of the Novel," *Novel* 31 (Summer 1998): 304–16.

3 GEORGE ELIOT AND THE PRODUCTION OF CONSUMERS

1 Lewes to John Blackwood, 25 April 1866, in George Eliot, *The George Eliot Letters*, ed. Gordon Haight (New Haven: Yale University Press, 1954–78), 8.374. All subsequent references to Eliot's correspondence will be cited as *Letters* (Haight's edition), Blackwood MSS. (National Library of Scotland), or Beinecke (George Eliot–G. H. Lewes Papers, Yale University).

2 *Zionism: an exposition by George Eliot from Daniel Deronda* (Boston: Zionist Bureau for New England, 1915).

3 *Adam Bede*, ed. Stephen Gill (Harmondsworth: Penguin, 1985), 33.397; [E. S. Dallas], review of *Adam Bede*, *The Times* (12 April 1859): 5. Richard Simpson, too, remarks on Eliot's "proverbs, aphorisms, or apologues, which she either distributes among her commentating characters, such as Mrs. Poyser, or else reserves for herself" ("George Eliot's Novels," *Home and Foreign Review* 3 [October 1863]: 522–49 [534]).

4 Amy Cruse, *The Victorians and their Books* (London: Allen Unwin, 1935), 279.

5 For the drowning fantasy, see John Blackwood to Eliot, 28 October 1871, *Letters*, 5.207.

6 The first edition of the *Sayings* appeared at Christmas 1871; a second, in 1873, was brought up to date by additions from *Middlemarch*; in 1880, a fourth added quotations from *Daniel Deronda* and *Theophrastus Such*. By 1896, the *Sayings* had gone through ten British editions. The *Wit and Wisdom of George Eliot* (Boston: Roberts, 1873) reproduces a shorter (uncredited) selection from Main's *Sayings*.

7 Main to John Blackwood, 3 June 1872 (Blackwood MS. 4294).

8 Alexander Main, ed., *Wise, Witty, and Tender Sayings in Prose and Verse Selected from the Works of George Eliot* (Edinburgh: Blackwood, 1872), ix, my emphasis.

9 Samuel Richardson, *Letters and Passages Restored from the Original Manuscripts of the History of CLARISSA* (London: S. Richardson, 1751), ix, my emphasis.

10 Main liked to harp on the comparison in his letters, repeating that "since Shakespeare left our earth there has appeared no such genius as George Eliot" (to George Simpson, 23 November 1872 [Blackwood MS. 4294]), and that there had been "nothing to match [*Middlemarch*] since William Shakespeare finished 'The Tempest' and laid down his pen" (to John Blackwood, 13 December 1872 [Blackwood MS. 4294]).

11 Main, *Sayings*, 4th edn. (Edinburgh: Blackwood, 1880), 350; George Eliot, *Middlemarch*, ed. W. J. Harvey (Harmondsworth: Penguin, 1965), 13.155; Main, *Sayings*, 294, Eliot, *Middlemarch* 33.349, my emphasis. All further references to the *Sayings* give page numbers from this edition except where otherwise specified.

12 Eliot to Main, 26 January 1872, Eliot, *Letters*, 5.239. Eliot was referring to "The Wit and Wisdom of George Eliot," *Spectator* 13 January 1872: 43–44, which repeated Main's Shakespearean comparison. Later Eliot would criticize Main's *Birthday Book* more directly, complaining of "certain small passages broken from their widely spaced dramatic connection in the

complete novel where they have value as characteristic dialogue over and above their general bearing" (17 December 1877, Eliot, *Letters*, 6.433).

13 This transposition makes it difficult to explain Eliot's encouragement of the anthology, as Rosemarie Bodenheimer does in an otherwise sensitive reading of Eliot's ambivalence, by "the pleasure that she took from a mind that responded directly to the appeals of her narrative voice," for Main's response consisted precisely of denying that Eliot's voice was a narrative one (*The Real Life of Mary Ann Evans: George Eliot, her Letters and Fiction* [Cornell: Cornell University Press, 1994], 245).

14 The *Sayings* include five of the fourteen songs contained in the poem, and forty-eight of the ninety-six epigraphs by Eliot herself. For the collection of songs, see Eliot, *Letters*, 8.425.

15 William Bennett, *The Book of Virtues* (New York: Simon and Schuster, 1993), 171, 182.

16 Main, *Sayings*, x.

17 Main to John Blackwood, 26 September 1874 (Blackwood MS. 4322); Blackwood showed no more interest in this than in any of the other proposals (including an exhaustive study of Scott's *Antiquary*) by which Main tried to turn the Eliot anthology into a stepping-stone for a literary career. Main's desire to bracket Eliot with Browning or Shelley was typical of her admirers: compare, for example, Frederic Harrison's statement that "I find myself taking up [*Felix Holt*] as I take up Tennyson or Shelley or Browning . . . I know whole families where the three volumes have been read chapter by chapter and line by line and reread and recited as are the stanzas of *In Memoriam*" (to Eliot, 19 July 1866, in George Eliot, *Selected Essays, Poems and Other Writings*, ed. A. S. Byatt and Nicholas Warren [Harmondsworth: Penguin, 1990], 241).

18 To William Blackwood, 4 November 1879, Eliot, *Letters*, 7.221. Arnold's *Poems of Wordsworth* appeared in the Golden Treasury series in 1879.

19 Virginia Woolf, "George Eliot," *The Common Reader*, 1st series (London: Hogarth Press, 1984), 162–72 (168). Ironically, Main dedicated his *Conversations of Dr. Johnson* to Mary Cowden Clarke, the author of the feminized and novelized *Girlhood of Shakespeare's Heroines* discussed in chapter 2. Their acquaintance suggests that Cowden Clarke's *Shakespeare Proverbs, or, the Wise Saws of our Wisest Poet Collected into a Modern Instance* (1847) may have supplied one precedent for Main's *Sayings*.

20 George Eliot to John Blackwood, 22 November 1877, Eliot, *Letters*, 6.423.

21 Main to John Blackwood, 5 October 1874 (Blackwood MS. 4322).

22 On the place of lyric in the anthology, see also Alastair Fowler, *Kinds of Literature: An Introduction to the Theory of Genres and Modes* (Cambridge: Harvard University Press, 1982), 231.

23 John Fiske to Mrs. John Fiske, 25 November 1873, Eliot, *Letters*, 5.465.

24 "Felix Holt," *Westminster Review* 86 [July 1866]: 200, quoted in Darrel Mansell, Jr., "George Eliot's Conception of Tragedy," *Nineteenth-Century Fiction* 22 [September 1967]: 155–72 (155); [E. S. Dallas], review of *Mill on the*

Floss, Times [19 May 1860]: 10–11 (10); Thomas Carlyle to the author of *Mary Barton,* 8 November 1848, in Angus Easson, ed., *Elizabeth Gaskell: The Critical Heritage* (London: Routledge, 1991), 72–73 (72); Edward Bulwer-Lytton, "On Certain Principles of Art in Works of Imagination" (1863), in David Skilton, ed., *The Early and Mid-Victorian Novel* (London: Routledge, 1993), 174–75 (174).

25 Main, *Sayings,* x; John Blackwood to William Blackwood, 2 November 1871, Eliot, *Letters,* 5.212.

26 *Telegraph,* 18 June 1872, quoted in Eliot, *Letters,* 5.277–78.

27 For Lewes's unsolicited loan to Main, see his letter of 19 December 1873, Eliot, *Letters,* 5.470.

28 "Wit and Wisdom," 44.

29 Main to Eliot and Lewes, 24 November 1873 and 24 February 1874 (Beinecke). Eliot's letter to Main of 11 September 1871 (quoted below) refers to "the passages which you have quoted from the Fifth Book." I have not found in the Blackwood archive the letter to which Eliot is responding, but since Haight identifies it as one of 31 August devoted to *The Spanish Gypsy* (Eliot, *Letters,* 5.184–85), it seems safe to assume that the quotations to which Eliot refers come from the poem.

30 George Jacob Holyoake, *The History of Co-operation,* 2 vols. (London: Fisher Unwin, 1906), 2.36.544; Lewes to Main, 31 May 1872, Eliot, *Letters,* 5.276. Holyoake misattributes the lines to William Morris, an error not corrected in the second edition even after Eliot called it to his attention: see Eliot, *Letters,* 7.193.

31 John Blackwood to Eliot, 31 December 1871, Eliot, *Letters,* 5.230. Lewes quotes Charles Ritter's reference to Main's "livre exquis qui est devenu mon bréviaire" in a letter to Mrs. William Cross, 15 June 1872, Eliot, *Letters,* 5.282.

32 Main, *Sayings,* 49, 291.

33 Main to John Blackwood, 15 January 1872 (Blackwood MS. 4294).

34 Main to John and William Blackwood, 4 January 1872 (Blackwood MS. 4294).

35 Eliot to Mrs. Peter Alfred Taylor, 17 March 1872, Eliot, *Letters,* 258.

36 On the endorsement of *Pamela* from the pulpit, see T. C. Duncan Eaves and Ben D. Kimpel, *Samuel Richardson: A Biography* (Oxford: Clarendon Press, 1971), 121.

37 Lewes to Main, 5 December 1872 and 26 September 1871, Eliot, *Letters,* 5.192 and 5.337.

38 In 1867, G. H. Lewes gave Antonin Roche permission to include three passages from Eliot's novels in his *English Prose and Poetry, Select Pieces from the Best Authors, for Reading, Composition, and Translation* (Eliot, *Letters,* 8.394). On 21 April 1868, George Eliot gave Carl Adolf Buchheim "full permission to extract from [*The Mill on the Floss*] any passage which he deemed suitable for his selections"; his *German Prose Composition, or Selections from Modern English Writers* (1868) excerpts the last paragraph of the novel (Eliot, *Letters,* 8.415).

And in 1879, William Blackwood forwarded a request from a professor at St. Andrews to include extracts of Eliot's work in a textbook. While Blackwood grumbled that "these compilations are regular robberies," Eliot's reply was surprisingly positive: "I think there is no objection to your giving the desired permission to Professor Meicklejohn, on the condition mentioned – namely that the extracts should be few and not exceeding six pages. Dr. Abbott and Professor Seeley introduced (with my permission) several well-chosen extracts in their 'English Lessons,' and I think that such indications from scholarly and tasteful men are really useful to the works from which they are taken" (William Blackwood to George Eliot, 30 December 1879; George Eliot to Blackwood, 31 December 1879 [Eliot, *Letters*, 7.236–37]). Later collections designed for schoolchildren include *Character Readings from George Eliot*, selected and arranged by Nathan Sheppard (New York: Harper's, 1883).

39 Main to George Simpson, 1 January 1874 (Blackwood MS. 4322).

40 "Examination for first appointments to the Cavalry and Infantry. English Composition," 15 August 1874 (Beinecke Library, Eliot IX.8).

41 *Birthday Greetings: Consisting of Poetical Extracts and Mottoes for Every Day of the Year* (London: Nimmo, 1878).

42 Chapters 7, 9, 27, 36, and 42 of *Felix Holt* and chapters 23, 57, and 60 of *Daniel Deronda* have two epigraphs – often one that is attributed followed by another that is not.

43 In that sense, *The Lifted Veil* could provide an even stronger case than *Middlemarch* for Michal Peled Ginsberg's argument that epigraphs resemble pseudonyms as rejections of origin and authority ("Pseudonyms, Epigraphs, and Narrative Voice: *Middlemarch* and the Problem of Authority," *ELH* 47 [1980]: 542–58).

44 Mary Cholmondeley, *Red Pottage* (1899; London: Virago, 1985), 263; on Cholmondeley's relation to Eliot more generally, see Elaine Showalter, *Sexual Anarchy: Gender and Culture at Fin de Siècle* (1990; London: Virago, 1992), 68. Marianne Novy has uncovered a second work of the 1890s that draws epigraphs from Eliot (one from "How Lisa Loved the King" and another from *Felix Holt*), Anna Julia Cooper's *A Voice from the South* (1892; New York: Greenwood, 1969): see *Engaging with Shakespeare: Responses of George Eliot and Other Women Novelists* (Athens: University of Georgia Press, 1994), 134.

45 "Recent Popular Novels," *Dublin University Magazine* 57 (February 1861): 192–208 (199); [A. C. Dicey], review of *Daniel Deronda, Academy* 10 (9 September 1876): 253–4 (253). Marian Evans herself complained, in a review of R. W. Mackay's *Progress of the Intellect*, that "some of his pages read like extracts from his common-place book, which must be, as Southey said of his own, an urn under the arm of a river-god, rather than like a digested result of study" (*Westminster Review* [January 1851], in Eliot, *Selected Essays*, 268–85 (273).

46 On this notebook (held at Yale), see J. R. Tye, "George Eliot's Unascribed Mottoes," *Nineteenth-Century Fiction* 22 (1967): 235–49 (236).

47 "I should like you to remember for a spring month the motto in *Deronda* beginning 'Fairy folks a-listening', and for a winter month the motto in *Middlemarch* beginning 'Surely the golden hours are turning grey'" (Eliot to Main, 4 December 1877, Eliot, *Letters*, 6.431). On the place of the epigraphs in Main's anthologies, see also David Leon Higdon, "George Eliot and the Art of the Epigraph," *Nineteenth-Century Fiction* 25 (1970): 127–51.

48 Margreta de Grazia, "Sanctioning Voice: Quotation Marks, the Abolition of Torture, and the Fifth Amendment," in Martha Woodmansee and Peter Jaszi, eds., *The Construction of Authorship: Textual Appropriation in Law and Literature* (Durham: Duke University Press, 1994), 288. For a related argument that inverted commas originate as a way of marking translation, see Antoine Compagnon, *La seconde main, ou le travail de la citation* (Paris: Seuil, 1979), 247; and on the ambiguity of the quotation mark, Marjorie Garber, "" " " (Quotation Marks)," *Critical Inquiry* 25 (Summer 1999): 653–79.

49 This absence would confirm Judith Wilt's argument that Scott "was not the novelist novelists used, he was the novelist novelists' characters used" ("Steamboat Surfacing: Scott and the English Novelists," *Nineteenth-Century Fiction* 35 [1981]: 459–86 [460]). Scott appears in the epigraph to chapter fifty-seven of *Middlemarch*, but not as its author, since the motto consists of Eliot's own narrative of children reading him. Here, the epigraph represents reading rather than recording it.

50 Main to John Blackwood, 13 September 1872 (Blackwood MS. 4294). Although Main's proposed index was no more successful than his *Spirit of British Poetry*, the genre remains popular to the present; see, for example, Phyllis Hartnoll, *Who's Who in George Eliot* (London: Hamish Hamilton, 1977), which indexes not only people but dogs and horses. It should be said that the debt of Eliot's editors to Scott's has occasionally been reversed, as when *The Scott Birthday Book* appeared a year after Main's *George Eliot Birthday Book*.

51 See Main to John Blackwood, 13 October 1871 and 13 September 1872 (Blackwood MS. 4279).

52 L. G. Seguin, *A Souvenir of George Eliot. Scenes and Characters from the Works of George Eliot: A Series of Illustrations by Eminent Artists*, with introductory essay and descriptive letterpress by L. G. Seguin (London: Alexander Strahan, 1888). See Ian Duncan, *Modern Romance and Transformations of the Novel: The Gothic, Scott, Dickens* (Cambridge: Cambridge University Press, 1992), 178–80, and Jane Millgate, *Scott's Last Edition* (Edinburgh: Edinburgh University Press, 1987), 89–107.

53 For Scott's masculinization of the novel, see Ina Ferris's *The Achievement of Literary Authority: Gender, History, and the Waverley Novels* (Ithaca: Cornell University Press, 1991).

54 [Eliza Lynn Linton], "George Eliot" (*Temple Bar*, April 1885), reprinted in *Prose by Victorian Women*, ed. Andrea Broomfield and Sally Mitchell (New York: Garland, 1996), 361–76 (374).

55 Eliot to John Blackwood, 18 April 1876, Eliot, *Letters*, 6.241.

56 David Carroll describes the bookmark in "George Eliot: The Sibyl of Mercia," *Studies in the Novel* 15 (1983): 10–25 (11).

57 Eliot to John Blackwood, 22 November 1877, Eliot, *Letters*, 6.423.

58 Lewes to John Blackwood, October 1871, Eliot, *Letters*, 5.195.

59 Eliot to Main, 4 December 1877, Eliot, *Letters*, 6.431.

60 William Blackwood to Eliot, 13 August 1878, Eliot, *Letters*, 7.58. For an analysis of Eliot's relation with the Blackwoods in this period, see John Sutherland, *Victorian Novelists and Publishers* (Chicago: University of Chicago Press, 1976), 188–205.

61 Lewes to William Blackwood, 19 July 1878, Eliot, *Letters*, 7.44.

62 Eliot to John Blackwood, 1 January 1872, Eliot, *Letters*, 5.231.

63 Lewes to Main, 2 January 1874, Eliot, *Letters*, 6.13.

64 Eliot to Main, 4 December 1877, Eliot, *Letters*, 6.431.

65 Lewes to Main, 31 October 1871, Eliot, *Letters*, 5.211.

66 Dicey, *"Daniel Deronda,"* 253.

67 Rosemary Ashton, *George Eliot* (Oxford: Oxford University Press, 1983), 94.

68 For the larger implications of Eliot's anxiety about self-marketing, see Catherine Gallagher, "George Eliot and *Daniel Deronda*: The Prostitute and the Jewish Question," in Ruth Bernard Yeazell, ed., *Sex, Politics, and Science in the Nineteenth-Century Novel* (Baltimore: Johns Hopkins University Press, 1986), 39–62.

69 Eliot, *Middlemarch*, 32.347, 60.653, 60.656.

70 To John Blackwood, 16 June 1874, Eliot, *Letters*, 5.57. Eliot was less apologetic, however, when she told Blackwood that "the two shilling series of Chapman and Hall is among those that make me shudder by the vitiating ugliness of the outside" (22 December 1866, Eliot, *Letters*, 8.393).

71 G. H. Lewes, *Ranthorpe* (London: Chapman and Hall, 1847), 4–5.

72 "It is in the highest sense lawful for [a writer] to get as good a price as he honourably can for the best work he is capable of; but not for him to force or hurry his production, or even do over again what has already been done, either by himself or others, so as to render his work no real contribution, for the sake of bringing up his income to the fancy pitch. In opposition to this, it is common to cite Walter Scott's case, and cry, 'Would the world have got as much innocent (and therefore salutary) pleasure out of Scott, if he had not brought himself under the pressure of money-need?' I think it would" ("Leaves from a Note-book," in George Eliot, *Essays*, ed. Thomas Pinney [London: Routledge and Kegan Paul, 1963], 441).

73 Eliot, *Middlemarch*, 27.302.

74 [William Thackeray], "Our Annual Execution," *Fraser's Magazine* (January 1839), reprinted in *The Oxford Thackeray*, ed. George Saintsbury, 17 vols. (Oxford: Oxford University Press, 1908), 2.359–79 (366). Thackeray suggests elsewhere that the binding itself is all that induces readers to get beyond the cover: "Let us not forget to applaud the India-rubber binding, by aid of which the book opens, and each leaf is displayed in the most satisfactory manner; if any inducement can tempt the reader to peruse the

contents of the *Keepsake*, the writers will surely have to thank Mr. Hand-cock's patent" ("The Annuals," *The Times* [2 November 1838], in *The Oxford Thackeray*, 2.349–58 [355]).

75 Wordsworth quoted in Alison Adburgham, *Women in Print: Writing Women and Women's Magazines from the Restoration to the Accession of Victoria* (London: Allen and Unwin, 1972), 245; Tennyson to William Henry Brookfield, 3 August 1831, quoted in Lee Erikson, *The Economy of Literary Form* (Baltimore: Johns Hopkins University Press, 1996), 41; Southey to G. D. Bedford, 8 December 1828, quoted in Erikson, *Economy*, 30. On the relation between gender, consumerism, and the annuals, see also Peter J. Manning, "Words-worth in the *Keepsake*, 1829" in *Literature in the Marketplace*, ed. John O. Jordan and Robert Patten (Cambridge: Cambridge University Press, 1995), 44–73 (69).

76 Eliot, *Middlemarch*, 27.304.

77 Eliot, *Middlemarch*, 27.244, my emphasis.

78 See, e.g., Henry James, "The Private Life" (1892), in *The Aspern Papers and Other Stories*, ed. Adrian Poole (Oxford: Oxford University Press, 1983), 111.

79 Like the first edition of the *Sayings*, the leather-bound edition of the *Birthday Book* sold for five shillings, but the price of enlarged editions of the *Sayings* jumped to six shillings from 1873 onward, while the clothbound *Birthday Book* was available for only 3s 6d. See Donald Hawes, "George Eliot's 'Sayings'," *George Eliot-George Henry Lewes Studies* 20–21 (September 1992): 49–57 (49).

80 George Eliot, "Silly Novels by Lady Novelists," *Westminster Review* (October 1856), in Eliot, *Selected Essays*, 140–63 (148), my emphasis.

81 Richard Brinsley Sheridan, *The Rivals* (1775), ed. Elizabeth Duthie (New York: Norton, 1979), 1.2.19; Charles Dickens, "Our English Watering-Place," in *American Notes and Reprinted Pieces* (London: Chapman and Hall, n.d.), 167; Thackeray, "Mr. and Mrs. Frank Berry," *Fraser's Magazine* (March 1843), in *The Oxford Thackeray*, 4.328. On Thackeray's satire, see Kate Flint's "Women, Men, and the Reading of *Vanity Fair*," in *The Practice and Representation of Reading in England*, ed. James Raven et al. (Cambridge: Cambridge University Press, 1996), 246–62. This obsession with the marks of female readers' bodies would support Ina Ferris's argument that nine-teenth-century critics associate women's reading with the body rather than the mind *(Achievement of Literary Authority*, 37–39); see also Peter de Bolla's argument that in the eighteenth century, "where the (male) reader was instructed by reading theory to give himself up to the page, to imitate as closely as possible the author, the woman reader in her practice makes every effort to make herself present to the text, within the text" (*The Discourse of the Sublime* [Oxford: Basil Blackwell, 1989], 269). The stereotype of the scribbl-ing female reader was not always negative, however: Kate Flint shows that Victorian advice literature compensated for a fear of female readers' passiv-ity by emphasizing the value of commonplacing, underlining, and note-taking (*The Woman Reader, 1837–1914* [Oxford: Clarendon Press, 1993],

90–96).

82 John Morley, review of J. W. Cross, *George Eliot's Life*, *Macmillan's* 51 (February 1885): 241–56, reprinted in Morley, *Nineteenth-Century Essays*, ed. Peter Stansky (Chicago: University of Chicago Press, 1970), 294–319 (298).

83 "She relishes minute analysis of character and motive, she loves clever dialogue, and cares not a jot whether it furthers the real progress of the story. With the story, on the other hand, man is mainly concerned, and the character-studies, the descriptions of scenery, and the irrelevant chatter he incontinently skips" ("He, She, and the Library List," *Academy* 54 [31 December 1893]: 553); on this passage, see Flint, *Woman Reader*, 182. Lewes, too, opposes female novelists' skill with "sentiment" and "detail" to men's talent for the "construction of plots" ("The Lady Novelists," *Westminster Review* 2 [1852]: 129–41 [133–4]).

84 Eliot, "Silly Novels," 148, 150, 154; Eliot to John Blackwood, 12 November 1873, *Letters*, 5.459; Lewes to Main, 19 February 1874, Eliot, *Letters*, 6.21.

85 Sarah Grand, *The Beth Book* (New York: Appleton, 1897), 500; Arnold Bennett, *Journals*, ed. Newman Flower (New York: Viking, 1932), 5, excerpted in Gordon Haight, ed., *A Century of George Eliot Criticism* (Boston: Houghton Mifflin, 1965), 169; E. A[rnold] Bennett, *Journalism for Women: A Practical Guide* (London: Bodley Head, 1898), 20.

86 [Dallas], review of *Mill on the Floss*, 10.

87 Frederic Harrison, *The Choice of Books and Other Literary Pieces* (London: Macmillan, 1886), 81.

88 Similarly, Woolf uses Main's *Sayings* to describe what classical literature is not: "A people who judged as much as the Athenians did by ear, sitting out-of-doors at the play or listening to argument in the marketplace, were far less apt than we are to break off sentences and appreciate them apart from the context. For them there were no Beauties of Hardy, Beauties of Meredith, Sayings from George Eliot. The writer had to think more of the whole and less of the detail" ("On Not Knowing Greek," *The Common Reader*, 1st series [London: Hogarth Press, 1984], 23–39 [34]). Thanks to Steve Monte for calling this essay to my attention.

89 Carroll, "Sibyl," 17. For the forms of wisdom literature in the nineteenth century, see Robert Preyer, "Victorian Wisdom Literature: Fragments and Maxims," *Victorian Studies* 6 (1963): 245–62.

90 "Our English Watering-Place," 167; Andrew Lang, "Mrs. Radcliffe's Novels," *Cornhill Magazine* n.s. 9 (1900): 24–43, excerpted in Deborah Rogers, ed., *The Critical Response to Ann Radcliffe* (Westport: Greenwood, 1994), 183.

91 Leonard Merrick, *Cynthia*, 2 vols. (London: Chatto and Windus, 1896), 1.29.

92 William M. Thackeray, "The Fashionable Authoress," in *The Oxford Thackeray*, 1.561–76 (570); Thackeray, "Our Annual Execution," 2.359.

93 Eliot, "Silly Novels," 157; Lewes to Main, 19 February 1874, Eliot, *Letters*, 6.21; Eliot to Main, 22 April 1873, Eliot, *Letters*, 5.404.

94 Eliot, *Middlemarch*, 1.29.

95 Eliot, *Middlemarch*, 83.870, 40.435, 43.470–71.

96 To Barbara Bodichon, 2 October 1876, Eliot, *Letters*, 6.290.

97 To John Blackwood, 12 November 1873, *Letters*, 5.459. Susan Meikle speculates that the concern about abstract "sayings" betrayed in this letter may explain Eliot's revision of the Finale of *Middlemarch*: "Fruit and Seed: The Finale to *Middlemarch*," in Anne Smith, ed., *George Eliot: Centenary Essays* (London: Vision, 1980), 181–95 (191).

98 Main to John Blackwood, 13 October 1871 (Blackwood MS. 4279). John Blackwood's letter to Eliot (11 November 1873, Eliot, *Letters*, 5.456) supports this hypothesis: he complains that Main's preface "has put the case rather too strong in favour of his compilation as compared with the Works."

99 See David Carroll's observation that "a sensitivity to the organic emphasizes the possibility and dangers of the inorganic, and in George Eliot's fiction this is always a very present danger" ("'Janet's Repentance' and the Myth of the Organic," *Nineteenth-Century Fiction* 35 [1980]: 331–48 [333]), and Gillian Beer's argument that in *Middlemarch*, the central metaphor of "the web [is] itself a product as much of strain and conflict as of supple interconnection" (*Darwin's Plots: Evolutionary Narrative in Darwin, George Eliot and Nineteenth-Century Fiction* [London: Routledge and Kegan Paul, 1983], 167). A useful corrective to a critical tradition that celebrates Eliot's organicism is J. Hillis Miller's argument that "in place of the concept of elaborate organic form, centered form, form organized around certain generalizable themes, George Eliot presents a view of artistic form as inorganic, acentered, and discontinuous" ("Narrative and History," *ELH* 41 [1974]: 455–73 [468]); but for a counterargument based on a more historically specific model of organicism, see Sally Shuttleworth, *George Eliot and Nineteenth-Century Science: The Make-Believe of a Beginning* (Cambridge: Cambridge University Press, 1984), 149.

100 See Susan Sniader Lanser's forceful argument that "Eliot's professed distrust of quotation and maxim stands in Archimedean tension with her formal practices" (*Fictions of Authority: Women Writers and Narrative Voice* [Ithaca: Cornell University Press, 1992], 83).

101 Hawes, "George Eliot's 'Sayings'," 52. These attacks on "men of maxims" and "general doctrines" reappear not only in the *Sayings* and in Hawes, but in various works of criticism beginning with Q. D. Leavis, *Fiction and the Reading Public* (London: Chatto and Windus, 1932), 257, who invokes it to justify her own scholarly method. For helpful discussions of the two passages, see Carroll, "Sibyl," 21–22, and Mary Jacobus, "Men of Maxims and *The Mill on the Floss*," in *Reading Woman: Essays in Feminist Criticism* (New York: Columbia University Press, 1986), 62–82 (67). Although Jacobus interprets the attack on "men of maxims" as a protest against specifically masculine rules and generalizations, the fact that the passage is immediately followed by Mrs. Glegg's decision to act on a general rule (loyalty to family) rather than responding to a particular case (Maggie's elopement) suggests that Eliot does not ultimately absolve women from the dangers of

the maxim. So does the representation of female readers' taste for "moral remarks" in "Silly Novels by Lady Novelists."

102 Eliot, *Daniel Deronda*, chapter 28.

103 Eliot to John Blackwood, 12 November 1873, Eliot, *Letters*, 5.458.

104 John Blackwood to Joseph Munt Langford, 24 November 1878, Eliot, *Letters*, 7.83; Main to [John Blackwood?], 30 May 1879 (Blackwood MS. 4395).

105 Ruby V. Redinger, *George Eliot: The Emergent Self* (New York: Knopf, 1975), 388, my emphasis.

106 See, e.g., Kate Dickinson Sweetser, *Boys and Girls from George Eliot* (New York: Harper Brothers, 1906), and Amy Cruse, *Stories from George Eliot* (London: Harrap, 1913).

107 Eliot to Main, 13 May 1874 and 19 March 1872, Eliot, *Letters*, 6.49 and 5.261; Lewes to Main, 21 February 1872, Eliot, *Letters*, 5.250.

108 Eliot to John Blackwood, 29 October 1871 and 1 January 1872, Eliot, *Letters*, 5.208, 5.231; see also Eliot to Main, 1 January 1873, Eliot, *Letters*, 5.358.

109 Eliot to Main, 11 September 1871, Eliot, *Letters*, 5.185.

110 Eliot to Main, 28 December 1871, Eliot, *Letters*, 5.229.

111 Eliot to Main, 4 November 1871, Eliot, *Letters*, 5.234.

112 On Eliot's reluctance to authorize dramatic adaptations of *Silas Marner*, see Eliot, *Letters*, 5.368, 8.303; two were eventually produced. For two compelling analyses of the events leading up to Marian Evans's avowal of the pseudonym, see Alexander Welsh, *George Eliot and Blackmail* (Cambridge: Harvard University Press, 1985), 128–31, and Bodenheimer, *Real Life of Mary Ann Evans*, 119–46.

113 Eliot to François d'Albert-Durade, 6 December 1859, *Letters*, 2.231.

114 Eliot to Charles Bray, 25 November 1859, Eliot, *Letters*, 3.214.

115 Eliot to John Blackwood, 16 October 1859, Eliot, *Letters*, 3.184.

116 *Athenaeum*, 2 July 1859, 20, quoted in Eliot, *Letters* 3.109.

117 "Wise, Witty and Tender Sayings of George Eliot," *Westminster Review* 41 (April 1872): 571–2.

118 14 March 1872, Eliot, *Letters*, 5.256. The review welds the two together so seamlessly as to make them indistinguishable to anyone who has not read *Middlemarch* itself: no inverted commas or different type mark Eliot's words off from the reviewer's, and sometimes the two are jostled together in a single sentence, as when the review cuts a quotation off without even a full stop: "Les principes et les scrupules lui faisaient l'effet d'autant d'aiguilles sur lesquelles on tremble de marcher ou de s'asseoir, et Célie avait bien raison; mais il est évident que l'auteur lui trouve un jugement court et borné." Up to "s'asseoir" the paragraph consists of verbatim translation, but only a comma, and no quotation mark, separates this from the reviewer's criticism – confirming Eliot's fear of a review mixing extracts with "matter of [the reviewer's] own" (Th. Bentzon, "Le roman de la vie de province en Angleterre: *Middlemarch*," *Revue des Deux Mondes* 103 [1 February 1873]: 667–90 [674]).

119 [Sir Walter Scott], review of *Tales of My Landlord, Quarterly Review* 15 (January 1817): 430–80, reprinted in John Hayden, *Scott: the Critical Heritage* (London: Routledge and Kegan Paul, 1970), 113–43 (118). See also Robert Mayo's argument that eighteenth-century reviews of fiction functioned effectively as abridgments (*The English Novel in the Magazines, 1740–1815* [Evanston: Northwestern University Press, 1962]), Paul Thomas Murphy's discussion of the role that literary excerpts played in radical nineteenth-century periodicals (*Toward a Working-Class Canon: Literary Criticism in British Working-Class Periodicals, 1816–1858* [Columbus: Ohio State University Press, 1994], 91), and James Engell's analysis of the relation between criticism and the periodical press more generally (*Forming the Critical Mind: Dryden to Coleridge* [Cambridge: Harvard University Press, 1989], 166–70).

120 William Hazlitt, *The Spirit of the Age* (1825; Plymouth: Northcote, 1991), 205. Because Victorian reviews appear in most recent criticism as sources of quotations about specific texts or stray generalizations about literature, a systematic history of the form of the Victorian review (apart from the much-discussed question of anonymity) has yet to be written. Good places to begin, however, include John Woolford, "Periodicals and the Practice of Literary Criticism, 1855–64," in Joanne Shattock and Michael Wolff, eds., *The Victorian Periodical Press: Samplings and Soundings* (Leicester: Leicester University Press, 1982), 109–42; Laurel Brake, "Literary Criticism in Victorian Periodicals," *Yearbook of English Studies* 16 (1986): 92–116; and B. E. Maidment, "Victorian Periodicals and Academic Discourse," in *Investigating Victorian Journalism*, ed. Laurel Brake, Aled Jones, and Lionel Madden (London: Macmillan, 1990), 143–54. Neither Isobel Armstrong's magisterial *Victorian Scrutinies: Reviews of Poetry 1830–1870* (London: Athlone Press, 1972) nor John Hayden's *Romantic Reviewers 1802–24* (Chicago: University of Chicago Press, 1968) focuses on the form of the review, but Nina Baym's *Novels, Readers, and Reviewers: Responses to Fiction in Antebellum America* (Ithaca: Cornell University Press, 1984) suggests a model for a history of the review as an institution, and Frank Donoghue's *The Fame Machine: Book Reviewing and Eighteenth-Century Careers* (Stanford: Stanford University Press, 1996) shows the importance of reviews in eighteenth-century British literary culture more persuasively than does Derek Roper's crudely teleological *Reviewing Before the 'Edinburgh', 1788–1802* (London: Methuen, 1978). See also Ferris's argument that the early-nineteenth-century review resembled the early-nineteenth-century novel in its ambivalent relation to the market (*Achievement of Literary Authority*, 30–31); and, on gender in the review, Nicola Diane Thompson, *Reviewing Sex: Gender and the Reception of Victorian Novels* (New York: New York University Press, 1996).

121 George Eliot, "Thomas Carlyle," *Leader* (27 October 1855), in Eliot, *Selected Essays*, 343–48 (345). The book under review is Thomas Ballantyne's *Passages Selected from the Writings of Thomas Carlyle*.

122 George Eliot, "Margaret Fuller and Mary Wollstonecraft," *Leader* (13 October 1855), in Eliot, *Selected Essays*, 332–38 (338).

123 George Eliot, "Evangelical Teaching: Dr Cumming," *Westminster Review* (October 1855), in Eliot, *Selected Essays*, 38–67 (42).

124 Samuel Taylor Coleridge, *Biographia Literaria*, ed. James Engell and W. Jackson Bate, 2 vols. (1817; Princeton: Princeton University Press, 1983), 1.61.

125 Similarly, John Barrell and Harriet Guest have shown that quoting "beauties" allowed eighteenth-century reviewers at once to bracket the larger political argument of long poems and to define the literary, because although reviews of works from a wide range of genres functioned partly to reproduce quotations, "only in the case of imaginative literature was it not also one of their functions to summarize and comment upon the argument (where there was one) of the work under review" ("On the Use of Contradiction," in Laura Brown and Felicity Nussbaum, eds., *The New Eighteenth Century* [New York: Methuen, 1987], 121–43 [141]). As that which gets reproduced through summary rather than synecdoche, plot functions in nineteenth-century reviews of novels rather as Barrell and Guest sug-gest "argument" does in eighteenth-century reviews of non-literary texts.

126 Edmund Yates, "The Novels of Wilkie Collins," *Temple Bar* 89 (August 1890): 528–32, excerpted in Norman Page, ed., *Wilkie Collins: The Critical Heritage* (London: Routledge and Kegan Paul, 1974), 273–77 (275).

127 T. H. Lister, "Dickens's Tales," *Edinburgh Review* 68 (October 1838), 75–97, in John Charles Olmsted, ed., *A Victorian Art of Fiction: Essays on the Novel in British Periodicals, 1830–1900*, 3 vols. (New York: Garland, 1979), 1.274.

128 [E. S. Dallas], review of *Felix Holt*, *Times* (26 June 1866): 3; [Simpson,] "George Eliot's Novels," 534, my emphasis. Nina Baym suggests that earlier American reviews may have been designed quite consciously as sources for commonplace-books (*Novels*, 122).

129 [John Chapman], review of *The Mill on the Floss*, *Westminster Review* 74 (July 1860): 24–33 (32–33, 29), my emphasis.

130 "Notes on Form in Art," in Eliot, *Selected Essays*, 231–36 (234).

131 *Contemporary Review* 20 (August 1872): 403–22, reprinted in Edward Dowden, *Studies in Literature 1789–1877* (London: Kegan Paul, 1883), 240–72 (241).

132 "Robert Browning's *Men and Women*," *Westminster Review* (January 1856), in Eliot, *Selected Essays*, 349–58 (355). This passage departs from an earlier review in which Evans labels quotations from *Westward Ho!* "specimens" of Kingsley's bad writing ("Westward Ho!" in Eliot, *Selected Essays*, 317). On the status of the "specimen" more generally, see James Chandler, *England in 1819: The Politics of Literary Culture and the Case of Romantic Historicism* (Chicago: University of Chicago Press, 1998), 156–57.

133 [Dallas], review of *Mill on the Floss*, 11.

134 "Central Criminal Court, October 31," *Times* (1 November 1888), p. 13.

135 See Peter Keating, *The Haunted Study: A Social History of the English Novel 1875–1914* (London: Secker and Warburg, 1989), 245–47.

136 Eliot, *Middlemarch*, 890.

137 [R. H. Hutton], "The Humour of *Middlemarch*," *Spectator* (14 December 1872): 182–83, reprinted in R. H. Hutton, *A Victorian Spectator: Uncollected Writings of R. H. Hutton*, ed. Robert Tener and Malcolm Woodfield (Bristol: Bristol Press, 1991), 197–202 (197).

138 [Dinah Mulock], review of *The Mill on the Floss*, *Macmillan's* 3 (April 1861): 441–48 (443), my emphasis.

139 [Henry James], review of *Felix Holt*, *Nation* 3 (16 August 1866): 127–8 (127); [A.V. Dicey], review of *Middlemarch*, *Nation* 16, excerpted in David Carroll, ed., *George Eliot: The Critical Heritage* (London: Routledge, 1971), 339–52 (346). My thinking about George Eliot's reception owes a lot to Carroll's suggestive anthology, whose argument about Eliot's sententiousness (explicit in the preface and implicit in its selections) is subtler than that of J. Russell Perkin's survey *A Reception-History of George Eliot's Fiction* (Rochester: University of Rochester Press, 1995).

140 Edwin Eigner and George Worth, *Victorian Criticism of the Novel* (Cambridge: Cambridge University Press, 1985), 5. Nina Baym argues that the 1840s drop in book prices in the United States caused the length of extracts to decrease as reviews ceased to be needed as a cheap substitute (*Novels*, 19).

141 *Monthly Review* 1 [August 1749]: 270, quoted in Donoghue, *Fame Machine*, 183; "The Works of Charles Lamb," *Blackwood's* 3 (August 1818): 601.

142 [Francis Jeffrey], review of *The Excursion*, *Edinburgh Review* 24 (November 1814), quoted in John O. Hayden, ed., *Romantic Bards and British Reviewers*, (London: Routledge and Kegan Paul, 1971), 39–52 (51); John Stoddart, review of William Wordsworth and S. T. Coleridge, *Lyrical Ballads*, *British Critic* 17 (February 1801), 125–31, quoted in *Lyrical Ballads*, ed. R. L. Brett and A. R. Jones (London: Routledge, 1991), 332. Compare the conversation of two characters in *Ranthorpe*: "'You mislead the public if you speak of a work as if its few merits were samples of the whole.' 'And,' rejoined Rixelton, 'does it not still more grossly mislead the public when a few faults are dwelt on as if they were samples of the whole?'"(35).

143 Barbara Johnson, *The Critical Difference: Essays in the Contemporary Rhetoric of Reading* (Baltimore: Johns Hopkins University Press, 1980), 111. See also Bakhtin's more general observation that "in the humanities – as distinct from the natural and mathematical sciences – there arises the specific task of establishing, transmitting, and interpreting the words of others (for example, the problem of sources in the methodology of the historical disciplines)" (M. M. Bakhtin, "Discourse in the Novel," in *The Dialogic Imagination*, trans. Michael Holquist and Caryl Emerson [Austin: University of Texas Press, 1981], 259–422 [351]).

144 James Boswell, *The Life of Samuel Johnson*, ed. R. W. Chapman (Oxford: Oxford University Press, 1980), 1230.

145 [Dicey], "*Middlemarch*," 351.

146 Henry James, '*Daniel Deronda*: A Conversation," *Atlantic Monthly* (December 1876), reprinted in Henry James, *The Critical Muse: Selected Literary Criticism*,

ed. Roger Gard (Harmondsworth: Penguin, 1987), 104–22 (113–14, 105);
Eliot, *Middlemarch*, 27.297.
147 Saintsbury, review of *Daniel Deronda*, *Academy* 10 (9 September 1876): 253–54
(253); [Dicey], "*Middlemarch*," 351; [Dallas], "*Adam Bede*," 5.
148 W. C. Brownell, *Victorian Prose Masters* (1901), excerpted in Gordon Haight,
ed., *A Century of George Eliot Criticism* (Boston: Houghton Mifflin, 1965),
170–80 (176).
149 Review of *Scenes of Clerical Life*, *Saturday Review* 5 (29 May 1858): 566–67
(567).
150 Edward Dowden, "The Interpretation of Literature," *Contemporary Review*
49 (May 1886): 701–19 (714); George Meredith, *The Pilgrim's Scrip: or, Wit and
Wisdom of George Meredith, with selections from his poetry* (Boston: Roberts, 1888),
xxvii; George Meredith, *The George Meredith Birthday Book*, ed. D[aisy]
M[eredith] (London: Archibald Constable, 1898). Compare Eliza Lynn
Linton's attack on Eliot's late novels for overdoing the "ponderous pedantry which, in the beginning and when sparingly used, had been like salt
to a roast, or a point of colour in a picture" ("George Eliot," 366).
151 Anthony Trollope, *An Autobiography*, ed. Michael Sadleir and Frederick
Page (Oxford: Oxford University Press, 1980), 218; Anthony Trollope, *Four
Lectures*, ed. Morris L. Parrish (London: Constable, 1938), 85.
152 Henry James, "The Art of Fiction" (1888) in Henry James, *The Art of Fiction
and other Essays* (New York: Oxford University Press, 1948), 3–23.
153 *Lady's Magazine* 43 (1812): 222, quoted in Ferris, *Achievement*, 38–39. The
comparison of fiction with sweets is conventional: Clara Reeve writes that
"a person used to [circulating-library novels] will be disgusted with every
thing serious or solid, as a weakened and depraved stomach rejects plain
and wholesome food" (*The Progress of Romance*, 2 vols. [Colchester: W.
Keymer, 1785], 2.79), and Vicesimus Knox advises against novel reading
because "when the sweetened poison is removed, plain and wholesome
food will always be relished" (*Essays Moral and Literary*, 3 vols. [1788; Dublin:
R. Marchbank, 1783], 1.71).
154 "Recent Popular Novels," 196.
155 "The Theory of Fiction," *Tinsley's Magazine* 13 (1873): 88–92, quoted in
Kenneth Graham, *English Criticism of the Novel 1865–1900* (Oxford: Clarendon Press, 1965), 72; John Blackwood to Eliot, 8 September 1872 and 8
February 1877, Eliot, *Letters* 5.307, 6.340; Blackwood to Main, 13 November
1873, Eliot, *Letters*, 5.460. Compare Isobel Armstrong's observation that
"however much they were preoccupied with the moral function of poetry,
critics almost invariably disclaimed didactic theory" (*Victorian Scrutinies*, 11).
156 Review of *Desperate Remedies*, *Saturday Review* 32 (30 September 1871): 441–
42, excerpted in R. G. Cox, ed., *Thomas Hardy: The Critical Heritage* (London:
Routledge and Kegan Paul, 1970), 6–8 (7); review of *Far from the Madding
Crowd*, *Saturday Review* 39 (9 January 1875): 57–58, excerpted in Cox, *Thomas
Hardy*, 39–45 (41); review of *Far from the Madding Crowd*, *Academy* 7 (2 January
1875): 9, excerpted in Cox, *Thomas Hardy*, 35–39 (36); "Concerning *Jude the*

196 *Notes to pages 150–53*

Obscure," Savoy Magazine (October 1896): 35–49, excerpted in Cox, *Thomas Hardy*, 300–15 (305).

157 "The Uses of Fiction," *Tinsley's Magazine* 6 (March 1870): 180–85, reprinted in Olmsted, *A Victorian Art of Fiction*, 3.3–8 (8).

158 David Masson, *British Novelists and Their Styles* (Cambridge: Macmillan, 1859), 308.

159 "Modern Novelists: Sir Edward Bulwer-Lytton," *Westminster Review* 27 (1865): 482–83, quoted in Graham, *English Criticism*, 86.

160 William Enfield, review of *The Mysteries of Udolpho, Monthly Review* 15 (November 1794), reprinted in Ioan Williams, ed., *Novel and Romance, 1700–1800. A Documentary Record* (London: Routledge and Kegan Paul, 1970), 395; review of *Gaston de Blondeville, Scots Magazine* n.s. 18 (1826): 703–4, excerpted in Rogers, *Critical Response*, 71–72 (72).

161 "Recent Popular Novels," 200; Walter Allen, *George Eliot* (London: Weidenfeld and Nicolson, 1965), 89, my italics.

162 Edith Jemima Simcox, "Women's Work and Women's Wages" (*Longman's Magazine*, July 1887), reprinted in Andrea Broomfield and Sally Mitchell, eds., *Prose by Victorian Women*, 565–82 (566).

163 Reviewers' move from condemning readers' taste for plot to attacking writers' taste for maxims may also reflect the shift that John Woolford has identified from early-nineteenth-century reviewers siding with readers against writers to late-nineteenth-century reviewers doing just the reverse ("Periodicals," 109–42).

164 See Gaye Tuchman with Nina E. Fortin, *Edging Women Out: Victorian Novelists, Publishers, and Social Change* (New Haven: Yale University Press, 1989).

165 Compare, for instance, criticism of Eliot for reducing the novel to a "vehicle" for "preaching" with the *Athenaeum*'s complaint that "it is no good expostulating with Sarah Grand about having a purpose in the sense of a doctrine to preach in her novels; she would say quite frankly that she cares nothing about novel-writing as an art, except in so far as it can be used as a vehicle for her doctrines" (*Athenaeum* [2 November 1897]: 393, quoted and discussed in Teresa Mangum, "Style Wars of the 1890s: The New Woman and the Decadent," in *Transforming Genre: New Approaches to British Fiction of the 1890s*, ed. Nikki Lee Manos and Meri-Jane Rochelson [New York: St. Martin's, 1994], 47–66 [48]).

166 Graham Martin, "*The Mill on the Floss* and the Unreliable Narrator," in Smith, *George Eliot*, 36–54 (37); W. J. Harvey, *The Art of George Eliot* (Oxford: Oxford University Press, 1969), 81. For an incisive critique of Martin's argument, see Bodenheimer, *Real Life*, 274–75. Isobel Armstrong challenges Harvey by arguing (like Dowden) that "the sayings can be detached from the novel" and that, far from inviting us to read more quickly, "the sage-like, discursive generalizations . . . slow down the novel in an almost processional way" (Isobel Armstrong, "*Middlemarch*: A Note on George Eliot's 'Wisdom,'" in *Critical Essays on George Eliot*, ed. Barbara Hardy

[London: Routledge and Kegan Paul, 1970]: 116–32 [116]). See also Lanser's argument that "postmodern critics who want to emphasize Eliot's deconstruction of authoritative discourse, and feminist critics who value women writers precisely for their rejection of authority as 'masculine,' seem to me to be overlooking the degree to which the rhetoric of Eliot's fiction arrogates authority in a project designed precisely to construct a narrative hegemony" (*Fictions*, 83); and J. P. Hunter's more general argument that "the penchant of critics to treat novels almost altogether in narrative terms, ignoring the non-narrative parts" has falsified our understanding of the eighteenth-century novel (*Before Novels* [New York: Norton, 1990], 54). Catherine Gallagher ruthlessly demolishes received ideas about the novel's subordination of the general to the particular in "George Eliot, Immanent Victorian," *Proceedings of the British Academy* 94 (1996): 157–72.

167 James, *"Daniel Deronda*: A Conversation," 109; Dorothea Barrett, *Vocation and Desire: George Eliot's Heroines* (London: Routledge, 1989), 3, 5.

168 Harvey, *Art*, 80.

169 Carroll, "Introduction," *Critical Heritage*, 32.

170 Stanley Fish, *Is There a Text in this Class?* (Cambridge: Harvard University Press, 1980), 178.

171 Lewes to John Blackwood, 25 April 1866, Eliot, *Letters* 8.374; Wilkie Collins, "The Unknown Public," *My Miscellanies* (New York: Harper, 1874), 126–42. For a suggestive analysis of novelists' fear of the mass public, see Patrick Brantlinger, *The Reading Lesson: The Threat of Mass Literacy in Nineteenth-Century Britain* (Bloomington: University of Indiana Press, 1998); on the changing position of literary fans in the 1890s, Margaret Diane Stetz, "Life's 'Half-profits': Writers and their Readers in Fiction of the 1890s," in *Nineteenth-Century Lives*, ed. Laurence S. Lockridge et al. (Cambridge: Cambridge University Press, 1989), 169–87; and, on the porous boundary separating production from reception, David Simpson's "Public Virtues, Private Vices: Reading Between the Lines of Wordsworth's 'Anecdote for Fathers'," in *Subject to History*, ed. David Simpson (Ithaca: Cornell University Press, 1991), 163–90 (176–77).

172 Pascal's aphorism forms the epigraph to Paul de Man, *Allegories of Reading: Figural Language in Rousseau, Nietzsche, Rilke and Proust* (New Haven: Yale University Press, 1979).

173 Ian Watt, *The Rise of the Novel: Studies in Defoe, Richardson, and Fielding* (Berkeley: University of California Press, 1957). This dynamic would confirm Roger Chartier's argument that the expansion of literacy lends significance to distinctions between different modes of reading: see *The Order of Books* (Stanford: Stanford University Press, 1994), 16. On the late-nineteenth-century divergence of high culture from mass art, see Andreas Huyssen, *After the Great Divide: Modernism, Mass Culture, Postmodernism* (Bloomington: Indiana University Press, 1986).

Bibliography

Abridgments and anthologies are listed under the editor's name, where known. Those for which I have been unable to identify an editor are listed by the author of their raw material (for abridgments and single-author anthologies) or by title (for those that compile the work of more than one author).

Abrams, M. H. et al., eds. *The Norton Anthology of English Literature*. 6th edn. New York: Norton, 1993.

Adburgham, Alison. *Women in Print: Writing Women and Women's Magazines from the Restoration to the Accession of Victoria*. London: Allen and Unwin, 1972.

Aikin, Janet. "'A Plot Discover'd'; or, the Uses of *Venice Preserv'd* within *Clarissa*." *University of Toronto Quarterly* 55 (Spring 1986): 219–34.

Allen, Walter. *George Eliot*. London: Weidenfeld and Nicolson, 1965.

Alliston, April. *Virtue's Faults: Correspondences in Eighteenth-Century British and French Women's Fiction*. Stanford: Stanford University Press, 1996.

Altick, Richard D. *The English Common Reader: A Social History of the Mass Reading Public 1800–1900*. Chicago: University of Chicago Press, 1957.

Altman, Janet Gurkin. *Epistolarity: Approaches to a Form*. Columbus: Ohio State University Press, 1982.

Analyse des ouvrages de Jean-Jacques Rousseau, de Genève, et de M. Court de Gebelin, Auteur du Monde primitif, par un solitaire. Genève: B. Chirol, 1785.

Armstrong, Isobel. "*Middlemarch*: A Note on George Eliot's 'Wisdom'." In *Critical Essays on George Eliot*, ed. Barbara Hardy. London: Routledge and Kegan Paul, 1970, 116–32.

Victorian Scrutinies: Reviews of Poetry 1830–1870. London: Athlone Press, 1972.

Armstrong, Nancy. *Desire and Domestic Fiction: A Political History of the Novel*. New York: Oxford University Press, 1987.

Ashfield, Andrew, ed. *Romantic Women Poets 1770–1838: An Anthology*. Manchester: Manchester University Press, 1995.

Ashton, Rosemary. *George Eliot*. Oxford: Oxford University Press, 1983.

Austen, Jane. *Complete Novels*. Oxford: Oxford University Press, 1994.

Bagehot, Walter. *Literary Studies*. 3 vols. Ed. Richard Holt Hutton. London: Longmans, Green, 1902.

Bakhtin, M. M. *The Dialogic Imagination*. Trans. Michael Holquist and Caryl Emerson. Austin: University of Texas Press, 1981.

Barbauld, Anna Laetitia, ed. *The British Novelists*. 50 vols. London: Rivington, 1810.

The Female Speaker; or, Miscellaneous Pieces in Prose and Verse . . . Adapted to the Use of Young Women. London: Joseph Johnson, 1811.

Barrell, John. *The Political Theory of Painting from Reynolds to Hazlitt*. New Haven: Yale University Press, 1986.

Barrell, John, and Harriet Guest. "On the Use of Contradiction." In Laura Brown and Felicity Nussbaum, eds. *The New Eighteenth Century*. New York: Methuen, 1987, 121–43.

Barrett, Dorothea. *Vocation and Desire: George Eliot's Heroines*. London: Routledge, 1989.

Barthes, Roland. *Image-Music-Text: Essays*. Trans. Stephen Heath. New York: Hill and Wang, 1977.

"Introduction to the Structural Analysis of Narratives." In *A Barthes Reader*, ed. Susan Sontag. New York: Hill and Wang, 1982, 251–95.

"La Rochefoucauld: 'Réflexions ou Sentences et Maximes'." *Nouveaux essais critiques*. Paris: Seuil, 1972, 69–87.

"Reflections on a Manual." Trans. Sandy Petrey. *PMLA* 112 (January 1997): 72–75.

S/Z. Trans. Richard Miller. Oxford: Blackwell, 1990.

Bartolomeo, Joseph F. *A New Species of Criticism: Eighteenth-Century Discourse on the Novel*. Newark: University of Delaware Press, 1994.

Bate, Jonathan. *Shakespearean Constitutions: Politics, Theatre, Criticism, 1730–1830*. Oxford: Clarendon Press, 1989.

Baym, Nina. *Novels, Readers, and Reviewers: Responses to Fiction in Antebellum America*. Ithaca: Cornell University Press, 1984.

Beckford, William. *Azemia: A Descriptive and Sentimental Novel; Interspersed with Pieces of Poetry . . . To which are added, Criticisms Anticipated*. London: Sampson Low, 1797.

Modern Novel Writing; or, the Elegant Enthusiast . . . A Rhapsodical Romance; Interspersed with Poetry. London: Robinson, 1796.

Beebee, Thomas O. *Clarissa on the Continent. Translation and Seduction*. University Park: Penn State University Press, 1990.

The Ideology of Genre: A Comparative Study of Generic Instability. University Park: Penn State University Press, 1994.

Beer, Gillian. *Darwin's Plots: Evolutionary Narrative in Darwin, George Eliot and Nineteenth-Century Fiction*. London: Routledge and Kegan Paul, 1983.

"Origins and Oblivion in Victorian Narrative." In *Sex, Politics, and Science in the Nineteenth-Century Novel*, ed. Ruth Bernard Yeazell. Baltimore: Johns Hopkins University Press, 1986, 63–87.

"Richardson, Milton, and the Status of Evil." *Review of English Studies* n.s. 19 (1968): 261–70.

Benedict, Barbara. *Making the Modern Reader: Cultural Mediation in Early Modern*

Anthologies. Princeton: Princeton University Press, 1996.

Bennett, E. A[rnold]. *Journalism for Women: A Practical Guide*. London: Bodley Head, 1898.

Bennett, William. *The Book of Virtues*. New York: Simon and Schuster, 1993.

Bennington, Geoffrey. *Sententiousness and the Novel: Laying Down the Law in Eighteenth-Century French Fiction*. Cambridge: Cambridge University Press, 1985.

Bentzon, T. "Le roman de la vie de province en Angleterre: *Middlemarch.*" *Revue des Deux Mondes* 103 (1 February 1873): 667–90.

Benveniste, Emile. *Problèmes de linguistique générale*. Paris: Gallimard, 1966.

Birthday Greetings: Consisting of Poetical Extracts and Mottoes for Every Day of the Year. London: Nimmo, 1878.

Blackwood MSS. National Library of Scotland.

Bodenheimer, Rosemarie. *The Real Life of Mary Ann Evans: George Eliot, her Letters and Fiction*. Cornell: Cornell University Press, 1994.

de Bolla, Peter. *The Discourse of the Sublime*. Oxford: Basil Blackwell, 1989.

Bonnell, Thomas. "Bookselling and Canon-Making: The Trade Rivalry over the English Poets, 1776–1783." *Studies in Eighteenth-Century Culture* 19 (1989): 53–89.

"John Bell's Poets of Great Britain." *Modern Philology* 85 (November 1987): 128–52.

Boswell, James. *The Life of Samuel Johnson*. Ed. R. W. Chapman. Oxford: Oxford University Press, 1980.

Bourdieu, Pierre. *Distinction: A Social Critique of the Judgement of Taste*. Trans. Richard Nice. Cambridge: Harvard University Press, 1984.

The Field of Cultural Production: Essays on Art and Literature. Ed. Randal Johnson. New York: Columbia University Press, 1994.

[Bowdler, Henrietta], ed. *The Family Shakespeare*. Bath: Thomas Crutwell, 1807.

Bowdler, Thomas, ed. *The Family Shakespeare, in which nothing is added to the original text; but those words and expressions are omitted which cannot with propriety be read aloud in a family*. London, 1818.

ed. *The Family Shakespeare*. London: Longman, 1863.

ed. *The Dramatic Works of William Shakespeare: Adapted for Family Reading*. London: Griffin, 1861.

"A Letter to the Editor of the British Critic." London: Longman, 1823.

Brake, Laurel. "Literary Criticism in Victorian Periodicals." *Yearbook of English Studies* 16 (1986): 92–116.

Brantlinger, Patrick. *The Reading Lesson: The Threat of Mass Literacy in Nineteenth-Century Britain*. Bloomington: University of Indiana Press, 1998.

Brewer, John. *The Pleasures of the Imagination: English Culture in the Eighteenth Century*. London: HarperCollins, 1997.

Bromwich, David. *Hazlitt: The Mind of a Critic*. New York: Oxford University Press, 1983.

Brooks, Cleanth. "The Heresy of Paraphrase" (1947). In *Critical Theory since Plato*, ed. Hazard Adams. New York: Harcourt Brace Jovanovich, 1971, 1033–41.

Brooks, Cleanth, and Robert Penn Warren, eds. *Understanding Fiction.* New York: F. S. Crofts, 1943.

Brooks, Peter. *Reading for the Plot: Design and Intention in Narrative.* New York: Knopf, 1984.

Brown, Homer Obed. *Institutions of the English Novel from Defoe to Scott.* Philadelphia: University of Pennsylvania Press, 1997.

Burrell, John Angus, abridger. *Clarissa.* By Samuel Richardson. New York: Random House, 1950.

Butler, Marilyn. "Culture's Medium: the Role of the Review." In *The Cambridge Companion to Romanticism,* ed. Stuart Curran. Cambridge: Cambridge University Press, 1993, 120–47.

"Revising the Canon." *Times Literary Supplement* 4 December 1987: 1349.

Buzard, James. *The Beaten Track: European Tourism, Literature, and the Ways of Culture, 1800–1918.* Oxford: Clarendon Press, 1993.

Bysshe, Edward, ed. *The Art of English Poetry.* 3rd edn. London: Samuel Buckley, 1708.

Cabinet of Poetry and Romance: Female Portraits from the Writings of Byron and Scott, with poetical illustrations. London: David Bogue, 1845.

Campbell, Douglas R., ed. *The Scott Birthday Record, containing extracts for every day in the year.* London: Henry Drane, 1897.

Carlyle, Thomas. *Critical and Miscellaneous Essays.* 6 vols. London: Chapman and Hall, 1888.

Carroll, David. "George Eliot: The Sibyl of Mercia." *Studies in the Novel* 15 (1983): 10–25.

"'Janet's Repentance' and the Myth of the Organic." *Nineteenth-Century Fiction* 35 (1980): 331–48.

ed. *George Eliot: The Critical Heritage.* London: Routledge, 1971.

Carroll, John. "Richardson at Work: Revisions, Allusions, and Quotations in *Clarissa.*" In *Studies in the Eighteenth Century II,* ed. R. F. Brissenden. Canberra: Australian National University Press, 1973, 53–72.

Castle, Terry. *Clarissa's Ciphers: Meaning and Disruption in Richardson's "Clarissa".* Ithaca: Cornell University Press, 1982.

Certeau, Michel de. *The Practice of Everyday Life.* Trans. Stephen F. Rendall. Berkeley: University of California Press, 1984.

Chandler, James. *England in 1819: The Politics of Literary Culture and the Case of Romantic Historicism.* Chicago: University of Chicago Press, 1998.

[Chapman, John]. Review of *The Mill on the Floss. Westminster Review* 74 (July 1860): 24–33.

Charles, Prince of Wales. *The Prince's Choice: A Personal Selection from Shakespeare.* London: Hodder and Stoughton, 1995.

Chartier, Roger. *The Order of Books.* Trans. Lydia Cochrane. Stanford: Stanford University Press, 1994.

Cholmondeley, Mary. *Red Pottage.* 1899. London: Virago, 1985.

Clery, E. J. *The Rise of Supernatural Fiction, 1762–1800.* Cambridge: Cambridge University Press, 1995.

Coleridge, Samuel Taylor. *Biographia Literaria*. 1817. Ed. James Engell and W.
    Jackson Bate. Princeton: Princeton University Press, 1983.
Collins, Wilkie. *My Miscellanies*. New York: Harper, 1874.
Compagnon, Antoine. *La seconde main, ou le travail de la citation*. Paris: Seuil,
    1979.
Connaughton, Michael E. "Richardson's Familiar Quotations: *Clarissa* and
    Bysshe's *Art of English Poetry*." *Philological Quarterly* 60 (1981): 183–95.
Cook, Elizabeth Heckendorn. *Epistolary Bodies: Gender and Genre in the Eighteenth-
    Century Republic of Letters*. Stanford: Stanford University Press, 1996.
Cope, Kevin L. "Richardson the Advisor." In *New Essays on Samuel Richardson*,
    ed. Albert J. Rivero. New York: St Martin's Press, 1996, 17–34.
Court, Franklin E. *Institutionalizing English Literature. The Culture and Politics of
    Literary Study 1750–1900*. Stanford: Stanford University Press, 1992.
Cowden Clarke, Charles. *Tales from Chaucer in Prose, Designed Chiefly for the Use of
    Young Persons*. London, 1833.
Cowden Clarke, Mary. *The Girlhood of Shakespeare's Heroines in a Series of Fifteen
    Tales*. London: W. H. Smith, 1850–52.
Cox, R. G., ed. *Thomas Hardy: The Critical Heritage*. London: Routledge and
    Kegan Paul, 1970.
Crane, Mary Thomas. *Framing Authority: Sayings, Self, and Society in Sixteenth-
    Century England*. Princeton: Princeton University Press, 1993.
Crawford, Robert. *Devolving English Literature*. Oxford: Clarendon Press, 1992.
Cross, J. W. *George Eliot's Life as Related in her Letters and Journals*. New York:
    Harper, 1885.
Cruse, Amy. *Stories from George Eliot*. London: Harrap, 1913.
    The Victorians and their Books. London: Allen and Unwin, 1935.
Culler, A. Dwight. "Edward Bysshe and the Poet's Handbook." *PMLA* 63
    (1948): 865–85.
Dallas, E. S., ed. [and abridger]. *Clarissa*. By Samuel Richardson. London:
    Tinsley, 1868.
    Review of *Adam Bede*. *Times* (12 April 1859): 5.
    Review of *Felix Holt*. *Times* (26 June 1866): 3.
    Review of *The Mill on the Floss*. *Times* (19 May 1860): 10–11.
Damrosch, David. "So Much to Read, So Little Time: Isn't That the Point?"
    Chronicle of Higher Education (16 April 1999): B7-B8.
Damrosch, Leo. "Generality and Particularity." In *The Cambridge History of
    Literary Criticism. Vol. 4: The Eighteenth Century*, ed. H. B. Nisbet and Claude
    Rawson. Cambridge: Cambridge University Press, 1997.
    *God's Plot and Man's Stories: Studies in the Fictional Imagination from Milton to
    Fielding*. Chicago: University of Chicago Press, 1985.
Darnton, Robert. *The Great Cat Massacre and Other Episodes in French Cultural
    History*. London: Allen Lane, 1984.
Dasenbrock, Reed Way. "English Department Geography." In *Literary Theory
    and Critical Teaching*, ed. Maria-Regina Kecht. Urbana: University of
    Illinois Press, 1992, 193–214.

Davis, Lennard. *Factual Fictions: The Origins of the English Novel.* New York: Columbia University Press, 1983.

Deane, Seamus, et al., eds. *Field Day Anthology of Irish Literature*, 3 vols. Derry: Field Day, 1991.

Defoe, Daniel. *Serious Reflections during the Life and Surprising Adventures of Robinson Crusoe.* London: W. Taylor, 1720.

de Grazia, Margreta. "Sanctioning Voice: Quotation Marks, the Abolition of Torture, and the Fifth Amendment." In *The Construction of Authorship: Textual Appropriation in Law and Literature*, ed. Martha Woodmansee and Peter Jaszi. Durham: Duke University Press, 1994, 218–302.

"Shakespeare in Quotation Marks." In *The Appropriation of Shakespeare*, ed. Jean I. Marsden. New York: Harvester Wheatsheaf, 1991, 57–72.

Shakespeare Verbatim: The Reproduction of Authenticity and the 1790 Apparatus. Oxford: Clarendon Press, 1991.

de Man, Paul. *Allegories of Reading: Figural Language in Rousseau, Nietzsche, Rilke and Proust.* New Haven: Yale University Press, 1979.

DeMaria, Robert. *Samuel Johnson and the Life of Reading.* Baltimore: Johns Hopkins University Press, 1997.

"Samuel Johnson and the Reading Revolution." *Eighteenth-Century Life* 16 (1992): 86–102.

[Dicey, A. V.]. Review of *Daniel Deronda. Academy* 10 (9 September 1876): 253–54.

Dickens, Charles. *American Notes and Reprinted Pieces.* London: Chapman and Hall, n.d.

Dobson, Michael. *The Making of the National Poet: Shakespeare, Adaptation and Authorship, 1660–1769.* Oxford: Clarendon Press, 1992.

D[obson], W[illiam] T. *Birthday Chimes: Selections from the Poems and Tales of Sir Walter Scott.* Edinburgh: Nimmo, 1891.

Dodd, William, ed. *The Beauties of Shakespear: regularly selected from each play. With a general index digesting them under proper heads. Illustrated with explanatory notes, and similar passages from ancient and modern authors.* London, 1752.

Donoghue, Frank. *The Fame Machine: Book Reviewing and Eighteenth-Century Careers.* Stanford: Stanford University Press, 1996.

Doody, Margaret Anne. *A Natural Passion: A Study of the Novels of Samuel Richardson.* Oxford: Clarendon Press, 1974.

"Shakespeare's Novels: Charlotte Lennox Illustrated." *Studies in the Novel* 19 (Fall 1987): 296–307.

The True Story of the Novel. London: HarperCollins, 1997.

Doody, Margaret Anne, and Florian Stuber. *"Clarissa* Censored." *Modern Language Studies* 18 (Winter 1988): 74–88.

Dowden, Edward. "The Interpretation of Literature." *Contemporary Review* 49 (May 1886): 701–19.

Studies in Literature 1789–1877. London: Kegan Paul, 1883.

Dufour, Théophile. *Recherches bibliographiques sur les oeuvres imprimées de J.-J. Rousseau.* Paris: Giraudin-Badin, 1925.

Duguid, Paul. "Material Matters: The Past and Futurology of the Book." In *The Future of the Book*, ed. Geoffrey Nunberg. Berkeley: University of California Press, 1996, 63–102.

Duncan, Ian. *Modern Romance and Transformations of the Novel: The Gothic, Scott, Dickens*. Cambridge: Cambridge University Press, 1992.

Dussinger, John. "Truth and Storytelling in *Clarissa*." In *Samuel Richardson: Tercentenary Essays*, ed. Margaret Anne Doody and Peter Sabor. Cambridge: Cambridge University Press, 1989, 40–50.

Eagleton, Terry. *Criticism and Ideology*. London: NLB, 1975.

Easson, Angus, ed., *Elizabeth Gaskell: The Critical Heritage*. London: Routledge, 1991.

Eaves, T.C. Duncan, and Ben D. Kimpel. *Samuel Richardson: A Biography*. Oxford: Clarendon Press, 1971.

Eger, Elizabeth. "Fashioning a Female Canon: Eighteenth-Century Women Poets and the Politics of the Anthology." In *Women's Poetry in the Enlightenment. The Making of a Canon, 1730–1820*. Ed. Isobel Armstrong and Virginia Blain. Basingstoke: Macmillan, 1999, 201–15.

Eigner, Edwin, and George Worth. *Victorian Criticism of the Novel*. Cambridge: Cambridge University Press, 1985.

George Eliot–G. H. Lewes Papers. Beinecke Library, Yale University.

Eliot, George. *Adam Bede*. 1859. Ed. Stephen Gill. Harmondsworth: Penguin, 1985.

Daniel Deronda. 1876. Ed. Barbara Hardy. Harmondsworth: Penguin, 1967.

Essays. Ed. Thomas Pinney. London: Routledge and Kegan Paul, 1963.

Felix Holt, the Radical. 1866. Ed. Peter Coveney. Harmondsworth: Penguin, 1972.

The George Eliot Letters. Ed. Gordon Haight. New Haven: Yale University Press, 1954–1978.

Middlemarch. 1872. Ed. W. J. Harvey. Harmondsworth: Penguin, 1965.

The Mill on the Floss. 1860. Ed. A. S. Byatt. Harmondsworth: Penguin, 1979.

Selected Essays, Poems and Other Writings. Ed. A. S. Byatt and Nicholas Warren. Harmondsworth: Penguin, 1990.

The Spanish Gypsy. Edinburgh: Blackwood, 1868.

Zionism: an exposition by George Eliot from Daniel Deronda. Boston: Zionist Bureau for New England, 1915.

Emmert, J. H., *The Novelist: or, a Choice Selection of the Best Novels*. Gottingen: Vandenhoek and Ruprecht, 1792.

Enfield, William. *Observations on Literary Property*. London: J. Johnson, 1774.

Review of *The Mysteries of Udolpho*. *Monthly Review* 15 (November 1794). In *Novel and Romance, 1700–1800. A Documentary Record*, ed. Ioan Williams. London: Routledge and Kegan Paul, 1970, 395.

ed. *The Speaker: or Miscellaneous Pieces, Selected from the Best English Writers, and disposed under proper heads, with a view to facilitate the improvement of youth in reading and speaking*. London: Joseph Johnson, 1774.

Engell, James. *Forming the Critical Mind: Dryden to Coleridge*. Cambridge: Harvard University Press, 1989.

Engels, Friedrich. *The Condition of the Working Class in England*. 1845. Trans. W. O Henderson and W. H. Chaloner. Stanford: Stanford University Press, 1968.

Engelsing, Rolf. "Die Perioden der Lesergeschichte in der Neuzeit." *Archiv für geschichte des Buchwesens* 10 (1970): 945–1002.

Erikson, Lee. *The Economy of Literary Form*. Baltimore: Johns Hopkins University Press, 1996.

"Exploralibus" [Eliza Haywood]. *The Invisible Spy*. 2 vols. Dublin: Robert Main, 1755.

Ezell, Margaret. *Writing Women's Literary History*. Baltimore: Johns Hopkins University Press, 1993.

Favret, Mary. *Romantic Correspondence: Women, Politics, and the Fiction of Letters*. Cambridge: Cambridge University Press, 1993.

Ferrier, Susan. *Destiny*. 3 vols. Philadelphia: Carey and Lea, 1831.

The Inheritance. 3 vols. 1824. London: Richard Bentley, 1882.

Marriage. 1818. Ed. Herbert Foltinek. Oxford: Oxford University Press, 1986.

Marriage. 1841. Ed. Rosemary Ashton. London: Virago, 1986.

Ferris, Ina. *The Achievement of Literary Authority: Gender, History, and the Waverley Novels*. Ithaca: Cornell University Press, 1991.

Fielding, Henry. *The History of Tom Jones*. Ed. R. P. C. Mutter. Harmondsworth: Penguin, 1966.

Fish, Stanley. *Is There a Text in this Class?* Cambridge: Harvard University Press, 1980.

Flesch, William. "Quoting Poetry." *Critical Inquiry* 18 (1991): 42–63.

Fliegelman, Jay. *Prodigals and Pilgrims: The American Revolution against Patriarchal Authority, 1750–1800*. Cambridge: Cambridge University Press, 1982.

Flint, Kate. *The Woman Reader, 1837–1914*. Oxford: Clarendon Press, 1993.

"Women, Men, and the Reading of *Vanity Fair*." In *The Practice and Representation of Reading in England*, ed. James Raven, Helen Small, and Naomi Tadmor. Cambridge: Cambridge University Press, 1996, 246–62.

Formey, Samuel. *L'esprit de Julie, ou Extrait de la Nouvelle Héloïse*. Berlin: Jean Jasperd, 1763.

Fowler, Alastair. *Kinds of Literature: An Introduction to the Theory of Genres and Modes*. Cambridge: Harvard University Press, 1982.

Gallagher, Catherine. "George Eliot and *Daniel Deronda*: The Prostitute and the Jewish Question." In *Sex, Politics, and Science in the Nineteenth-Century Novel*, ed. Ruth Bernard Yeazell. Baltimore: Johns Hopkins University Press, 1986, 39–62.

"George Eliot, Immanent Victorian." *Proceedings of the British Academy* 94 (1996): 157–72.

Garber, Marjorie. ""''(Quotation Marks)." *Critical Inquiry* 25 (Summer 1999): 653–79.

Genette, Gérard. *Figures* 3. Paris: Seuil, 1972.

Seuils. Paris: Seuil, 1987.

Ginsberg, Michal Peled. "Pseudonyms, Epigraphs, and Narrative Voice: *Middlemarch* and the Problem of Authority." *ELH* 47 (1980): 542–58.

Graham, Kenneth. *English Criticism of the Novel, 1865–1900.* Oxford: Clarendon Press, 1965.

Grand, Sarah. *The Beth Book.* New York: Appleton, 1897.

Griffith, Elizabeth. *The Morality of Shakespeare's Drama Illustrated.* London: T. Cadell, 1775.

Gross, Robert A. "Much Instruction from Little Reading: Books and Libraries in Thoreau's Concord." *Proceedings of the American Antiquarian Society* 97 (April 1987): 129–88.

Guillory, John. "Canon." In *Critical Terms for Literary Study*, ed. Frank Lentricchia and Thomas McLaughlin. Chicago: University of Chicago Press, 1990, 233–49.

Cultural Capital: The Problem of Literary Canon Formation. Chicago: University of Chicago Press, 1993.

Haas, Sabine. "Victorian Poetry Anthologies." *Publishing History* 17 (1985): 51–64.

Haight, Gordon, ed. *A Century of George Eliot Criticism.* Boston: Houghton Mifflin, 1965.

Halpern, Richard. *The Poetics of Primitive Accumulation: English Renaissance Culture and the Genealogy of Capital.* Ithaca: Cornell University Press, 1991.

Harris, Jocelyn. "Learning and Genius in *Sir Charles Grandison*." In *Studies in the Eighteenth Century* IV, ed. R. F. Brissenden and J. C. Eade. Canberra: Australian National University Press, 1979, 167–91.

"Richardson: Original or Learned Genius?" In *Samuel Richardson: Tercentenary Essays*, ed. Margaret Anne Doody and Peter Sabor. Cambridge: Cambridge University Press, 1989, 188–202.

Harrison, Frederic. "The Life of George Eliot." In *The Choice of Books and Other Literary Pieces.* London: Macmillan, 1886.

Hart, Francis R. *Lockhart as Romantic Biographer.* Edinburgh: Edinburgh University Press, 1971.

Hartnoll, Phyllis. *Who's Who in George Eliot.* London: Hamish Hamilton, 1977.

Harvey, W. J. *The Art of George Eliot.* Oxford: Oxford University Press, 1969.

Hawes, Donald. "George Eliot's 'Sayings.'" *George Eliot-George Henry Lewes Studies* 20–21 (September 1992): 49–57.

Hawkes, Terence. *That Shakespeherian Rag.* London: Methuen, 1986.

Hayden, John O. *Romantic Reviewers 1802–1824.* Chicago: University of Chicago Press, 1968.

Scott: the Critical Heritage. London: Routledge and Kegan Paul, 1970.

Romantic Bards and British Reviewers. London: Routledge and Kegan Paul, 1971.

Hazen, Allen T. "The *Beauties of Johnson*." *Modern Philology* 35 (February 1938): 289–95.

Hazlitt, William, *The Spirit of the Age.* 1825. Plymouth: Northcote, 1991.

ed. *Select British Poets, or New Elegant Extracts from Chaucer to the Present Time.* London: Wm. C. Hall, 1824.

Higdon, David Leon. "George Eliot and the Art of the Epigraph." *Nineteenth-Century Fiction* 25 (1970): 127–51.

Hohendahl, Peter Uwe. *Building a National Literature: The Case of Germany, 1830–1870.* Ithaca: Cornell University Press, 1989.

Holyoake, George Jacob. *The History of Co-operation.* 2 vols. London: Fisher Unwin, 1906.

Horkheimer, Max, and Theodor Adorno. *Dialectic of Enlightenment.* Trans. John Cumming. New York: Continuum, 1994.

Howells, William Dean. *Heroines of Fiction.* 2 vols. New York: Harper, 1901.

Howitt, Mary, abridger. *Sir Charles Grandison.* By Samuel Richardson. London: Routledge, 1873.

Hughes, Linda K., and Michael Lund. *The Victorian Serial.* Charlottesville: University Virginia Press, 1991.

Hunter, J. Paul. *Before Novels.* New York: Norton, 1990.

Hutton, R. H. *A Victorian Spectator: Uncollected Writings of R. H. Hutton.* Ed. Robert Tener and Malcolm Woodfield. Bristol: Bristol Press, 1991.

Huyssen, Andreas. *After the Great Divide: Modernism, Mass Culture, Postmodernism.* Bloomington: Indiana University Press, 1986.

Hyatt, Alfred H., ed. *The Pocket George Eliot, Being Passages Chosen from the Works of George Eliot.* London: Chatto & Windus, 1907.

Jacobus, Mary. *Reading Woman: Essays in Feminist Criticism.* New York: Columbia University Press, 1986.

James, Henry. "The Art of Fiction." 1888. In *The Art of Fiction and other Essays.* New York: Oxford University Press, 1948, 3–23.

The Aspern Papers and Other Stories. Ed. Adrian Poole. Oxford: Oxford University Press, 1983.

"*Daniel Deronda*: A Conversation." In *The Critical Muse: Selected Literary Criticism.* Ed. Roger Gard. Harmondsworth: Penguin, 1987, 104–22.

Review of *Felix Holt. Nation* 3 (16 August 1866): 127–28.

Jaszi, Peter. "On the Author Effect: Contemporary Copyright and Collective Creativity." In *The Construction of Authorship: Textual Appropriation in Law and Literature,* ed. Martha Woodmansee and Peter Jaszi. Durham: Duke University Press, 1994, 29–56.

Jauss, Hans Robert. *Toward an Aesthetic of Reception.* Trans. Timothy Bahti. Minneapolis: University of Minnesota Press, 1982.

[Jeffrey, Francis]. Review of *The Giaour. Edinburgh Review* 21 (July 1813). In *The Romantics Reviewed: Byron,* 2 vols., ed. Donald Reiman. New York: Garland, 1972, 2.842–47.

Review of *Thalaba. Edinburgh Review* 1 (October 1802): 63–83.

Johnson, Barbara. *The Critical Difference; Essays in the Contemporary Rhetoric of Reading.* Baltimore: Johns Hopkins University Press, 1980.

Johnson, Claudia L. *Equivocal Beings: Politics, Gender, and Sentimentality in the 1790s.* Chicago: University of Chicago Press, 1995.

Johnson, Glen M. "Richardson's 'Editor' in *Clarissa*," *Journal of Narrative Technique* 10 (1980): 99–114.

Johnson, Samuel. *Lives of the Poets*. Ed. Arthur Waugh. Oxford: Oxford University Press, 1975.

"Preface to Shakespeare." 1765. In *Shakespeare Criticism: A Selection*, ed. D. Nichol Smith. London: Oxford University Press, 1949, 77–124.

Kaplan, Carey, and Ellen Cronan Rose. *The Canon and the Common Reader*. Knoxville: University of Tennessee Press, 1990.

Kaye-Smith, Sheila, ed. *Samuel Richardson*. London: Herbert and Daniel, 1911.

Keating, Peter. *The Haunted Study: A Social History of the English Novel, 1875–1914*. London: Secker and Warburg, 1989.

Kelly, Gary. "Reading Aloud in *Mansfield Park*." *Nineteenth-Century Fiction* 37 (1982): 29–49.

[Kelly, John.] *Pamela's Conduct in High Life*. London: Ward and Chandler, 1741.

Kermode, Frank, and John Hollander. *Oxford Anthology of English Literature*. New York: Oxford University Press, 1973.

Kernan, Alvin. *Printing Technology, Letters, and Samuel Johnson*. Princeton: Princeton University Press, 1987.

Keymer, Tom. *Richardson's "Clarissa" and the Eighteenth-Century Reader*. Cambridge: Cambridge University Press, 1992.

"Richardson's *Meditations*: Clarissa's *Clarissa*." In *Samuel Richardson: Tercentenary Essays*, ed. Margaret Anne Doody and Peter Sabor. Cambridge: Cambridge University Press, 1989, 89–109.

Kinkead-Weekes, Mark. "*Clarissa* Restored?" *Review of English Studies*, n.s. 10 (May 1959): 156–71.

Samuel Richardson: Dramatic Novelist. Ithaca: Cornell University Press, 1973.

Kittler, Friedrich A. *Discourse Networks 1800/1900*. Trans. Michael Metteer. Stanford: Stanford University Press, 1990.

Klancher, Jon P. *The Making of English Reading Audiences, 1790–1832*. Madison: University of Wisconsin Press, 1987.

Knox, Vicesimus, *Essays Moral and Literary*. 1778. 2 vols. Dublin: R. Marchbank, 1783.

Winter Evenings, or, Lucubrations on Life and Letters. 2 vols. London: Charles Dilly, 1790.

ed. *Elegant Epistles: Being a Copious Collection of Familiar and Amusing Letters, Selected for the Improvement of Young Persons, and for General Entertainment*. London: Longman, 1795.

ed. *Elegant Extracts: or useful and entertaining Passages in Prose Selected for the Improvement of Scholars in Classical and other Schools*. 2nd edn. London: C. Dilly, 1783.

ed. *Elegant Extracts in Prose, Selected for the Improvement of Young Persons*. 10th edn. London, 1816.

ed. *Elegant Extracts: or Useful and Entertaining Pieces of Poetry, Selected for the Improvement of Youth in Speaking, Reading, Thinking, Composing; and in the Conduct of Life*. London: C. Dilly, [1784?].

Kucich, Greg. "Gendering the Canons of Romanticism: Past and Present." *Wordsworth Circle* 27 (Spring 1996): 95–102.

Lamb, Charles. "On the Tragedies of Shakespeare, considered with reference to their fitness for Stage Representation." 1811. In *Shakespeare Criticism: A Selection*, ed. D. Nichol Smith. London: Oxford University Press, 1949, 190–212.

Lamb, Charles [and Mary]. *Tales from Shakespeare, Designed for the Use of Young Persons*. 1807. 2nd edn. London: M. J. Godwin, 1809.

Lanser, Susan Sniader. *Fictions of Authority: Women Writers and Narrative Voice*. Ithaca: Cornell University Press, 1992.

Lauter, Paul. *Canons and Contexts*. New York: Oxford University Press, 1991.

Leavis, Q. D. *Fiction and the Reading Public*. London: Chatto and Windus, 1932.

[Lennox, Charlotte.] *Shakespear Illustrated: or the Novels and Histories on which the plays of Shakespear are founded*. London: A. Millar, 1753.

[Lewes, G. H.] "The Lady Novelists." *Westminster Review* 2 (1852): 129–41.

Ranthorpe. London: Chapman and Hall, 1847.

[Linton, Eliza Lynn]. "George Eliot." *Temple Bar*, April 1885. Reprinted in *Prose by Victorian Women*, ed. Andrea Broomfield and Sally Mitchell. New York: Garland, 1996, 361–76.

Lockhart, J. G. *Memoirs of the Life of Sir Walter Scott, Bart*. 7 vols. Philadelphia: Carey, Lea, Blanchard, 1838.

Memoirs of the Life of Sir Walter Scott. By J. G. Lockhart. Condensed and revised by the editor of "The Chandos Classics." 1869. London: Frederick Warne, n.d.

The Life of Sir Walter Scott, Bart. Abridged from the larger work by J. G. Lockhart. 1848. Edinburgh: Adam & Charles Black, 1871.

Lonsdale, Roger. "Gray and 'Allusion': The Poet as Debtor." In *Studies in the Eighteenth Century* IV, ed. R. F. Brissenden and J. C. Eade. Canberra: Australian National University Press, 1979, 31–56.

ed. *New Oxford Book of Eighteenth-Century Verse*. Oxford: Oxford University Press, 1984.

Macauley, Elizabeth. *Tales of the Drama*. Chiswick: C. Whittingham, 1822.

MacDiarmid, Hugh. *Selected Poems*. Ed. Alan Riach and Michael Grieve. Harmondsworth: Penguin, 1994.

Maidment, B. E. "Victorian Periodicals and Academic Discourse." In *Investigating Victorian Journalism*, ed. Laurel Brake, Aled Jones, and Lionel Madden. London: Macmillan, 1990, 143–54.

Main, Alexander, ed. *Conversations of Dr. Johnson (founded chiefly upon Boswell)*. London: Chapman and Hall, 1874.

The George Eliot Birthday Book. Edinburgh: Blackwood, 1878.

Wise, Witty, and Tender Sayings in Prose and Verse Selected from the Works of George Eliot. Edinburgh: Blackwood, 1872.

Wit and Wisdom of George Eliot. Boston: Roberts, 1873.

Mandell, Laura, ed. *Romanticism on the Net* 7 (August 1997).

Mangum, Teresa. "Style Wars of the 1890s: The New Woman and the

Decadent." In *Transforming Genre: New Approaches to British Fiction of the 1890s*, ed. Nikki Lee Manos and Meri-Jane Rochelson. New York: St. Martin's, 1994, 47–66.

Manning, Peter J. "Wordsworth in the *Keepsake*, 1829." In *Literature in the Marketplace*, ed. John O. Jordan and Robert Patten. Cambridge: Cambridge University Press, 1995, 44–73.

Mansell, Darrel Jr. "George Eliot's Conception of Tragedy." *Nineteenth-Century Fiction* 22 (September 1967): 155–72.

Marotti, Arthur. *Manuscript, Print, and the English Renaissance Lyric*. Ithaca: Cornell University Press, 1995.

Martin, Graham. "*The Mill on the Floss* and the Unreliable Narrator." In *George Eliot: Centenary Essays*, ed. Anne Smith. London: Vision, 1980, 36–54.

Mason, William. *Poems of Mr. Gray. To which are prefixed Memoirs of his Life and Writings*. York: A. Ward, 1775.

Masson, David. *British Novelists and Their Styles*. Cambridge: Macmillan, 1859.

Mayo, Robert. *The English Novel in the Magazines, 1740–1815*. Evanston: Northwestern University Press, 1962.

McGann, Jerome J. "The Monks and the Giants: Textual and Bibliographical Studies and the Interpretation of Literary Works." In *Textual Criticism and Literary Interpretation*, ed. Jerome J. McGann. Chicago: University of Chicago Press, 1985, 180–200.

"Rethinking Romanticism." *ELH* 59 (1992): 725–54.

The Romantic Ideology. Chicago: University of Chicago Press, 1983.

McKeon, Michael. *The Origins of the English Novel*. Baltimore: Johns Hopkins University Press, 1987.

"Prose Fiction: Great Britain." In *The Cambridge History of Literary Criticism. Vol. 4: The Eighteenth Century*, ed. H. B. Nisbet and Claude Rawson. Cambridge: Cambridge University Press, 1997, 238–63.

McKillop, Alan Dugald. *Samuel Richardson: Printer and Novelist*. Chapel Hill: University of North Carolina Press, 1936.

"Wedding Bells for Pamela." *Philological Quarterly* 28 (1949): 323–25.

Meikle, Susan. "Fruit and Seed: The Final to *Middlemarch*." In *George Eliot: Centenary Essays*, ed. Anne Smith. London: Vision, 1980, 181–95.

Mercier, Louis-Sebastien. *L'an deux mille quatre cent quarante. Rêve s'il en fût jamais*. 1771. Londres, 1785.

M[eredith], D[aisy], ed. *The George Meredith Birthday Book*. London: Archibald Constable, 1898.

Meredith, George. *The Pilgrim's Scrip: or, Wit and Wisdom of George Meredith, with selections from his poetry*. Boston: Roberts, 1888.

Merrick, Leonard. *Cynthia*. 2 vols. London: Chatto and Windus, 1896.

Messerli, Douglas, ed. *From the Other Side of the Century: A New American Poetry*. Los Angeles: Sun and Moon Press, 1994.

ed. *"Language" Poetries: An Anthology*. New York: New Directions, 1987.

Michael, Ian. *The Teaching of English from the Sixteenth Century to 1870*. Cambridge: Cambridge University Press, 1987.

Miller, J. Hillis. "Narrative and History." *ELH* 41 (1974): 455–73.

Millgate, Jane. *Scott's Last Edition: A Study in Publishing History*. Edinburgh: Edinburgh University Press, 1987.

Moments with George Eliot. London: Seigle, Hill & Co, n.d.

More, Hannah. *Coelebs in Search of a Wife*. 2 vols. London: T. Cadell, 1808.

Florio: A Tale, for Fine Gentlemen and Fine Ladies. London: T. Cadell, 1786.

Strictures on the Modern System of Female Education. 2 vols. London: T. Cadell, 1799.

Moretti, Franco. *Modern Epic: The World-System from Goethe to García Márquez*. London: Verso, 1996.

Morley, John. Review of J. W. Cross, *George Eliot's Life*, *Macmillan's* 51 (February 1885): 241–56. Reprinted in Morley, *Nineteenth-Century Essays*, ed. Peter Stansky. Chicago: University of Chicago Press, 1970, 294–319.

Moss, Ann. *Printed Commonplace-Books and the Structuring of Renaissance Thought*. Oxford: Clarendon Press, 1996.

[Mulock, Dinah.] Review of *The Mill on the Floss*. *Macmillan's* 3 (April 1861): 441–48.

Murphy, Paul Thomas. *Toward a Working-Class Canon: Literary Criticism in British Working-Class Periodicals, 1816–1858*. Columbus: Ohio State University Press, 1994.

Murphy, Peter T. "Climbing Parnassus, and Falling Off." In *At the Limits of Romanticism: Essays in Cultural, Feminist, and Materialist Criticism*, ed. Mary A. Favret and Nicola J. Watson. Bloomington: Indiana University Press, 1994, 40–58.

Poetry as an Occupation and an Art in Britain, 1760–1830. Cambridge: Cambridge University Press, 1993.

Newcomb, Robert. "Franklin and Richardson." *Journal of English and Germanic Philology* 57 (1958): 27–35.

Novy, Marianne. *Engaging With Shakespeare: Responses of George Eliot and Other Women Novelists*. Athens: University of Georgia Press, 1994.

O'Brien, P. *Warrington Academy, 1757–86*. Wigan: Owl Books, 1989.

Olmsted, John Charles, ed. *A Victorian Art of Fiction: Essays on the Novel in British Periodicals, 1830–1900*. 3 vols. New York: Garland, 1979.

Ong, Walter, S.J. *Interfaces of the Word*. Ithaca: Cornell University Press, 1977.

Rhetoric, Romance, and Technology. Ithaca: Cornell University Press, 1971.

Page, Norman, ed. *Wilkie Collins: The Critical Heritage*. London: Routledge and Kegan Paul, 1974.

Palgrave, Francis Turner, ed. *The Golden Treasury of the Best Songs and Poems in the English Language*. 1861. Ed. Christopher Ricks. Harmondsworth: Penguin, 1991.

P[almer], C[ecil]. *The Thomas Hardy Calendar: a quotation from the works of Thomas Hardy for every day in the year*. London: C. Palmer, [1921].

Patey, Douglas Lane. "Aesthetics and the Rise of the Lyric in the Eighteenth Century." *SEL* 33 (1993): 587–608.

"The Eighteenth Century Invents the Canon." *Modern Language Studies* 18 (Winter 1988): 17–37.

Peacock, Thomas Love. *Crotchet Castle*. Ed. Raymond Wright. Harmondsworth: Penguin, 1969.

Percy, Thomas. *Reliques of Ancient English Poetry*. Dublin: P. Wilson, 1766.

Perkin, J. Russell. *A Reception-History of George Eliot's Fiction*. Rochester: University of Rochester Press, 1995.

Perloff, Marjorie. "Why Big Anthologies Make Bad Textbooks." *Chronicle of
Higher Education* 45 (16 April 1999): B6–B7.

Peters, Julie Stone. *Congreve, the Drama and the Printed Word*. Stanford: Stanford
University Press, 1990.

Piglia, Ricardo. "Notas sobre *Facundo*." *Punto de Vista* 3 (1980): 15–17.

Pinch, Adela. *Strange Fits of Passion: Epistemologies of Emotion, Hume to Austen*.
Stanford: Stanford University Press, 1996.

Pope, Alexander. *Correspondence*. 5 vols. Ed. George Sherburn. Oxford: Clarendon Press, 1956.

Preyer, Robert. "Victorian Wisdom Literature: Fragments and Maxims."
Victorian Studies 6 (1963): 245–62.

Price, Leah. "The *Life of Charlotte Brontë* and the Death of Miss Eyre." *Studies in
English Literature* 35 (1995): 757–68.

   "*Sir Charles Grandison* and the Executor's Hand." *Eighteenth-Century Fiction* 8
(April 1996): 329–42.

Radcliffe, Ann. *The Italian*. 1797. Ed Frederick Garber. Oxford: Oxford University Press, 1968.

   The Mysteries of Udolpho. 1794. Ed. Bonamy Dobrée. Oxford: Oxford University Press, 1970.

   Poems of Mrs Ann Radcliffe. London: J. Smith, 1816.

   The Romance of the Forest. 1791. Ed. Chloe Chard. Oxford: Oxford University
Press, 1986.

Ramsay, Allan, ed. *The Tea-Table Miscellany*. Edinburgh: Thomas Ruddiman,
1723.

"Recent Popular Novels." *Dublin University Magazine* 57 (February 1861): 192–
208.

Redinger, Ruby V. *George Eliot: The Emergent Self*. New York: Knopf, 1975.

R[eeve], C[lara]. *The Progress of Romance*. 2 vols. Colchester: W. Keymer, 1785.

Reiss, Timothy. *The Meaning of Literature*. Ithaca: Cornell University Press, 1992.

Review of George Eliot, *Scenes of Clerical Life*. *Saturday Review* 5 (29 May 1858):
566–67.

Review of Ann Radcliffe, *The Mysteries of Udolpho*. *British Critic* 4 (August 1794):
110–21.

Review of *The Poetical Works of Ann Radcliffe*. *Edinburgh Review* 59 (1834): 327–41.

Richardson, Alan. *Literature, Education, and Romanticism: Reading as Social Practice,
1780–1832*. Cambridge: Cambridge University Press, 1994.

Richardson, Samuel. *The Case of Samuel Richardson . . . with Regard to the Invasion of
his Property in The History of Sir Charles Grandison*. London: S. Richardson,
1753.

   Clarissa, or the History of a Young Lady. 1747–8. Ed. Angus Ross. Harmondsworth: Penguin, 1985.

Clarissa. 2nd edn. 7 vols. London: Samuel Richardson, 1749.

Clarissa. 3rd edn., 1751. 8 vols. Ed. Florian Stuber. New York: AMS, 1990.

Clarissa, or, The history of a young lady . . . abridged from the works of Samuel Richardson. London: Newbery, n.d. [1769?].

The History of Sir Charles Grandison. 1754. Ed. Jocelyn Harris. London: Oxford University Press, 1972.

The History of Sir Charles Grandison, abridged from the works of Samuel Richardson. London: Newbery, n.d. [1769?].

The history of Sir Charles Grandison, and the Hon. Miss Byron. London: C. Cooke, n.d. [1780?].

Letters and Passages Restored from the Original Manuscripts of the History of CLARISSA. To which is subjoined, A Collection of such of the Moral and Instructive SENTIMENTS, CAUTIONS, APHORISMS, REFLECTIONS and OBSER-VATIONS contained in the History, as are presumed to be of general Use and Service. London: S. Richardson, 1751.

Meditations from the Sacred Books . . . mentioned in the HISTORY OF CLARISSA as drawn up by her for her own use. To each of which is prefixed, A Short Historical Account, Connecting it with the Story. London: J. Osborn, 1750.

PAMELA: OR, VIRTUE Rewarded. 4 vols. 6th edn. London: S. Richardson, 1742.

The Paths of Virtue Delineated: or, the History in Miniature of the Celebrated Pamela, Clarissa Harlowe, and Sir Charles Grandison, Familiarised and Adapted to the Capacities of Youth. London: R. Baldwin, 1756.

Selected Letters of Samuel Richardson. Ed. John Carroll. Oxford: Clarendon Press, 1964.

Sir Charles Grandison [abridgment]. London: Field and Tuer, [1886].

Richter, David H. *The Progress of Romance: Literary Historiography and the Gothic Novel*. Columbus: Ohio State University Press, 1996.

Riding, Laura, and Robert Graves. *A Pamphlet Against Anthologies*. London: Jonathan Cape, 1927.

Ritson, Joseph, ed. *Scottish Songs*. London: J. Johnson, 1794.

Robertson, Fiona. *Legitimate Histories: Scott, the Gothic, and the Authorities of Fiction*. Oxford: Clarendon Press, 1994.

Rogers, Deborah, ed. *The Critical Response to Ann Radcliffe*. Westport: Greenwood, 1994.

Rogers, Pat. "Classics and Chapbooks." In *Books and their Readers in Eighteenth-Century England*, ed. Isabel Rivers. New York: St Martin's Press, 1982, 27–45.

Roper, Derek. *Reviewing Before the 'Edinburgh', 1788–1802*. London: Methuen, 1978.

Rose, Mark. *Authors and Owners: The Invention of Copyright*. Cambridge: Harvard University Press, 1993.

Ross, Trevor. "Copyright and the Invention of Tradition." *Eighteenth-Century Studies* 25 (1992): 1–27.

"The Emergence of 'Literature': Making and Reading the English Canon in the Eighteenth Century," *ELH* 63 (1996): 397–422.

"Just When *Did* 'British Bards Begin t'Immortalize?'" *Studies in Eighteenth-Century Culture* 19 (1989): 383–98.

Rothenberg, Jerome, and Pierre Joris, eds. *Poems for the Millennium*. 2 vols. Berkeley: University of California Press, 1995–98.

Rousseau, Jean-Jacques. *Confessions, autres textes autobiographiqes*. Ed. Bernard Gagnebin. Paris: Gallimard, 1959.

Esprit, Maximes et Principes de Monsieur Jean-Jacques Rousseau. Neuchâtel, 1764.

Julie ou La Nouvelle Héloïse. Lettres de deux amants habitants d'une petite ville au pied des Alpes. Recueillies et publiées par Jean-Jacques Rousseau. 1761. Paris: Garnier-Flammarion, 1967.

Les Pensées de J.-J. Rousseau, citoyen de Genève. Paris: Prault, 1763.

Runge, Laura L. "Gendered Strategies in the Criticism of Early Fiction." *Eighteenth-Century Studies* 28 (1995): 363–78.

Rushdie, Salman, and Elizabeth West, eds. *The Vintage Book of Indian Writing, 1947–1997*. London: Vintage, 1997.

Saintsbury, George. *Collected Essays and Papers 1875–1920*. London: Dent, 1923.

Review of *Daniel Deronda*. *Academy* 10 (9 September 1876): 253–54.

abridger. *Letters from Sir Charles Grandison: selected . . . with connecting notes by George Saintsbury*. By Samuel Richardson. London: G. Allen, 1895.

Schor, Naomi. *Reading in Detail: Aesthetics and the Feminine*. New York: Methuen, 1987.

Scott, Sir Walter. *The Abbottsford Miscellany: A Series of Selections from the Works of Sir Walter Scott*. Edinburgh: Adam and Charles Black, 1855.

Beauties of Sir Walter Scott, Bart.: being a selection from his writings and life: comprising historical, descriptive, and moral pieces, lyrical and miscellaneous poetry. 2nd edn. Edinburgh: Cadell, 1849.

Biographical Memoirs of Eminent Novelists, and other Distinguished Persons, 2 vols. 1834. Freeport: Essay Index, 1972.

The Genius and Wisdom of Sir Walter Scott, Comprising Moral, Religious, Political, Literary, and Social Aphorisms, Selected Carefully from his Various Writings: With a Memoir. London: W. S. Orr, 1839.

Ivanhoe. 1819. Ed. A. N. Wilson. Harmondsworth: Penguin, 1984.

The Poetry contained in the Novels, Tales and Romances of the Author of Waverley. Edinburgh: Constable, 1822.

Portraits of the Principal Female Characters in the Waverley Novels; to which are added, Landscape Illustrations. London: Charles Tilt, 1833.

Quentin Durward. 1823. Ed. Susan Manning. Oxford: Oxford University Press, 1992.

Redgauntlet. 1824. Ed. Kathryn Sutherland. Oxford: Oxford University Press, 1985.

Rob Roy. 1817. Ed. Eric Anderson. New York: Knopf, 1995.

Waverley; or, 'Tis Sixty Years Since. 1814. Ed. Andrew Hook. Harmondsworth: Penguin, 1972.

The Waverley Keepsake: Seventy Engravings from Real Scenes Described in the Novels. London: David Bogue, 1853.

The Waverley Poetical Birthday Book. London: Eyre and Spottiswoode, 1883.

The Waverley Proverbial Birthday Book: Being a Collection of the Proverbs and other Wise Sayings to be Found in the Waverley Novels. London: Remington, 1890.

ed. *Minstrelsy of the Scottish Border.* Ed. Thomas Henderson. 4 vols. Edinburgh: Blackwood, 1902.

Seguin, L. G., ed. *A Souvenir of George Eliot. Scenes and Characters from the Works of George Eliot: A Series of Illustrations by Eminent Artists.* With introductory essay and descriptive letterpress by L. G. Seguin. London: Alexander Strahan, 1888.

Sénelier, Jean. *Bibliographie générale des oeuvres de J.-J. Rousseau.* Paris: Presses Universitaires de France, 1950.

Shakespeare, William. *The Beauties of Shakespeare, selected from his plays and poems.* London: G. Kearsley, 1783.

Sheppard, Nathan, ed. *Character Readings from George Eliot.* New York: Harper's, 1883.

Sherburn, George, abridger. *Clarissa.* By Samuel Richardson. Boston: Houghton Mifflin, 1962.

Sheridan, Richard Brinsley. *The Rivals.* 1775. Ed. Elizabeth Duthie. New York: Norton, 1979.

Showalter, Elaine. *Sexual Anarchy: Gender and Culture at Fin de Siècle.* 1990. London: Virago, 1992.

Shuttleworth, Sally. *George Eliot and Nineteenth-Century Science: The Make-Believe of a Beginning.* Cambridge: Cambridge University Press, 1984.

Simcox, Edith Jemima. "Women's Work and Women's Wages." *Longman's Magazine* (July 1887). Reprinted in *Prose by Victorian Women,* ed. Andrea Broomfield and Sally Mitchell. New York: Garland, 1996, 565–82.

Simpson, David. "Public Virtues, Private Vices: Reading Between the Lines of Wordsworth's 'Anecdote for Fathers'." In *Subject to History,* ed. David Simpson. Ithaca: Cornell University Press, 1991, 163–90.

Simpson, Richard. "George Eliot's Novels." *Home and Foreign Review* 3 (October 1863): 522–49.

Siskin, Clifford. *The Work of Writing: Literature and Social Change in Britain, 1700–1830.* Baltimore: Johns Hopkins University Press, 1998.

Skilton, David, ed., *The Early and Mid-Victorian Novel.* London: Routledge, 1993.

Small, Ian. *Conditions for Criticism.* Oxford: Clarendon Press, 1991.

Smith, Anne, ed., *George Eliot: Centenary Essays.* London: Vision, 1980.

Smith, Barbara Herrnstein. "Narrative Versions, Narrative Theories." In *On Narrative,* ed. W. J. T. Mitchell. Chicago: University of Chicago Press, 1981, 209–39.

Spacks, Patricia Meyer. *Boredom: The Literary History of a State of Mind.* Chicago: University of Chicago Press, 1995.

"The Privacy of the Novel." *Novel* 31 (Summer 1998): 304–16.

The Beauties of Sterne: Including all his Pathetic Tales, and Most Distinguished Observa-
tions on Life, Selected for the Heart of Sensibility. London: T. Davies, 1782.

Stetz, Margaret Diane. "Life's 'Half-profits': Writers and their Readers in
Fiction of the 1890s." In *Nineteenth-Century Lives*, ed. Laurence S. Lockridge
et al. Cambridge: Cambridge University Press, 1989, 169–87.

Stevick, Philip, abridger. *Clarissa.* By Samuel Richardson. San Francisco:
Rinehart, 1971.

Stewart, Garett. *Dear Reader: The Conscripted Audience in Nineteenth-Century British*
Fiction. Baltimore: Johns Hopkins University Press, 1996.

Stewart, Susan. *On Longing.* Baltimore: Johns Hopkins University Press, 1984.

Stoneman, Patsy. *Brontë Transformations.* London: Harvester, 1996.

Sullivan, Sir Edward. *Tales from Scott.* London: Elliot Stock, 1894.

Sutherland, John. "Publishing History: A Hole at the Center of Literary
Sociology." In *Literature and Social Practice*, ed. Philippe Desan et al.
Chicago: University of Chicago Press, 1989, 267–82.

Victorian Novelists and Publishers. Chicago: University of Chicago Press, 1976.

Sweetser, Kate Dickinson. *Boys and Girls from George Eliot.* New York: Harper
Brothers, 1906.

Tadmor, Naomi. "'In the even my wife read to me': Women, Reading, and
Household Life in the Eighteenth Century." In *The Practice and Representa-*
tion of Reading in England, ed. James Raven, Helen Small, and Naomi
Tadmor. Cambridge: Cambridge University Press, 1996, 162–74.

[Talfourd, Thomas Noon]. "Memoir of the Life and Writings of Mrs. Radcliffe." In Ann Radcliffe, *Gaston de Blondeville . . . to which is prefixed a memoir of*
the author, 2 vols. London: Henry Colburn, 1826, 1.1–132.

Tatin, Jean-Jacques. "La dissemination du texte Rousseau: Le 'Contrat-social'
dans les recueils de 'Pensées de J.-J. Rousseau'." *Littérature* 69 (1988): 19–27.

Taylor, Gary. *Reinventing Shakespeare: A Cultural History from the Restoration to the*
Present. New York: Weidenfeld and Nicholson, 1989.

Terry, Richard. "The Eighteenth-Century Invention of English Literature: A
Truism Revisited." *British Journal for Eighteenth-Century Studies* 19 (Spring
1996): 47–62.

Thackeray, W. M. *The Oxford Thackeray.* Ed. George Saintsbury, 17 vols.
Oxford: Oxford University Press, 1908.

Thomas, Max W. "Reading and Writing the Renaissance Commonplace
Book: A Question of Authorship?" In *The Construction of Authorship: Textual*
Appropriation in Law and Literature, ed. Martha Woodmansee and Peter Jaszi.
Durham: Duke University Press, 1994, 410–16.

Thompson, Ann, and Sasha Roberts, eds. *Women Reading Shakespeare 1660–1900:*
An Anthology of Criticism. Manchester: Manchester University Press, 1997.

Thompson, Nicola Diane. *Reviewing Sex: Gender and the Reception of Victorian Novels.*
New York: New York University Press, 1996.

Trollope, Anthony. *An Autobiography.* Ed. Michael Sadleir and Frederick Page.
Oxford: Oxford University Press, 1980.

Four Lectures. Ed. Morris L. Parrish. London: Constable, 1938.

Trumpener, Katie. *Bardic Nationalism: the Romantic Novel and the British Empire.* Princeton: Princeton University Press, 1997.

Tuchman, Gaye with Nina E. Fortin. *Edging Women Out. Victorian Novelists, Publishers, and Social Change.* New Haven: Yale University Press, 1989.

Turner, James. "Novel Panic: Picture and Performance in the Reception of *Pamela.*" *Representations* 48 (Fall 1994): 70–96

Tye, J. R. "George Eliot's Unascribed Mottoes." *Nineteenth-Century Fiction* 22 (1967): 235–49.

Uphaus, Robert W. "Vicesimus Knox and the Canon of Eighteenth-Century Literature." *The Age of Johnson* 4 (1991): 345–61.

"The Uses of Fiction." *Tinsley's Magazine* 6 (March 1870): 180–85. In *A Victorian Art of Fiction: Essays on the Novel in British Periodicals, 1830–1900,* ed. John Charles Olmsted, 3 vols. New York: Garland, 1979, 3.3–8.

Veblen, Thorstein. *The Theory of the Leisure Class.* Harmondsworth: Penguin, 1994.

Versini, Laurent. *Le roman épistolaire.* Paris: Presses Universitaires de France, 1979.

Viswanathan, Gauri. *Masks of Conquest: Literary Study and British Rule in India.* New York: Columbia University Press, 1989.

Ward, Mrs. Humphry. *Clarissa Harlowe, a New and Abridged Edition.* By Samuel Richardson. London: Routledge, 1868.

Warner, William B. *Licensing Entertainment: The Elevation of Novel Reading in Britain, 1684–1750.* Berkeley: University of California Press, 1998.

Reading Clarissa: The Struggles of Interpretation. New Haven: Yale University Press, 1979.

Watson, Nicola J. *Revolution and the Form of the British Novel 1790–1825: Intercepted Letters, Interrupted Seductions.* Oxford: Clarendon Press, 1994.

Watt, Ian. *The Rise of the Novel: Studies in Defoe, Richardson, and Fielding.* Berkeley: University of California Press, 1957.

Weinbrot, Howard W. "*Clarissa,* Elias Brand and Death by Parentheses." In *New Essays on Samuel Richardson,* ed. Albert J. Rivero. New York: St Martin's Press, 1996, 117–40.

Welsh, Alexander. *George Eliot and Blackmail.* Cambridge: Harvard University Press, 1985.

The Hero of the Waverley Novels. New Haven: Yale University Press, 1963.

Widdowson, Peter. *Hardy in History: A Study in Literary Sociology.* London: Routledge, 1989.

Williams, Ioan, ed. *Novel and Romance, 1700–1800. A Documentary Record.* London: Routledge and Kegan Paul, 1970.

Wilt, Judith. "Steamboat Surfacing: Scott and the English Novelists." *Nineteenth-Century Fiction* 35 (1981): 459–86.

"Wise, Witty and Tender Sayings of George Eliot." *Westminster Review* 41 (April 1872): 571–72.

"The Wit and Wisdom of George Eliot." *Spectator* 13 January 1872: 43–44.

"The Works of Charles Lamb." *Blackwood's* 3 (August 1818): 601.

Woodmansee, Martha. *The Author, Art, and the Market*. New York: Columbia University Press, 1994.

Woolf, Virginia. *The Common Reader*. 1st series. London: Hogarth Press, 1984.

Review of *A Treasury of English Prose*, ed. Logan Pearsall Smith. *Athenaeum*, 30 January 1920. In *The Essays of Virginia Woolf*, 4 vols, ed. Andrew McNeillie. London: Hogarth Press, 1988, 3.171–76.

Woolford, John. "Periodicals and the Practice of Literary Criticism, 1855–64." In *The Victorian Periodical Press: Samplings and Soundings*, ed. Joanne Shattock and Michael Wolff. Leicester: Leicester University Press, 1982, 109–42.

Wordsworth, William, and S. T. Coleridge. *Lyrical Ballads*. Ed. R. L. Brett and A. R. Jones. London: Routledge, 1991.

Wright, Julia. "'The Order of Time': Nationalism and Literary Anthologies, 1774–1831." *Papers on Language and Literature* 33 (Fall 1997): 339–65.

Yates, Edmund. "The Novels of Wilkie Collins." *Temple Bar* 89 (August 1890): 528–32. In *Wilkie Collins: The Critical Heritage*, ed. Norman Page. London: Routledge and Kegan Paul, 1974, 273–77.

Yeazell, Ruth Bernard. "Podsnappery, Sexuality and the English Novel." *Critical Inquiry* 9 (December 1982): 339–57.

Index